IMAGES
of America

BROOKFIELD

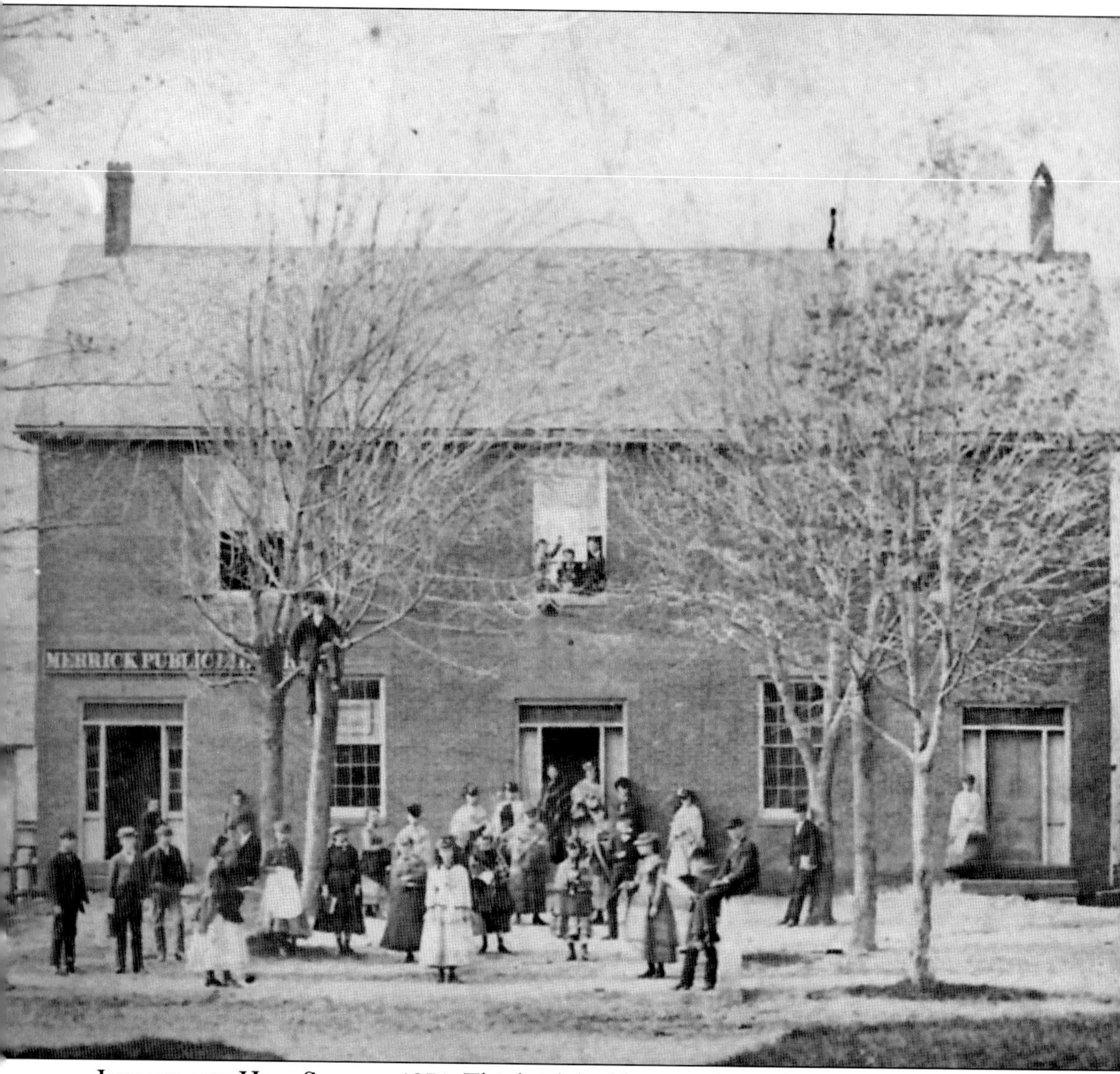

LIBRARY AND HIGH SCHOOL, 1871. This brick building was located on Central Street between the town hall and the Congregational Church, where the fire station now stands. It was used as the high school and library before each had separate buildings. The Merrick Public Library sign, which is about 15 feet long, now rests in the current library's upstairs gallery. (Courtesy of Michael Seery.)

ON THE COVER: OLIVER CROSBY HOUSE, 1927. Costumed townspeople gather on the lawn of 13 West Main Street to celebrate the installation of the Gen. Henry Knox monument. The house, with its distinguished fan window over the front door, was built in 1797 after architect Asher Benjamin's design and was first occupied by Oliver and Sally Crosby and Daniel and Olive Bullard. (Courtesy of Loana Nichols Gadaire and Paula Gadaire Woodard.)

IMAGES
of America

BROOKFIELD

Brenda Metterville, Kate Simpson,
and Andrea Faugno

ARCADIA
PUBLISHING

ISBN 978-0-7385-9134-6

Published by Arcadia Publishing
Charleston, South Carolina

Printed in the United States of America

Library of Congress Control Number: 2011938363

For all general information, please contact Arcadia Publishing:
Telephone 843-853-2070
Fax 843-853-0044
E-mail sales@arcadiapublishing.com
For customer service and orders:
Toll-Free 1-888-313-2665

Visit us on the Internet at www.arcadiapublishing.com

This book is dedicated to the people of Brookfield, yesterday and today.

Contents

Acknowledgments

We would like to thank the many people who shared their photographs, family histories, and memories of living and working in Brookfield. For every photograph we were able to include in this book, there were too many we were not able to include. We wish we had room for all of them as well as the full stories and histories that accompany them. Our archive of photographs and notes is available for viewing at the Merrick Public Library.

Thank you to our library community for their kind patience while we worked on this project. A special thank you to the Board of Trustees; Friends of the Library; Robert Wilder; Ron Couture; Barbara Wilson; James Pronto; Julia Taylor; Jessica Magnuson; and Mikayla Harnois; and to John Kinnear of Digital-Vistas, who scanned all of the Blanchard Means Foundation photographs as well as many others. Thank you, also, to the people who brought us items we were regrettably unable to use.

We strove to make the information in this book as accurate as possible and have relied on both written and oral records. In many cases, we turned to Brookfield town reports, tax valuations, and anniversary booklets—including those from 1910, 1960, and 1973. We also used written interviews with residents; the 1889 Brookfield Business Guide and Social Directory; print and microfilm versions of the *Brookfield Times, Brookfields' Union, County Courier, Spencer Leader/Spencer New Leader*, and *Worcester Telegram & Gazette* as well as *Team-Mates* newsletters from the McLaurin-Jones Company; St. Mary's Church 100th anniversary booklet; National Register of Historic Places registration forms compiled by the Brookfield Historical Commission; and the *Massachusetts Heritage Landscape Inventory Program, Brookfield Reconnaissance Report* (MHLIP). Other sources are listed in the bibliography in more detail. Please note that the Merrick Public Library is abbreviated as MPL.

INTRODUCTION

The history presented in this book is a snapshot of life in Brookfield, focusing mainly on the late 1800s to mid-1900s. Brookfield grew from a small group of families to a town bustling with people and industry. Its location on the Boston Post Road, centered 60 miles from Boston and 90 miles from Albany, provided a stream of people passing through town. Inns abounded from the 1850s until the 1920s, with the railroad, trolley, and other modes of transportation stimulating advantages for livelihood and families. The Quaboag River and lakes Quaboag and Quacumquasit enriched lives both with opportunities for water-powered businesses and for times of recreation and relaxation. Farming to manufacturing embroider a rich and fascinating historical legend with fodder for wonderful tales.

Brookfield was originally part of the Quaboag Plantation, initiated by a group of families from Ipswich who petitioned the General Court in 1660 for a land grant in central Massachusetts. The terms of the agreement were for 20 families to be settled there within three years, which took longer to do than expected. By 1673, the township was granted, but soon after, the settled families encountered hostility from the Native Americans and were attacked and burned out, abandoning the land for almost a decade. The second settlement was established in 1686, and despite continued conflict, the settlers persevered and remained in the township, by now renamed Brookfield. By 1718, the General Court awarded local governance of the land to the settlers, and they held their first town meeting. In the intervening years, the area was sectioned off into the six separate towns that now make up the original land grant, Brookfield, East Brookfield, North Brookfield, New Braintree, Warren, and West Brookfield.

From such a difficult beginning, the town prospered. In 1839, the Boston & Albany Railroad opened its line through Brookfield, and by the 1880s, seven trains a day were stopping at the depot by the river. The town became a hubbub of factories producing boots, shoes, heels, bricks, bicycles, and boxes and of stores selling lumber, produce, meat, clothing, rugs, and more. The streets of Brookfield teamed with people. Some of these people were famous, such as Gen. George Washington, Revolutionary War general Marquis de Lafayette, and Gen. Henry Knox, who passed through Brookfield during important revolutionary campaigns, and Franklin Delano Roosevelt, who visited the Brookfield Inn during his presidential campaign. Some were infamous, such as East Main Street resident Bathsheba Ruggles Spooner, who was hanged in Worcester in 1778, along with three Revolutionary War soldiers, for killing her husband, Joshua Spooner, and disposing of his body in the family well. Much was made of the trial and subsequent hangings, especially of a woman who, as she claimed but was not believed, was pregnant at the time.

Other Brookfield people included Maj. George Holbrook, a bell maker who had apprenticed with Paul Revere. He came to town in 1797 at the age of 30 to forge bells and resided in the Lewis Mansion. Stage star and summer visitor Louise Galloway Bassett married here and opened the Louise Galloway Tea House in the 1920s. Brookfield's Elm Hill Farm, home of a large apple orchard and cattle operation, was the birthplace of the cow chosen as the Borden Company's mascot,

Elsie the Cow, who became famous worldwide and is still used in the company's advertising. The farm had in earlier days been owned by Charles P. Blanchard, who while not famous in the outside world, was a great benefactor to the town of Brookfield and left his mark, both with many of the photographs seen in this book that capture daily scenes of life in Brookfield around 1890 and with legacies he left to the town, such as the Grand Army of the Republic book still held in the library today.

Brookfield people remember where they came from. On Thanksgiving Day in 1828, Joseph Ives Foot, pastor of the First Church in Brookfield, delivered the following historic discourse in which he reflected on the beginnings of Brookfield:

> Whilst national blessings ought to be gratefully remembered, it is equally important, that particular favors should not be forgotten. This place was originally the residence of Indians. These ponds and brooks and hills and plains were calculated to attract the attention of the sons of the forest and to supply them with the necessaries of life.

Charles Oliver Howe, who was born on a large working farm in July 1822, one of seven children, wrote about Brookfield in his 1895 recollection *What I Remember*. He noted that while Thanksgiving and Independence Day were days with no restraint, "we lived plainly for the most part all other for the 365 days." He said he "could write volumes telling the story of my young life in staid old Brookfield, of the 'orchards, the meadows, the deep tangled wildwood, and all the loved haunts my infancy knew.' " Ella Bartlett, interviewed by Louise Bassett as part of the Federal Writers' Project in 1939, also reminisced about what it was like to grow up and live in Brookfield:

> School started at nine, or about then. It wasn't a crime to be late. . . . children walked to school—sometimes near two miles—except in awful deep snow weather, then some farmer would have his ox sled started out and he'd collect all th' children along th' way. There'd be two, three men on th' sled 'cause lots of times snowdrifts would have to be shoveled away. . . . They'd get to school with th' sled all full of children, all shoutin' and callin'. . . . Th' children . . . always walked, but they hardly missed a day durin' the winter. . . . Th' children today, think they're killed if they have to walk six blocks.
>
> Brookfield, in the 1870s and 1880s was doing wonderful business. . . . We were a real dressy town in those days. . . . The main road from Worcester to Springfield ran right through the center of town then, and the two hotels were always full. Then too, people would drive over here from Spencer and the likes that on a Sunday to have dinner.

The town today bustles in different ways. Gone are the many factories and stores, the train depot, and the streets crowded with pedestrians. But the people are still here. The townspeople are steadfast, true, committed, and proud, and they have a sense of humor. When Jacob J. Knight was commissioned by the Brookfield Community Club to paint a picture of the Apple Country Fair, held every Columbus Day weekend, he portrayed Brookfield as a historic, bucolic, folksy, united, and fun town. The evolution from a booming industrial town with farms, camps on the ponds, a historical common, and beloved benefactors who gifted our community with beautiful architecture—from our cemetery gate to our beloved public library—to our quiet town of today is presented in snippets throughout this collection. Apologies are made for any omissions, deletions, misspellings, or other errors; all such instances are purely unintentional.

One

EARLY DAYS

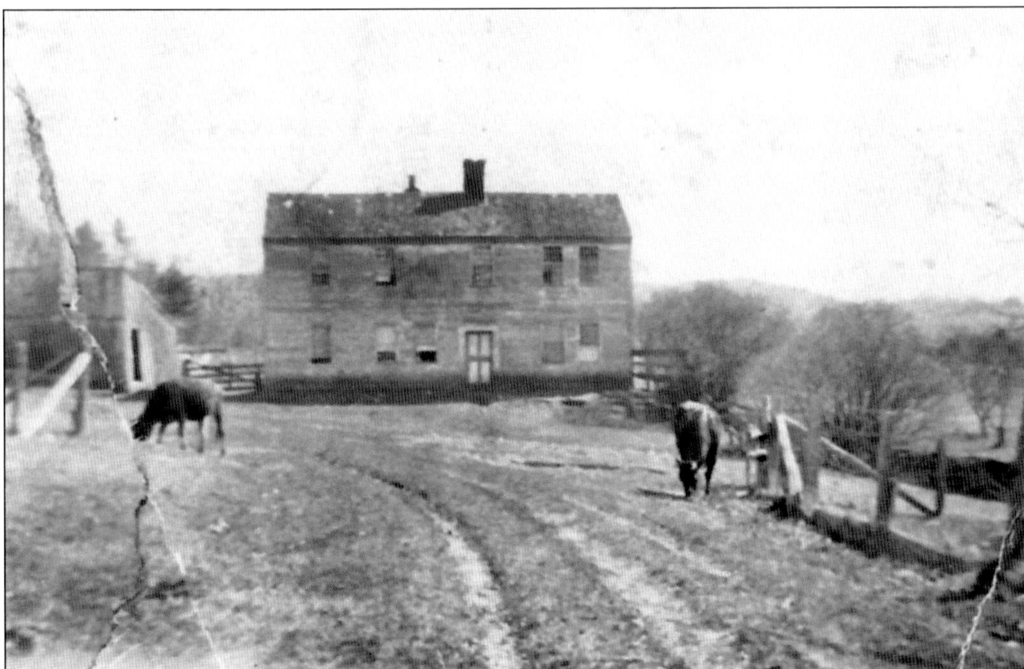

WALKER HOMESTEAD, C. 1900. This c. 1698 saltbox, located on the south side of the river high atop Martin Road, is one of the oldest buildings in town, constructed during the second settlement of the Quaboag Plantation. The Walker family owned it for the first half of its existence. This view, with cows grazing, was taken during Rachael Bolshaw's ownership. (Courtesy of Paul and Kris Casucci.)

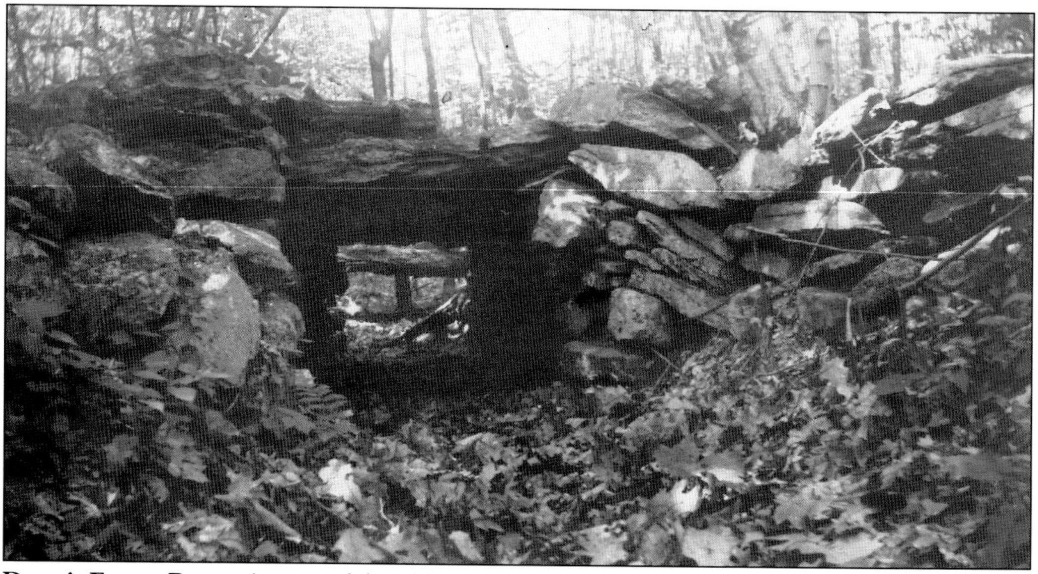

Devil's Elbow Road. As part of the old military highway known as the Bay Path, Devil's Elbow Road was once connected to the early settlement on Foster Hill in West Brookfield and contains several remnants of its historic past. It has been estimated that the old stone bridge, above, dates from about 1675. It is made of four eight-inch-thick stone slabs, each measuring seven feet long and three feet wide. The entrance to an old root cellar, below, dates from about 1700 and is evidence of long-ago homesteads, such as that of Judah Trumble. (Above, courtesy of White's Landing on behalf of Winifred Broughton; below, courtesy of Robert and Nancy Cronin Wilder.)

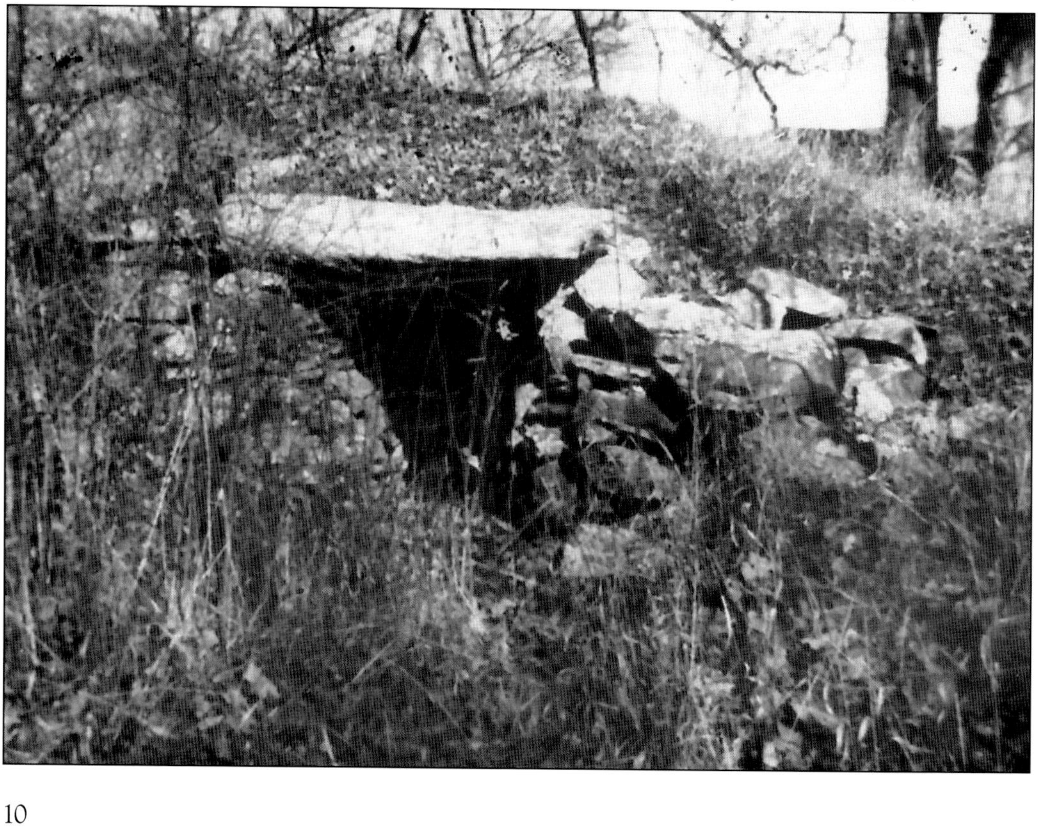

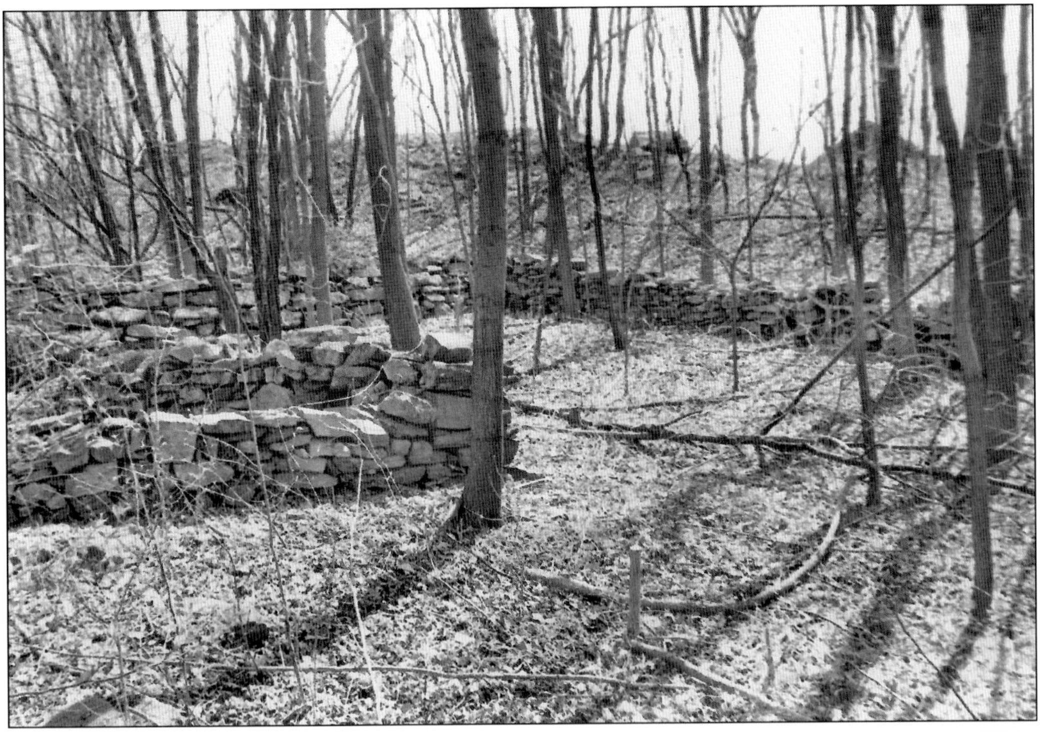

TOWN POUND. Located on West Brookfield Road, the pound was very likely constructed at the same time as the early Quaboag Plantation buildings on Foster Hill Road and is one of the oldest remaining physical artifacts of the early settlement. Used to keep stray animals from eating or damaging crops, the pound was built around 1686. (Courtesy of White's Landing on behalf of Winifred Broughton.)

THE

DYING DECLARATION

OF

JAMES BUCHANAN, EZRA ROSS,

AND WILLIAM BROOKS,

Who were executed at Worcester, July 2, 1778,

FOR THE MURDER OF

Mr. Joshua Spooner.

ON February 8th, 1778, we, *James Buchanan* and *William Brooks* left Worcester with an intent to go to Springfield to work. In passing Mr. Spooner's we were called in by *Alexander Cummings*, who we thought was a British soldier. Having stood some time by the fire, he told us his master was gone from home, but he would go and call his mistress, for she had a great regard for the army, as her father was in it and one of her brothers. He called her, and she came down, and appeared glad to see us. She asked us whether we came from the Hill? We told her we did, and were going to *Canada*, as I, *Buchanan*, had left my family there. She ordered Breakfast for us, and as soon as it was ready we were desired to go into the sitting-room. We were very much surprised at this, for we should have thought ourselves well dealt by to have received any favours she might see fit to bestow on us in the kitchen. However, we all breakfasted together. The weather being very bad, we were asked to stay till it cleared up. As we had but little money, we accordingly stayed. The weather continuing very bad, we stayed there that day and night. I (Buchanan) am not positive whether it was the first or second day, she told me, when by ourselves, that she and her husband did not agree—that he was gone a journey to Prince-

SPOONER MURDER CONFESSION. The murder of Joshua Spooner in 1778 outside his home on East Main Street led to one of the century's most sensationalized trials. Three British soldiers, James Buchanan, Ezra Ross, and William Brooks, were hanged for the crime, as was the victim's wife, Bathsheba Ruggles Spooner. The remains of the well in which Joshua Spooner's body was disposed are still visible today. (Courtesy of MPL.)

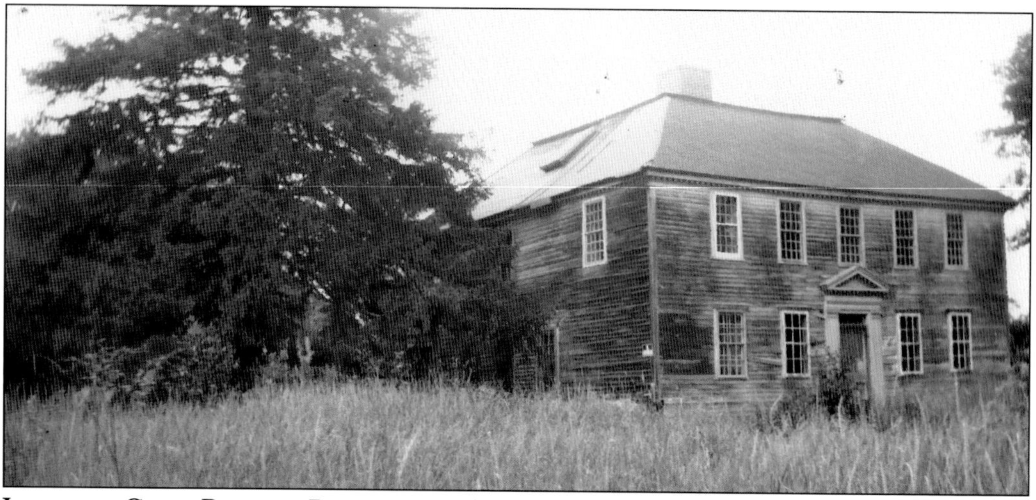

LAWRENCE CROSS ROAD AT ROUTE 148. This building is believed by some to be the Banister Garrison, built by Joseph Banister in 1704 as a bulletproof shelter with underground passages. Others believe the garrison was located on East Main Street, and this building is the Jennings house, constructed in 1785 in an earlier style. The building was dismantled in 1975. (Courtesy of White's Landing on behalf of Winifred Broughton.)

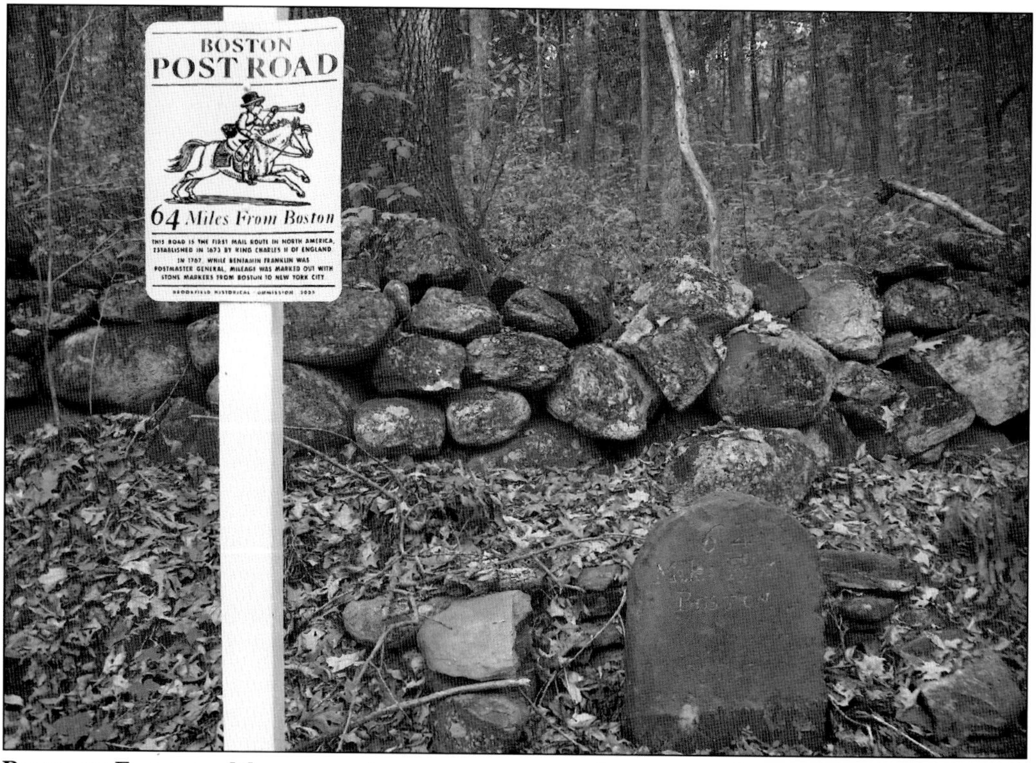

BENJAMIN FRANKLIN MILESTONE. In an attempt to regulate postage fees in the 1760s, Benjamin Franklin, assistant postmaster general, directed that red sandstone markers be placed every mile from Boston to New York. Although the Boston Post Road has changed greatly over the last 250 years, Brookfield's three markers remain standing. The one pictured here is located on East Main Street. (Photograph by and courtesy of Kate Simpson.)

Two

Families, Farms, and Homes

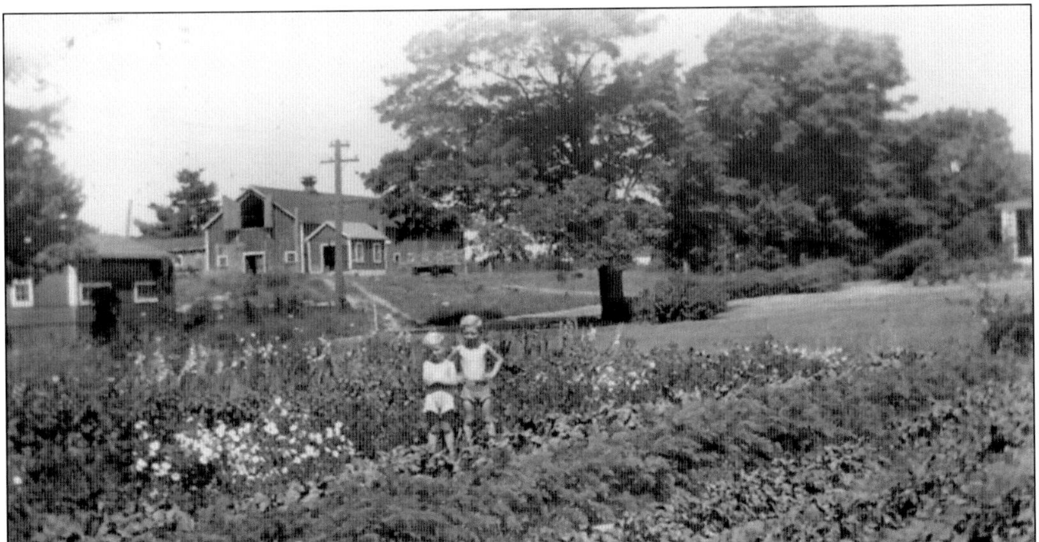

Bennett Farm, 1949. Erwin Achilles was hired as the Bennett farm manager in 1925. Here, his sons Harrison "Archie" (age four, on left) and Horace (age five) stand in their mother Alice's flower garden near the fork of Rice Corner and Rice Corner Cross Roads. She loved flowers, and her garden was the envy of the neighborhood. All of her seven children became excellent weeders. (Courtesy of Gloria Achilles Faugno.)

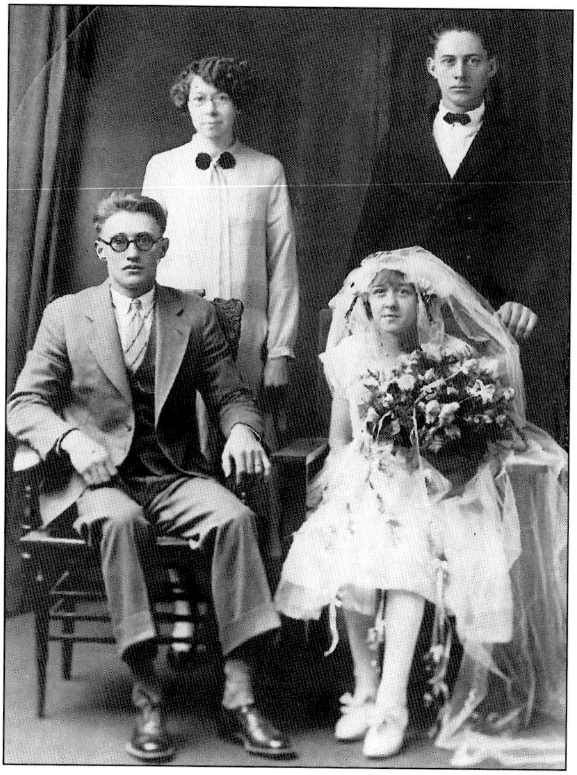

Christmas Eve Wedding, 1925. Alice Wilson became the bride of Erwin Achilles in a wedding held in Sturbridge. The attendants were the bride's sister Goldie Wilson and the groom's good friend. The family worked at Sibley farm, now known as Jeppson's Oakholm Farm, and at Bennett farm. In time, seven children were added to their family, Olive, Gloria, Ralph, Shirley, Glenora, Horace, and Harrison Achilles. (Courtesy of Gloria Achilles Faugno.)

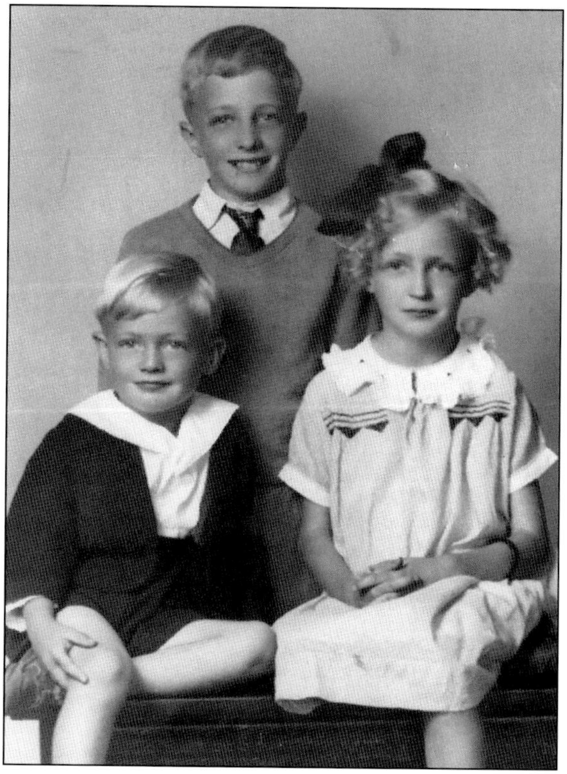

Steadman Family, 1932. Clayton and Hilda Steadman raised their children Wilfred (front left), Phyllis (front right), and John on Rice Corner Road. The children graduated from Brookfield High School. Wilfred Steadman graduated from the University of Massachusetts, Amherst, in 1951 and was an engineer at Norton Company until 1987. He married Brookfield resident Barbara Sheldon in 1952, and they had one son, Dana Steadman. (Courtesy of Wilfred and Barbara Steadman.)

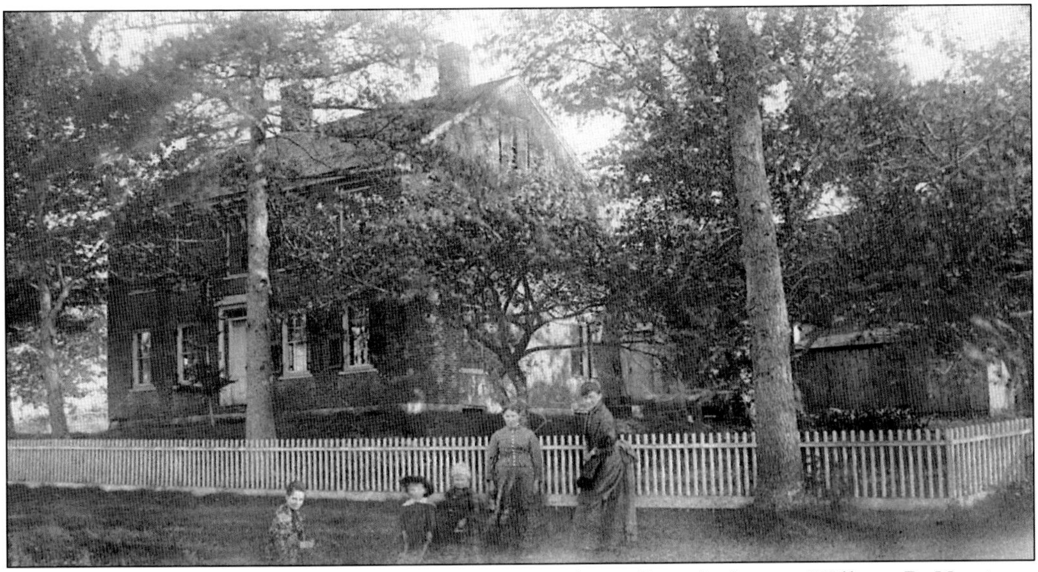

Long Hill Road, 1886. This home, built in 1839 by well-to-do farmer William B. Hastings, remained in the Hastings family for over 100 years. It is a Greek Revival–style house with two large chimneys, four fireplaces, and wide pine floors. The large kitchen was fitted with a cistern next to the sink to pipe water directly from the well. (Courtesy of Cipro family.)

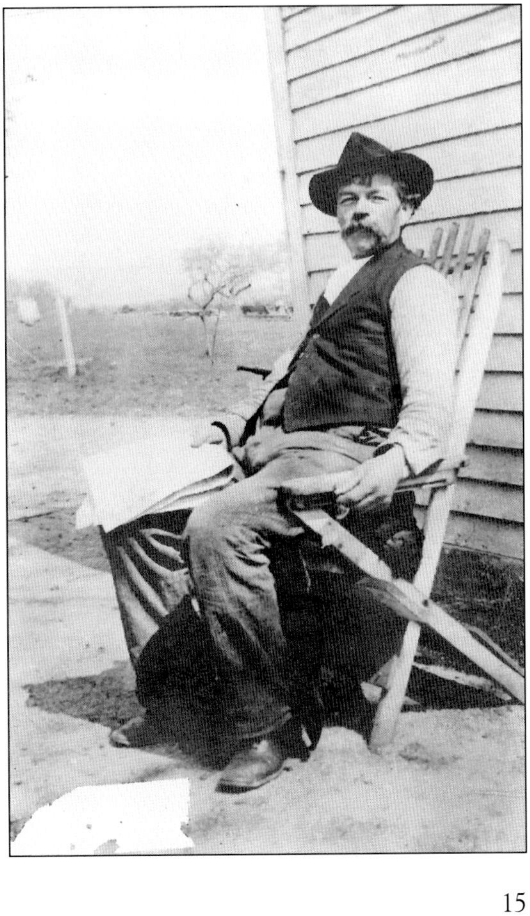

Theodore Eaton. In 1886, Theodore Eaton and Katie Belle Whittemore were married in the Brookfield Methodist Church (no longer standing). While not much is known about Theodore Eaton, his wife ran a millinery shop in the center of Brookfield as a young woman and later a dressmaking business from their home until the 1950s. In 1917, Theodore Eaton died at age 66. (Courtesy of Ruggles family.)

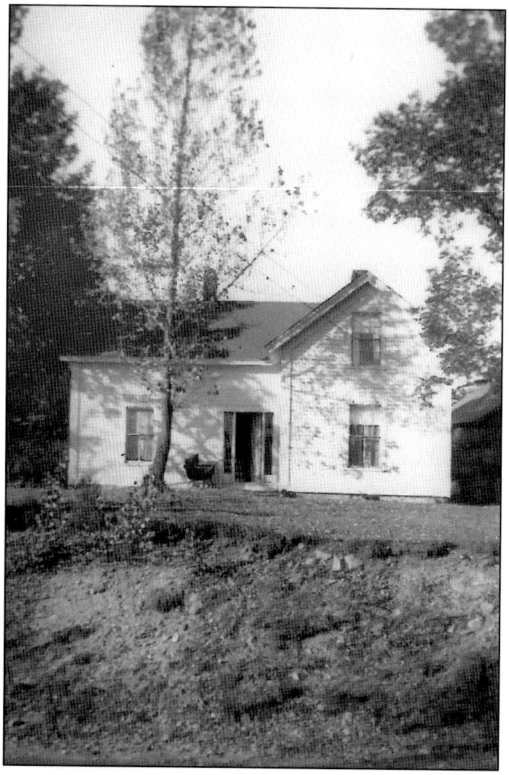

28 Lake Road, 1949. Whitley and Barbara Shailer purchased this home in 1948 to raise their family. Here, the front door is open in order to check on baby Faye as she sleeps in the carriage outside. Faye Shailer Mahoney currently lives at 32 Lake Road, not far from where she grew up, and her sister Rachel Shailer Bracconnier lives at the homestead with her husband, Gary. (Courtesy of Paul Shailer.)

A 1947 Ford. Paul Shailer sits in his first car in front of his Lake Road home. Friend Gordon "Peeky" Richards worked at Brookfield Motors in 1958, and when this vehicle was traded in, he called Shailer, who purchased it for $25. Shailer was only 15 at the time and did not receive his driver's license for another year. (Courtesy of Paul Shailer.)

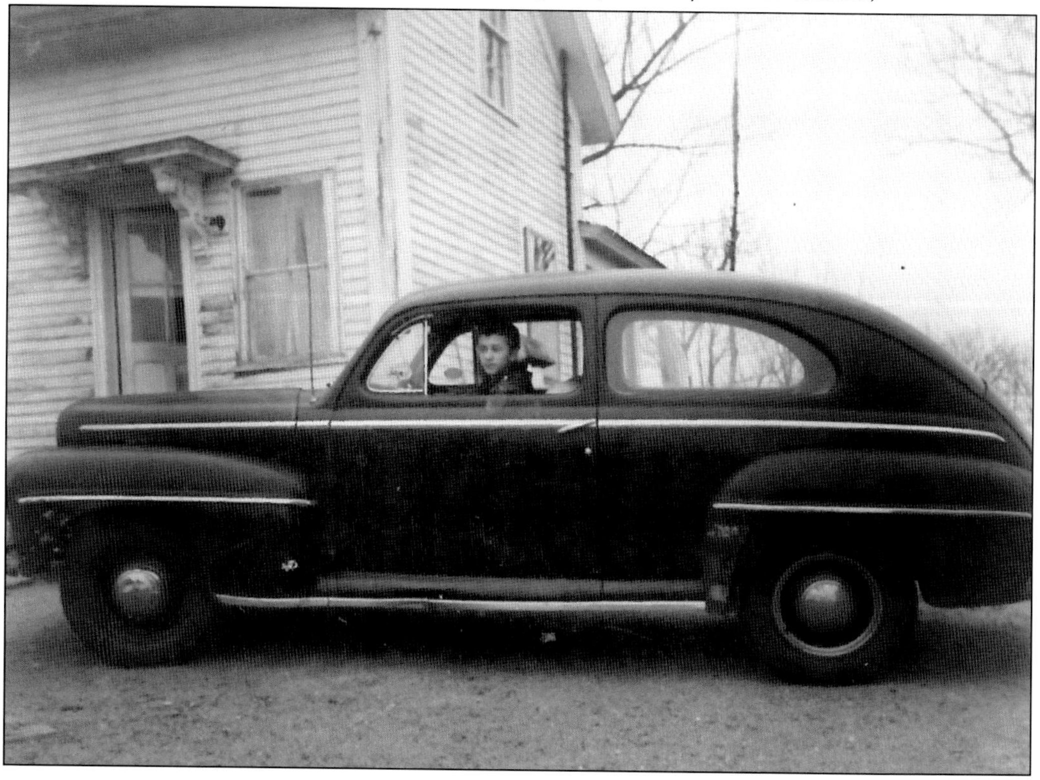

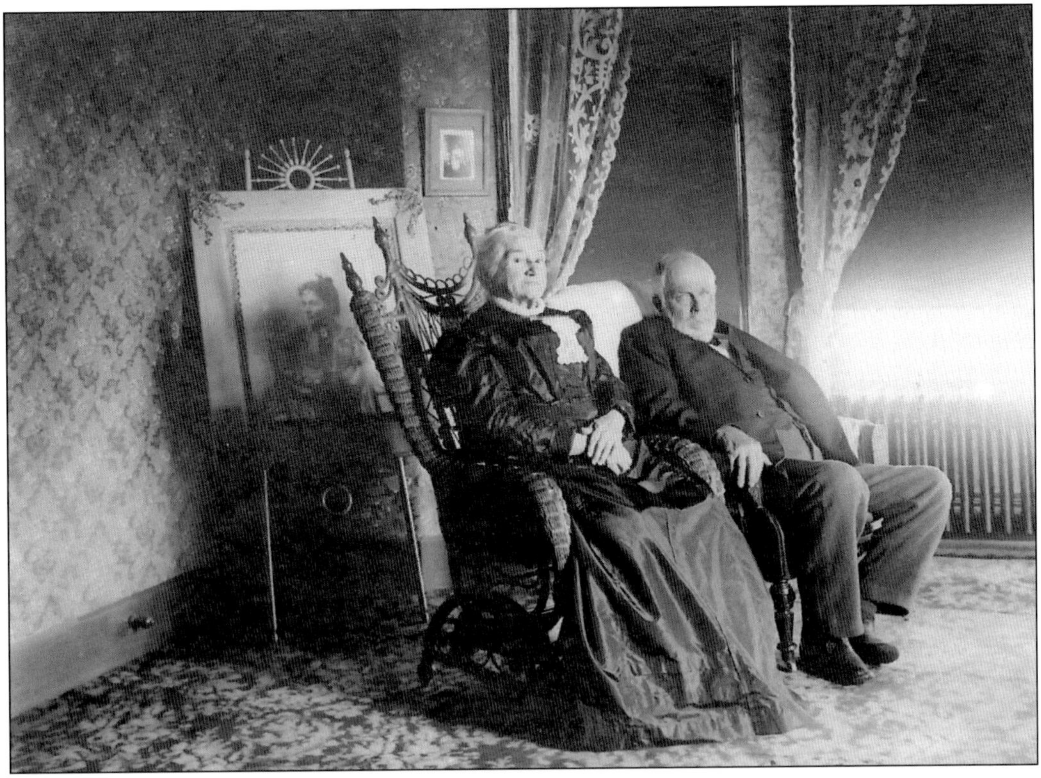

Charles and Martha Rice. The 1889 business directory advertises Rice's Mills, with Charles F. Rice, proprietor, as "headquarters for Baled Hay and Straw, Grain, Meal, Feed, Wood, & etc. Sawing done at any time." Here, the couple is seen in their finery c. 1900. The significance of the painting in the background is not known. (Courtesy of Loana Nichols Gadaire and Paula Gadaire Woodard.)

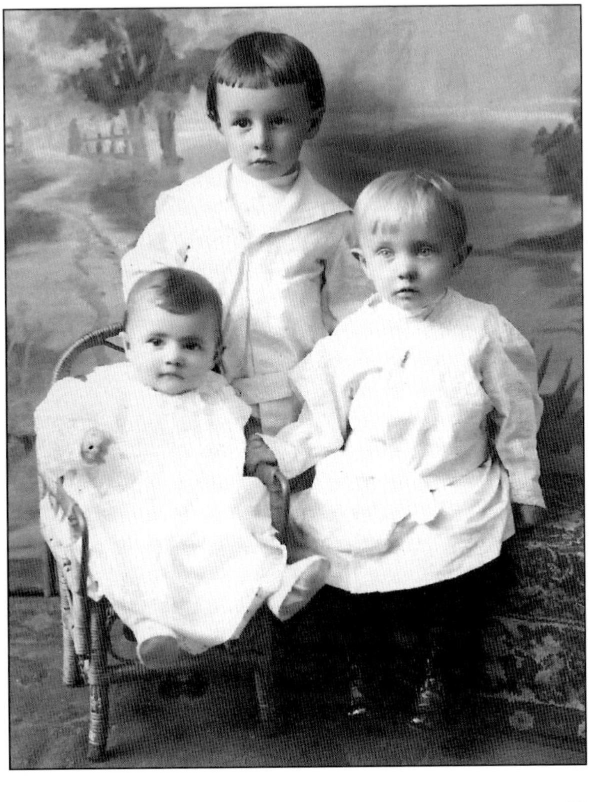

Nichols Family, 1910. Loana Nichols (left) is pictured with her brothers Julius Nichols (above) and Estes Nichols (right). Loana Nichols married Paul Gadaire and raised Bruce, Douglas, Russell, Paula, Laurel, and George Gadaire. She lived to the age of 98. Estes Nichols succumbed to polio shortly after this photograph was taken after playing in drain water near their Main Street home. (Courtesy of Loana Nichols Gadaire and Paula Gadaire Woodard.)

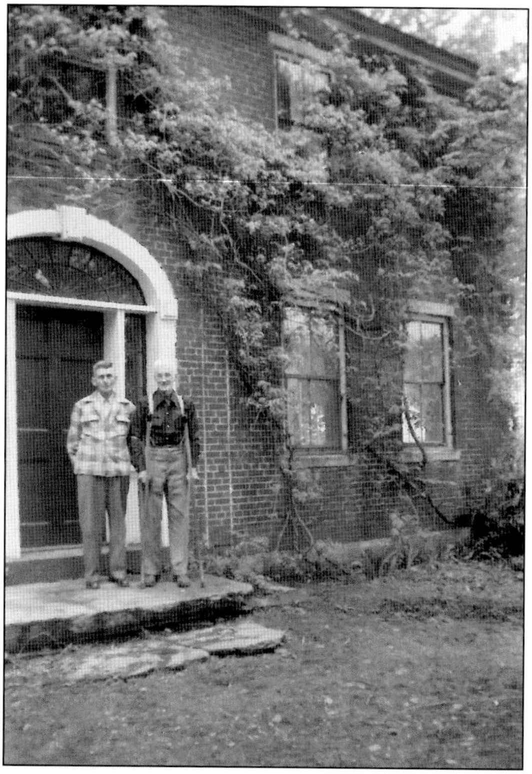

Coes Farm, 1949. Robert Craig managed a dairy farm on Lake Road with views encompassing both the Quaboag River and Lake Quaboag to the north. In the farmhouse doorway are Robert Craig's father-in-law, Herbert Campbell (left), and Herbert Campbell's brother Fred of New Brunswick, Canada. Built in 1816 for Samuel Ward, this brick Federal-style home has granite windowsills and lintels and an elliptical fanlight. (Courtesy of Marguerite Craig Ericson.)

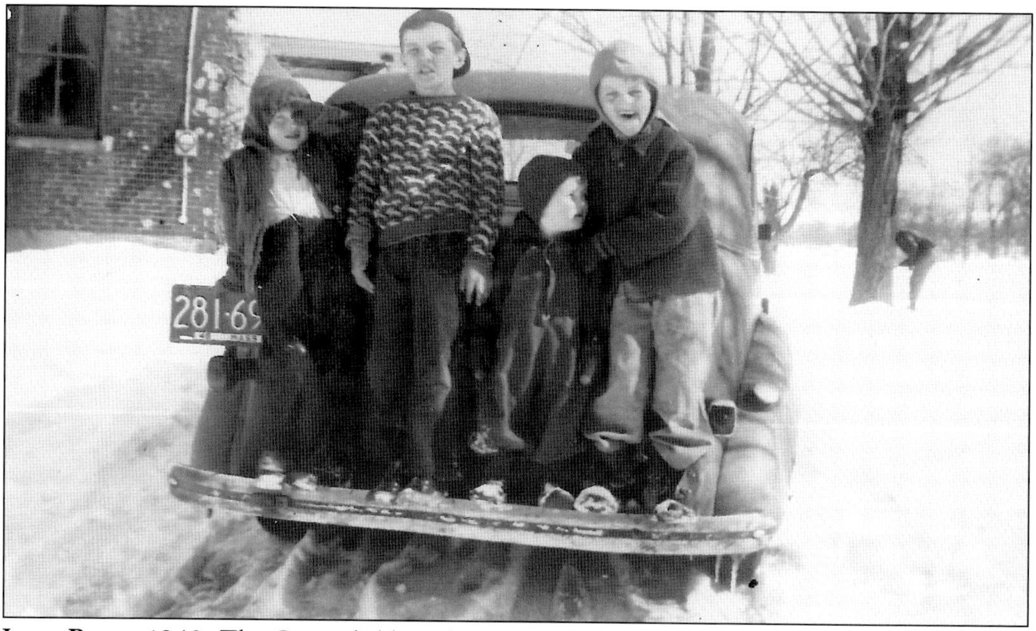

Lake Road, 1948. The Craig children, living at Coes farm, ride on the bumper of this 1932 Chevrolet. From left to right are Marguerite "Maggie," Robert "Bud," John "Jack," and Roderick "Rod." They were most impressed with the two horns sported by the car: a city horn (ah-oo-gah) and a country horn (toot-toot). Their father, Robert Craig, checks a tapped sugar maple in the background. (Courtesy of Marguerite Craig Ericson.)

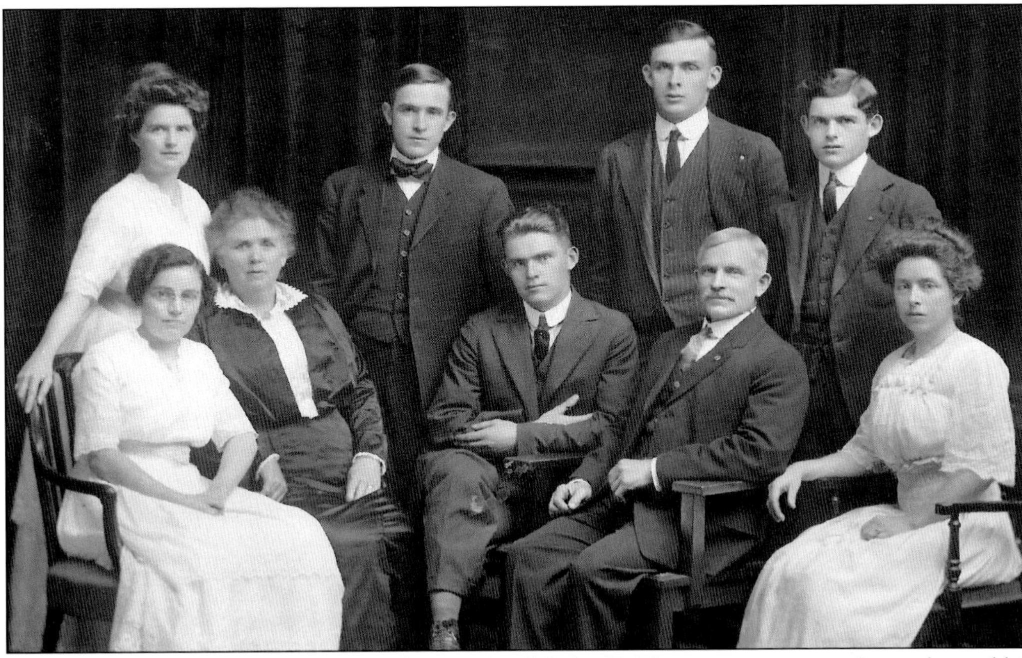

KIMBALL STREET, 1920. Emigrating from Ireland, John F. Clancy was a mason by trade, and his wife, Catherine Harrington, ran the household, instilling impeccable table manners and a love of learning in her children. Seated are, from left to right, (first row) Annie, Catherine, John, John F., and Mary; (second row) Nellie, William, Henry, and James Raymond Clancy. Henry became the father of George, longtime fire chief. (Courtesy of Barbara Clancy.)

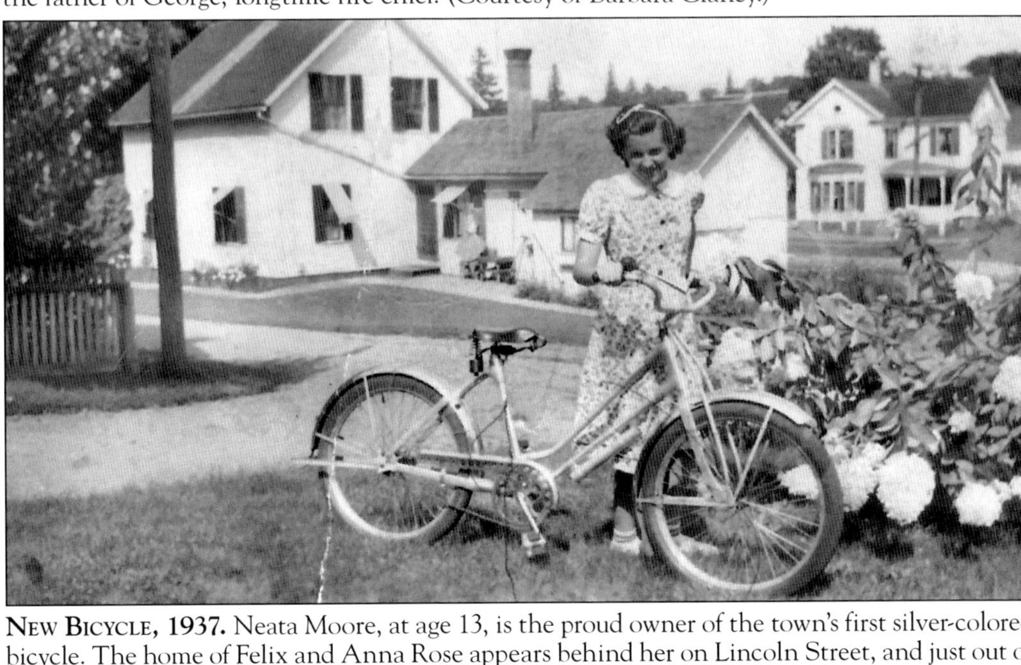

NEW BICYCLE, 1937. Neata Moore, at age 13, is the proud owner of the town's first silver-colored bicycle. The home of Felix and Anna Rose appears behind her on Lincoln Street, and just out of the frame on the right stood a barn for the Roses' cows, horses, and chickens. The livestock were pastured in a field farther down Pleasant Street, bordered by Hyde, Kimball, and Mill Streets. (Courtesy of Neata Moore Campbell.)

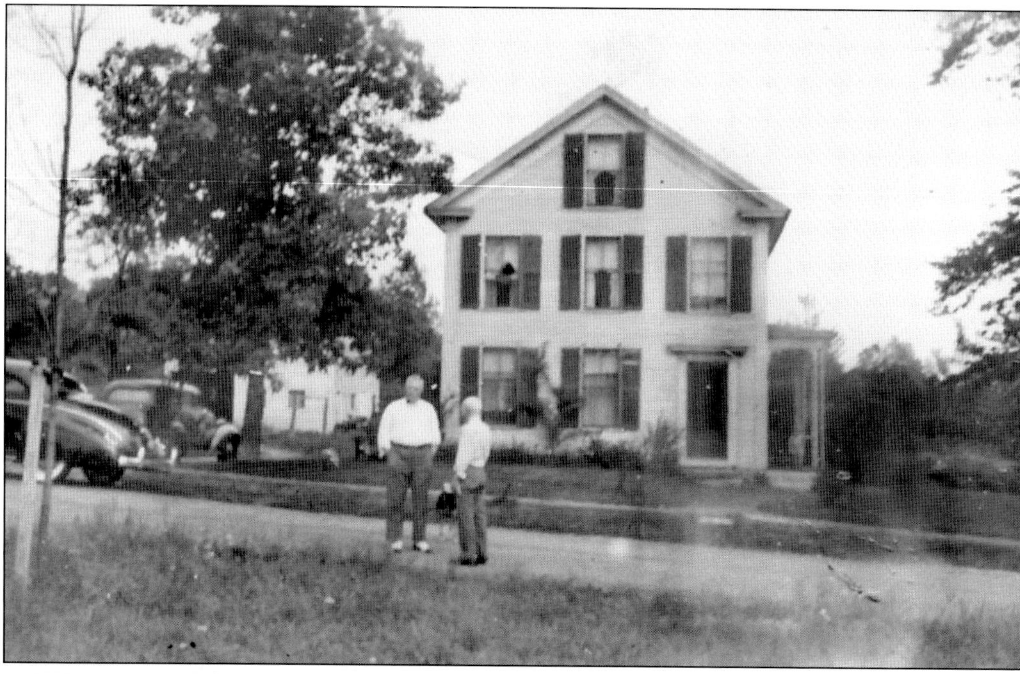

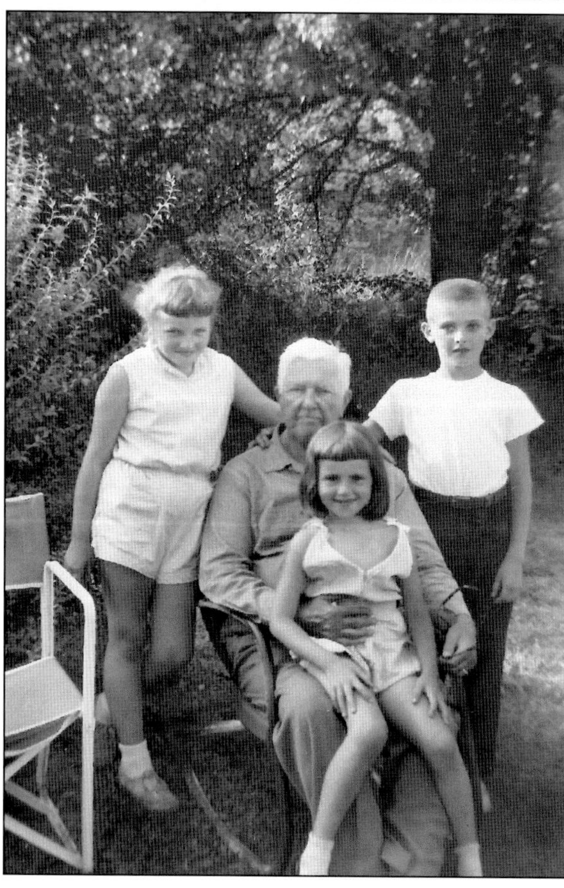

KIMBALL STREET. Above, Andrew J. Leach (left) chats with an unidentified neighbor at his home near the intersection of Hyde Street around 1939. Leach, at various turns, served on the Democratic Town Committee and the Citizen's Town Committee, was elected as selectman and measurer of leathers, and headed an American Legion minstrel show. He was employed by McLaurin-Jones Company. The house on Kimball Street remained in the family for many years, as his daughter Mary Leach, principal of the elementary school, lived there until after her retirement. Mary Leach was also a tireless supporter of community endeavors. At left, Andrew Leach enjoys a sunny afternoon in 1956 with his grandchildren, including sisters Margaret and Katherine Docwra (in lap) and Andrew Leach. (Both, courtesy of Docwra family.)

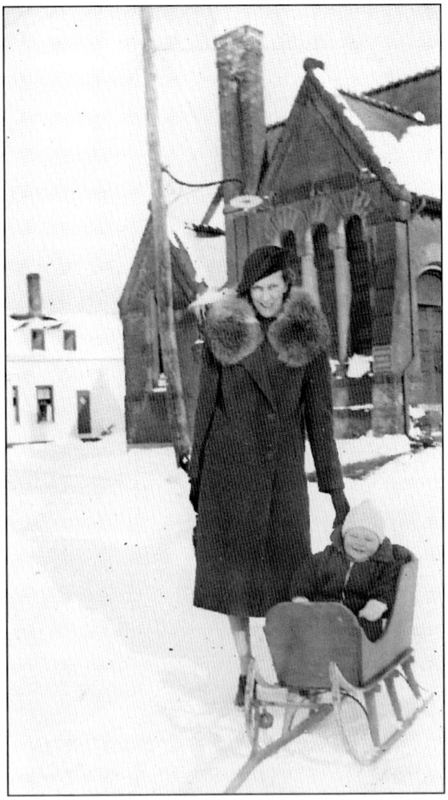

Heirloom Sleigh, 1938. David Clark Mellen, born in August 1937, smiles in front of the library in the sleigh his great-grandfather John W. Livermore crafted in his Central Street furniture store. Enjoying the winter day with him is his mother Grace Clark Mellen's friend Phyllis Wheeler of Rutland. The sleigh is still in family hands, now in the state of Virginia. (Courtesy of Claudia Mellen Golemboski.)

Gadaires and Mellens, 1939. Sitting on the stoop are Jean Ann Gadaire (back left) and Clifford Gadaire (back right) with David Mellen (front left) and Claudia Mellen (front right), for whom they often babysat. Both families resided on the corner of Lincoln and Sherman Streets, in separate apartments, across from St. Mary's Church. (Courtesy of Claudia Mellen Golemboski.)

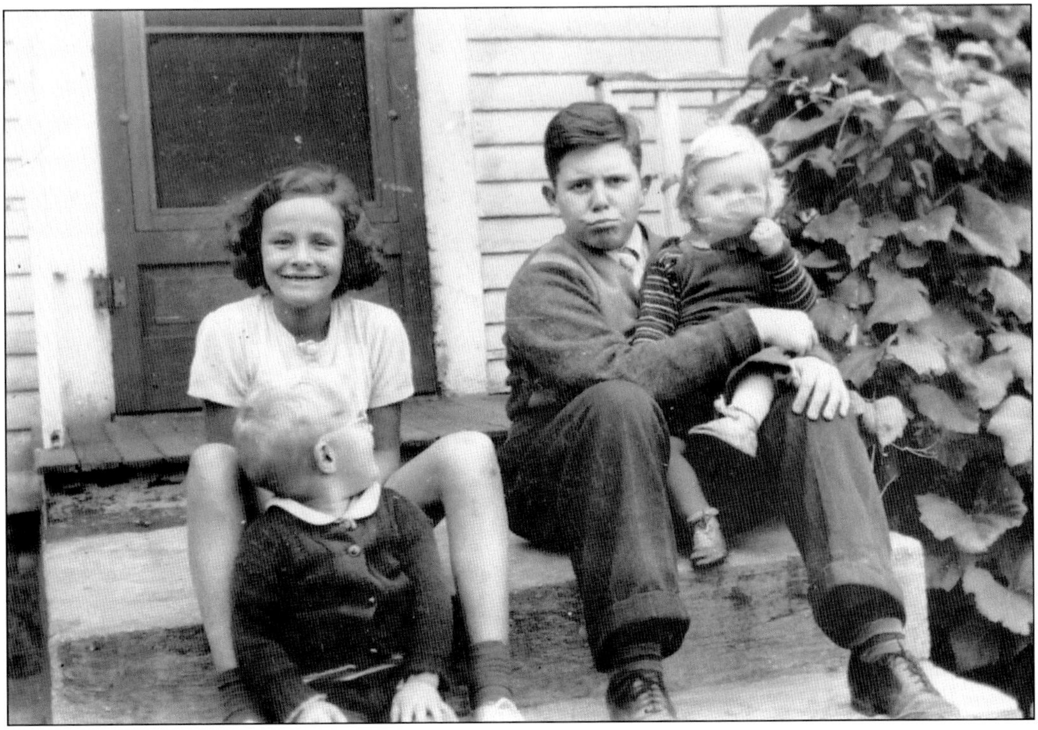

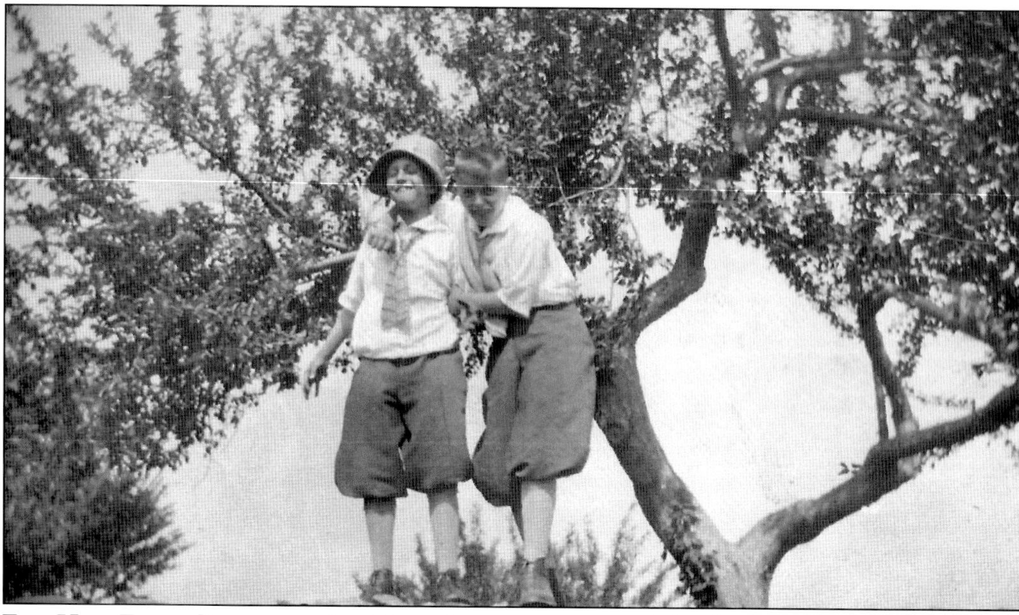

Elm Hill Farm Orchard. The Noyes boys, Alton and Arland, moved to Brookfield from Coventry, Vermont. Here, they are seen among the apple trees on Elm Hill. Their grandfather Gilbert Ware, with whom they made their home on Howard Street, worked at the farm. Alton Noyes served in the Navy and later became office manager at McLaurin-Jones Company after a stint working in finance in Manhattan. (Courtesy of May-Boyce Collection.)

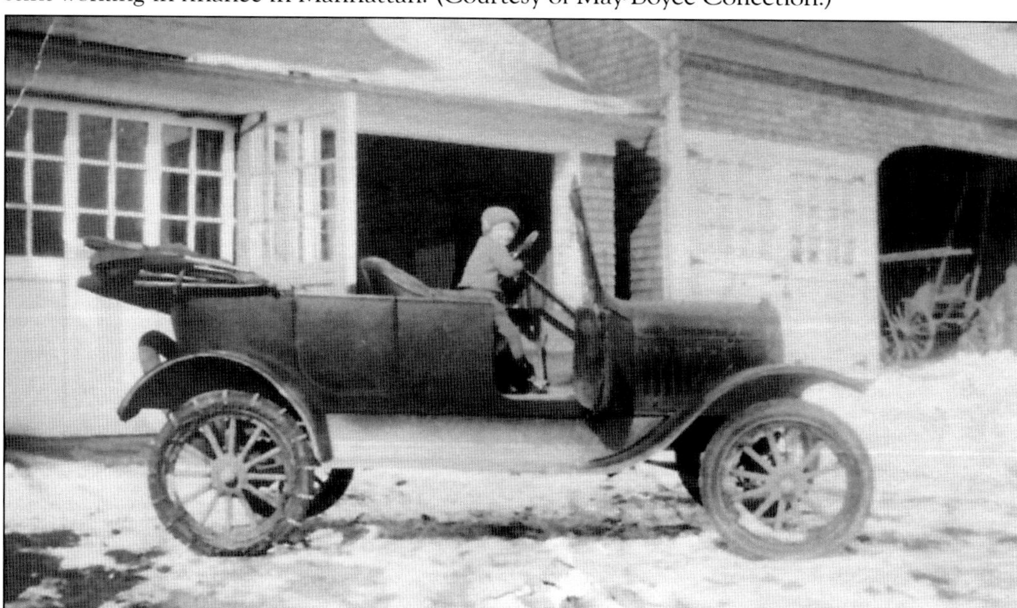

Ford at Elm Hill Farm. Barbara Vivian Boyce poses in a work vehicle around 1915. Her father, Lee Boyce, was a teacher in New York State before becoming the farm superintendent at Elm Hill Farm. In later years, farm vehicles were sent to Brookfield High School to transport industrious students to the orchard to pick and polish apples after school. (Courtesy of May-Boyce Collection.)

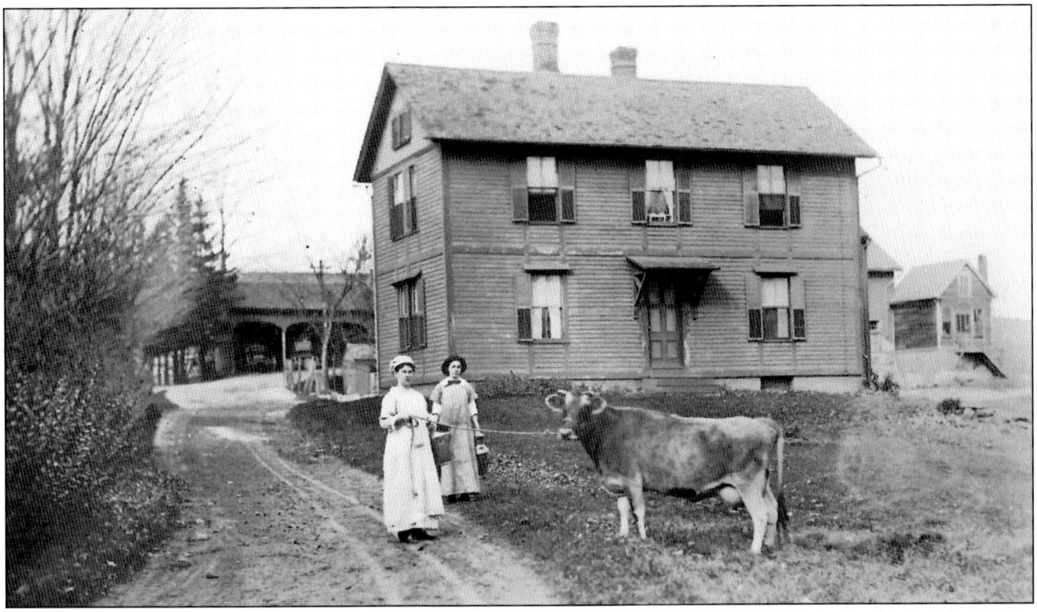

Elm Hill Farm Tenant House. This late-1800s photograph shows the tenant house before a porch and ell were added. From the 1930s, farm superintendent Lee Boyce lived here with his family—his office and a milk room were in the back. The manure building at right, used for storing fertilizer until it could be spread on the fields, featured a scooper on a track. (Courtesy of Brookfield Historical Commission.)

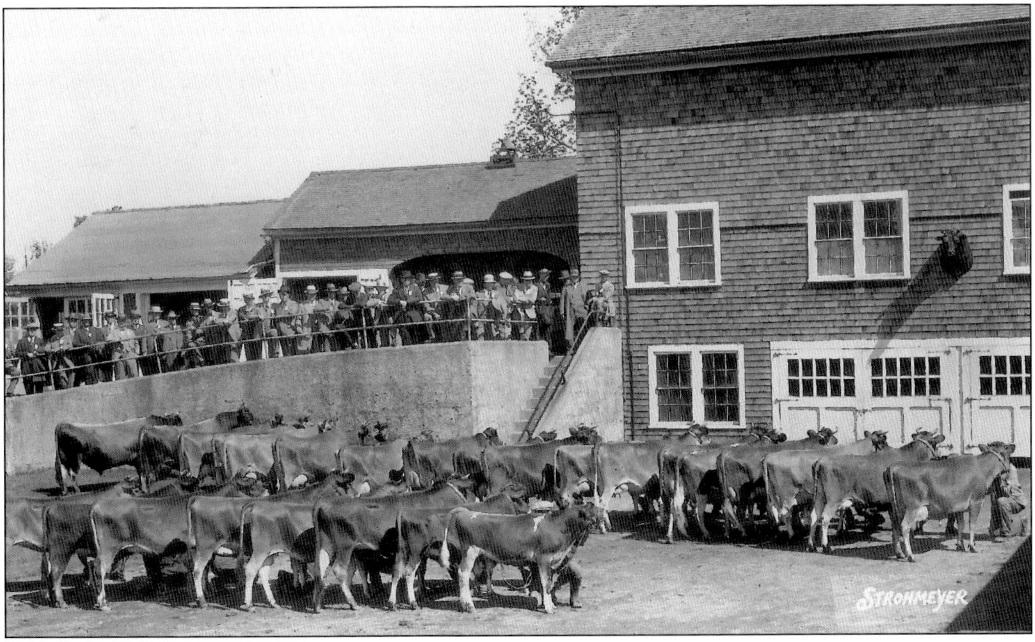

Jerseys on Display. The "gold medal cows," sons and daughters of champion bull Xenia Sultan, warrant rapt attention at Elm Hill Farm during the late 1930s. The farm hosted both large groups, such as the American Jersey Cattle Club, who were at times served breakfast on the grounds, and individuals, such as Red Sox player Robert Moses "Lefty" Grove, himself a cattle owner. (Photograph by Strohmeyer; courtesy of Howard Whitcomb.)

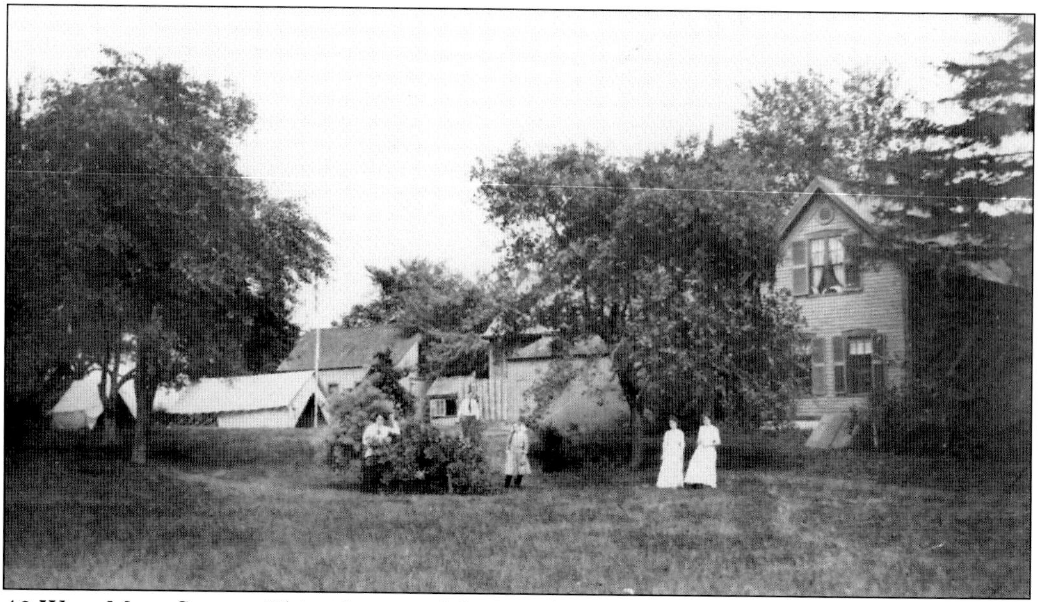

40 WEST MAIN STREET. This side view of the Burt house, with several outbuildings, shows tents set up for visiting family members on July 17, 1912. From left to right are Grace, Henry, and Ethel Burt, Marion Farrar, and Helen Burt. For many years, the barn that later became Dave's Appliance was turned into a haunted house for local children to visit on Halloween. (Courtesy of Trish Caron.)

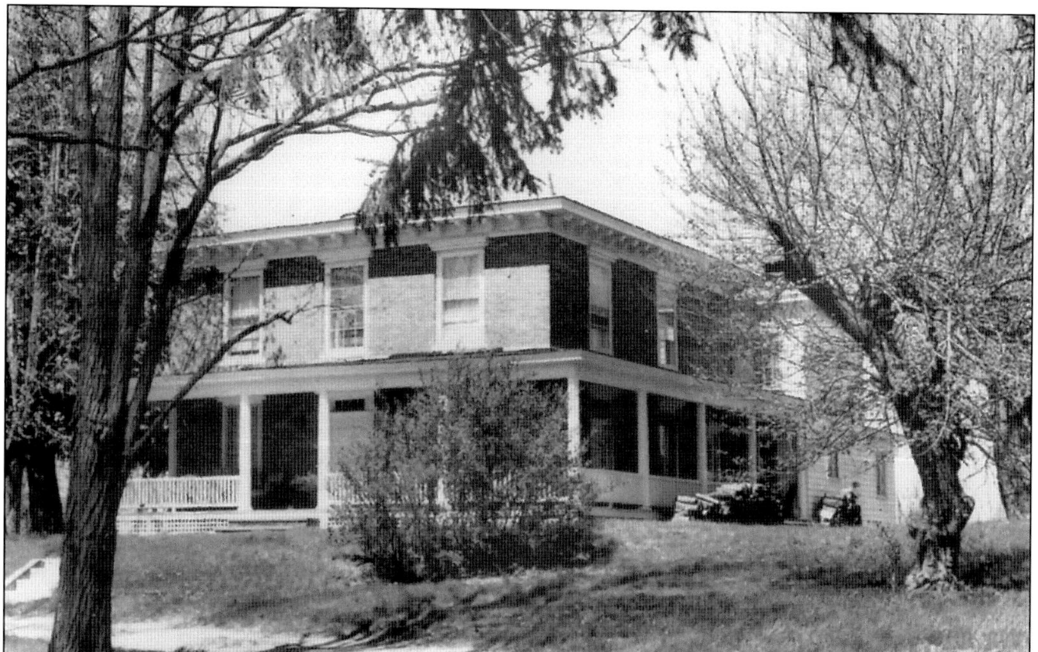

38 WEST MAIN STREET, C. 1950. This brick Greek Revival–style house was built just before the Civil War by Daniel Adams, a prosperous farmer and member of the Masons. A 44-foot-square house with floor-to-ceiling windows, wraparound porch, transom window, and summer kitchen, it was deeded to Daniel's son George, also a farmer, in late 1860. (Courtesy of Thomas and Jennifer Rettig.)

BOYNTON AND PRIZIO FAMILIES. Phillip Henry and Julia Stone Boynton, shown at right in their wedding portrait, were married on April 15, 1909. They had seven children and made their home on Mill Street. Julia died at age 27, resulting in all of the children being sent to live with friends of the family. One daughter, Grace Boynton Prizio, is now Brookfield's oldest resident. She eloped with William Gabrial Prizio, and they married in Wilton, New Hampshire, on January 7, 1930; the couple, shown below, had another ceremony a year later in St. Mary's Church in Brookfield and lived on Quaboag Street. (Both, courtesy of Grace Boynton Prizio and Linda Prizio Lincoln.)

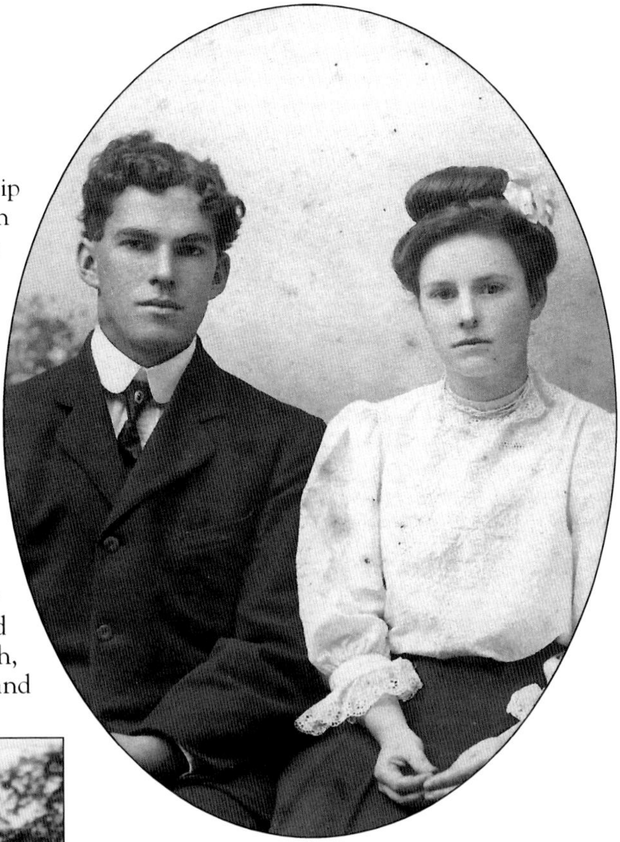

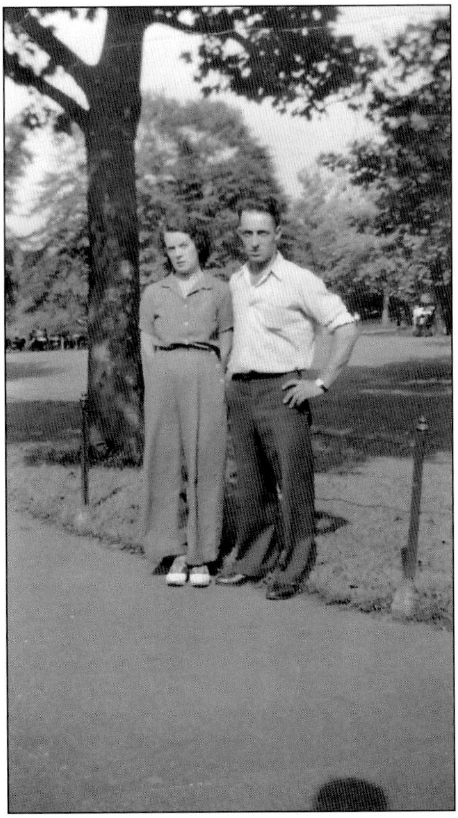

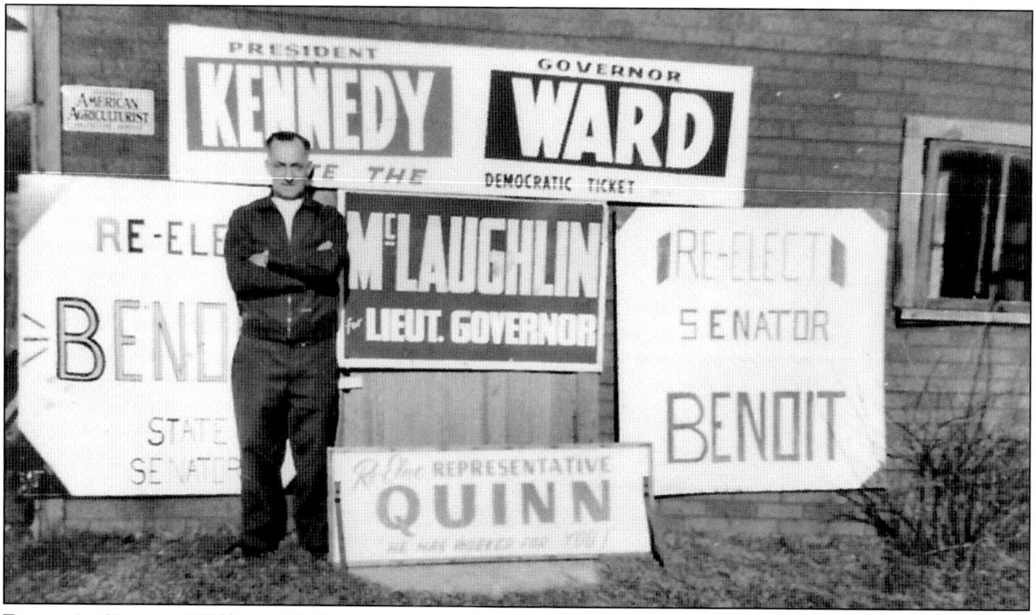

PRIZIO'S GROVE. William G. Prizio was well versed in Democratic political action committees. These campaign signs from the early 1960s showcase material used to promote candidates. Prizio's Grove, a family picnic and recreation area on Quaboag Street, held clambakes and other events for town businesses. The barn is still standing. (Courtesy of Grace Boynton Prizio and Linda Prizio Lincoln.)

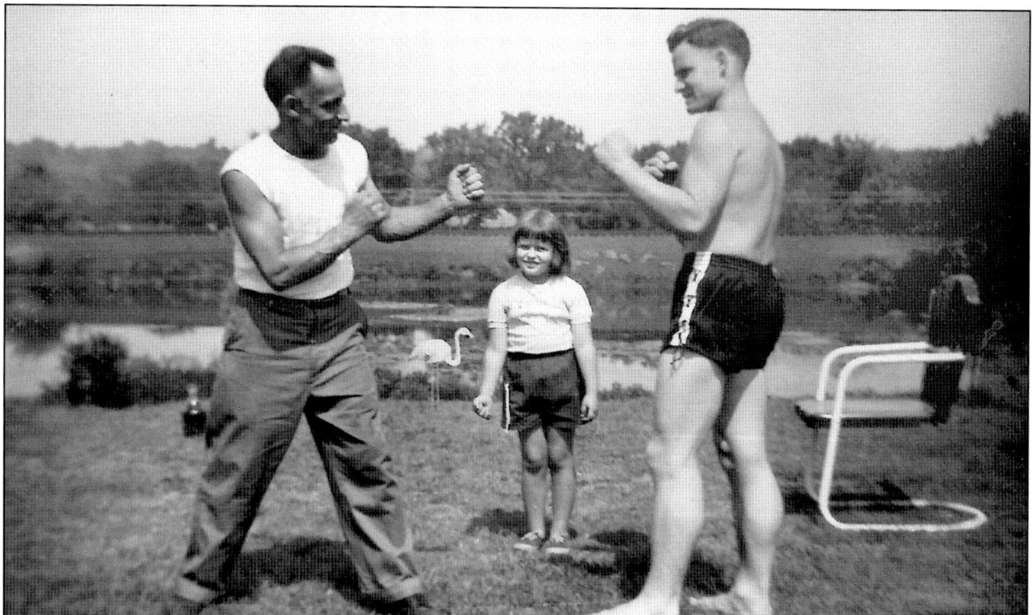

PRIZIO FAMILY. Linda Mae Prizio delights in a mock battle between her father, William G. Prizio (left), and brother William C. Prizio in their yard at 22 Quaboag Street. William C. Prizio enlisted in the Army in 1956 and served in Germany for three years. Linda Prizio married Gary Lincoln and served as town clerk for over two decades. (Courtesy of Grace Boynton Prizio and Linda Prizio Lincoln.)

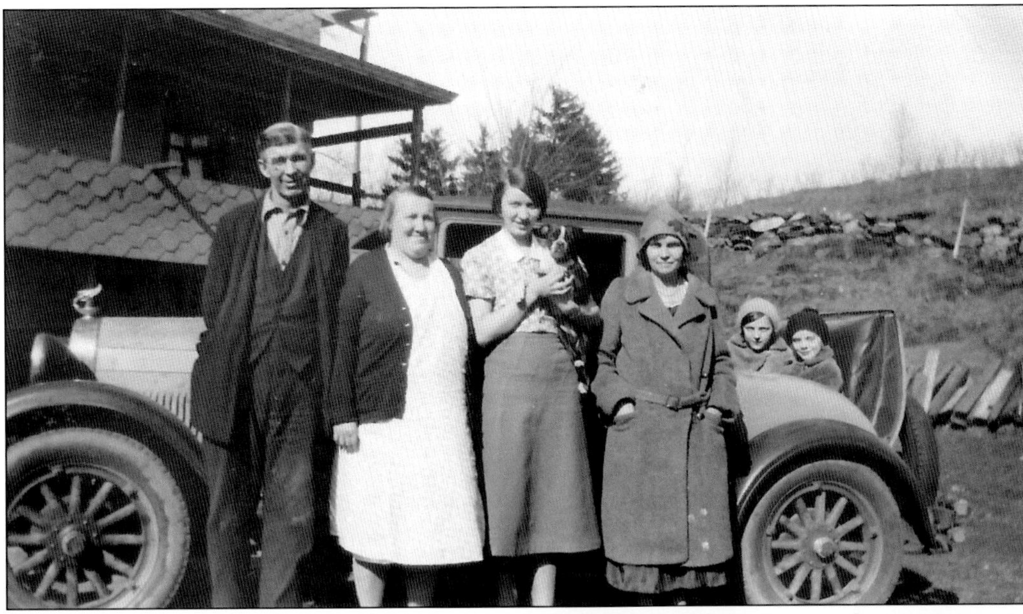

HAYDEN AVENUE. The photograph above, taken in 1934, shows the Menard family at their Hayden Avenue home, the last house on the south side, with Twichell's Grove in the background. From left to right are parents Moses and Flora, their daughters Lillian and Louise, and two neighborhood children in the jump seat of Louise's fiancé Waldo Bemis's Essex. Siblings not present include Mildred and Evon Amelia Menard. The Menards all attended Brookfield High School. Louise Menard, an avid photographer, married Waldo Bemis in 1935 and took the photograph at right of her husband with her sister Lillian Menard in front of the same family home on Hayden Avenue. Louise went on to work at Gavitt Wire Company on Central Street. (Photographs by Louise Menard Bemis; courtesy of Sheila Pronto McCarthy.)

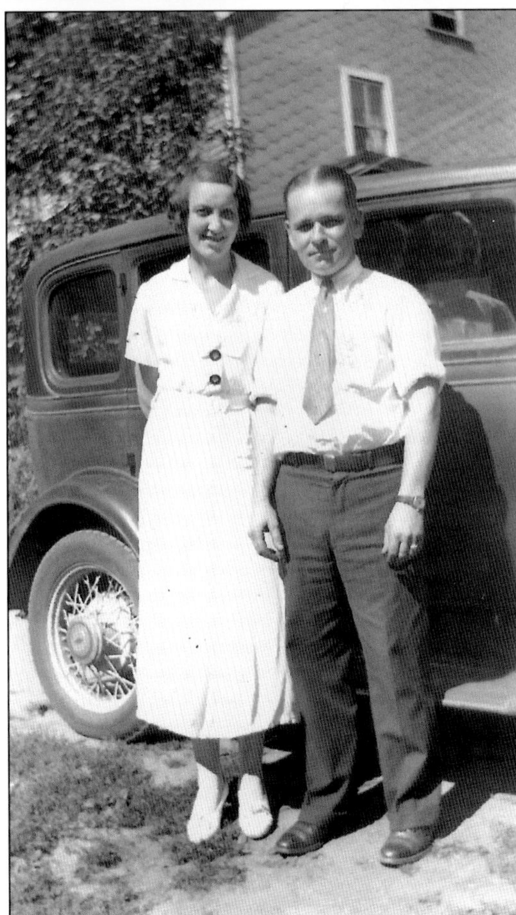

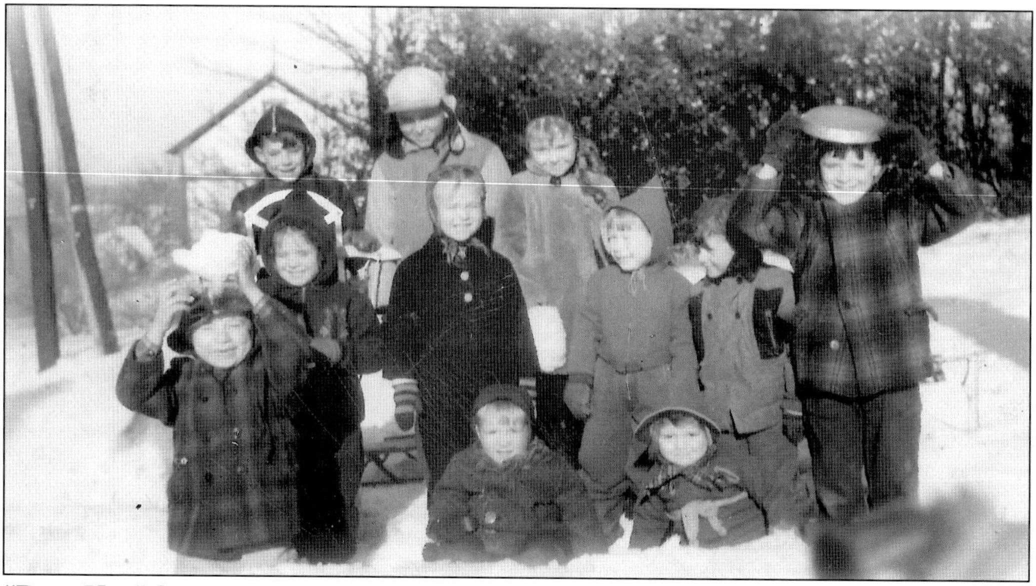

"Dixie Hill" Sledders, 1949. Snow plowers often left Dixie Hill, also known as Grove Street, untouched after a storm for the neighborhood's enjoyment. Taking a break from sledding are, from left to right, (first row) Anthony Faugno, Clifford Fournier, and Laurel Gadaire; (second row) Paula Gadaire, Janet Brown, Alfred Pratt, Martin Faugno, and Bruce Gadaire; (third row) Russell Gadaire, Rufus Streeter, and Elinor Reed. (Courtesy of Loana Nichols Gadaire and Paula Gadaire Woodard.)

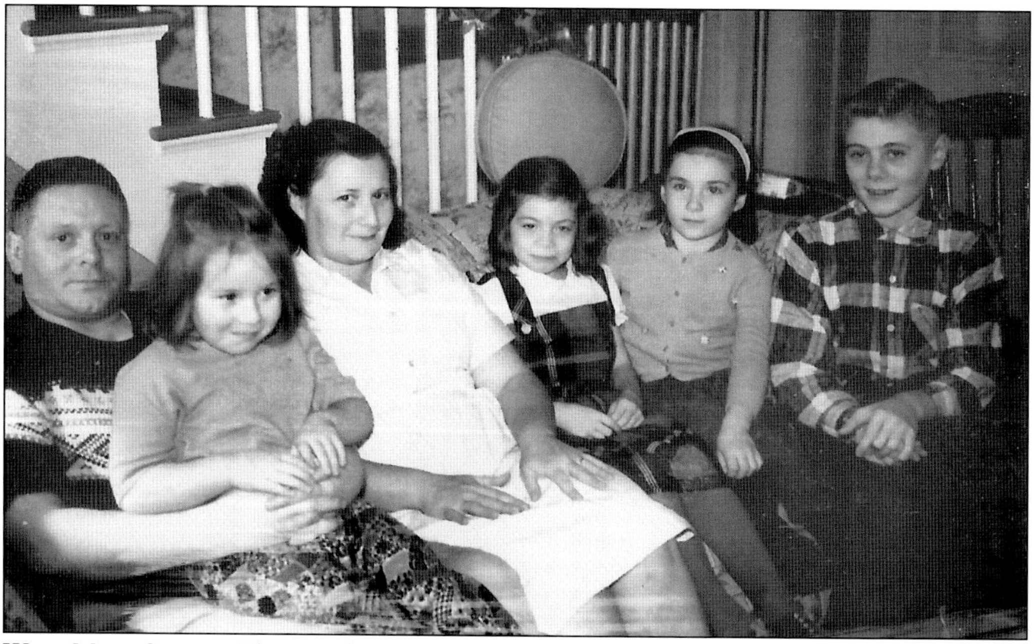

West Main Street. The Ruggles family of Maple Street celebrates the Christmas holiday at grandmother Carrie Ruggles's home, known as the Ruggles farm. Here, the family gathers for a photograph around 1960. From left to right are father Robert K. Ruggles Jr., Carole, mother Marian Steadman Ruggles, Beatrice, Mary, and Robert K. Ruggles III. (Photograph by Lewis Ayers; courtesy of Ruggles family.)

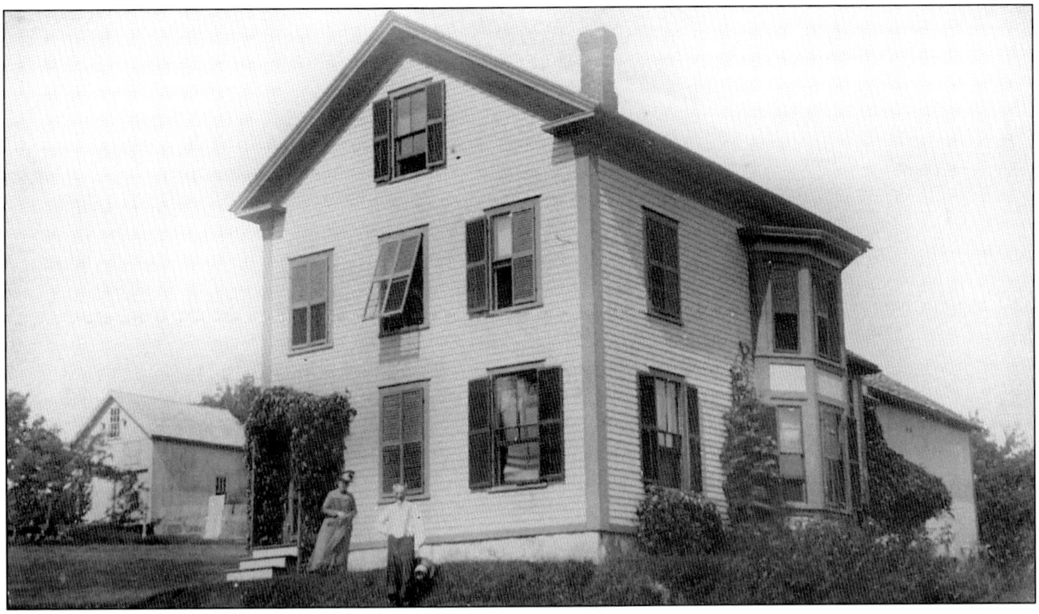

Howard Street. The Gass and Holcomb families lived in this house in the late 1800s when this photograph was taken. The Greek Revival–style home was built in 1865 by George Oakes, a local grocer who later managed the town's first telephone office. It still stands as the southernmost home on the east side of Howard Street. (Courtesy of longtime resident.)

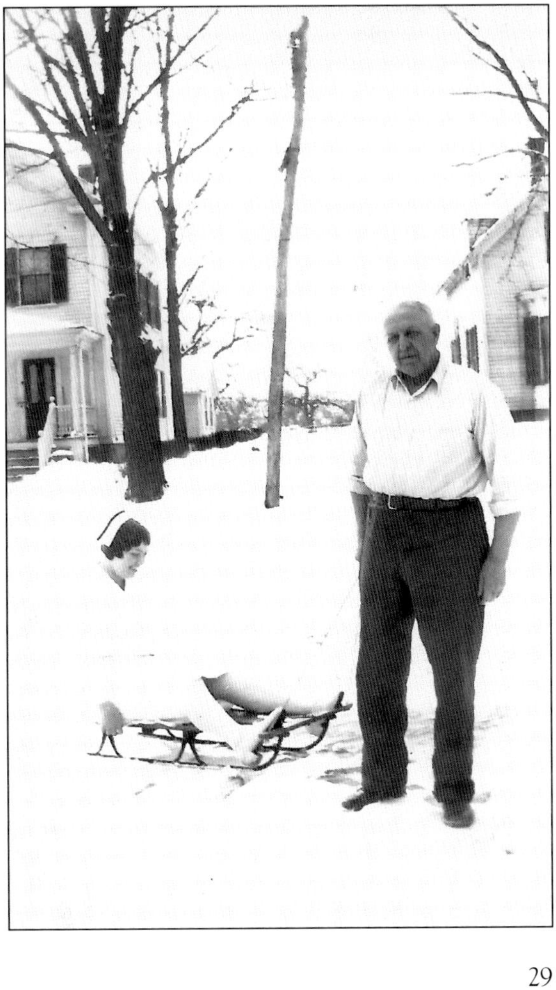

Lincoln Street, 1932. Ernest A. Colburn, a prominent business owner in the town center, takes a break from caring for his invalid wife by giving her nurse Ann Carlson Dahl a short ride one mild wintry day. Bertha Colburn appears to be enjoying the scene from their porch, as seen on the next page. (Photograph by Louise Menard Bemis; courtesy of Sheila Pronto McCarthy.)

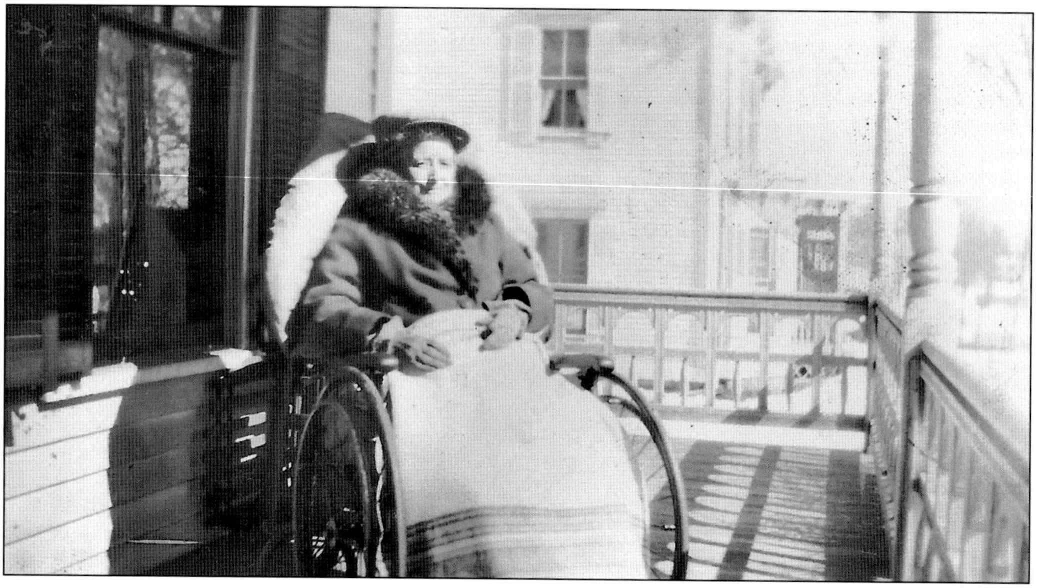

Colburn Home, 1932. Bertha Colburn, shown above, was an invalid for some time before her death on November 21, 1932. Her husband, Ernest Colburn, owned the stables where the fire department kept their horses, at the rear of the Central House on Central Street. He advertised his business as Colburn's Livery, Board, and Feed Stable and offered carriages for meeting trains as well as carriages furnished for weddings and sleighing parties for up to 30 people. Town records of 1898 show that Colburn paid taxes on seven horses, eight vehicles, one omnibus, one wagonette, harnesses, and robes. By 1916, he owned this house on Lincoln Street, shown below, and a lake cottage as well. (Photographs by Louise Menard Bemis; courtesy of Sheila Pronto McCarthy.)

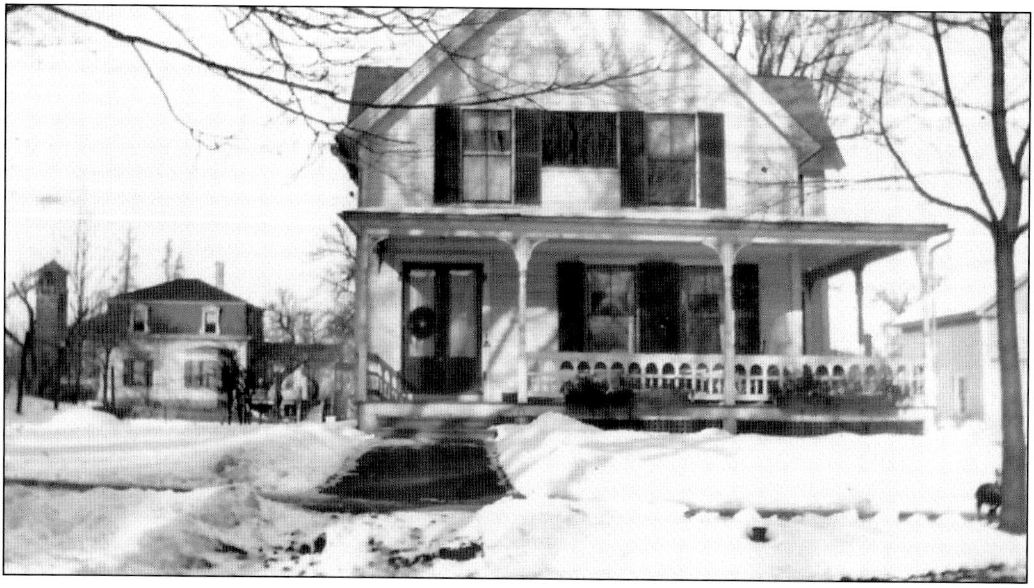

Three

Around Town

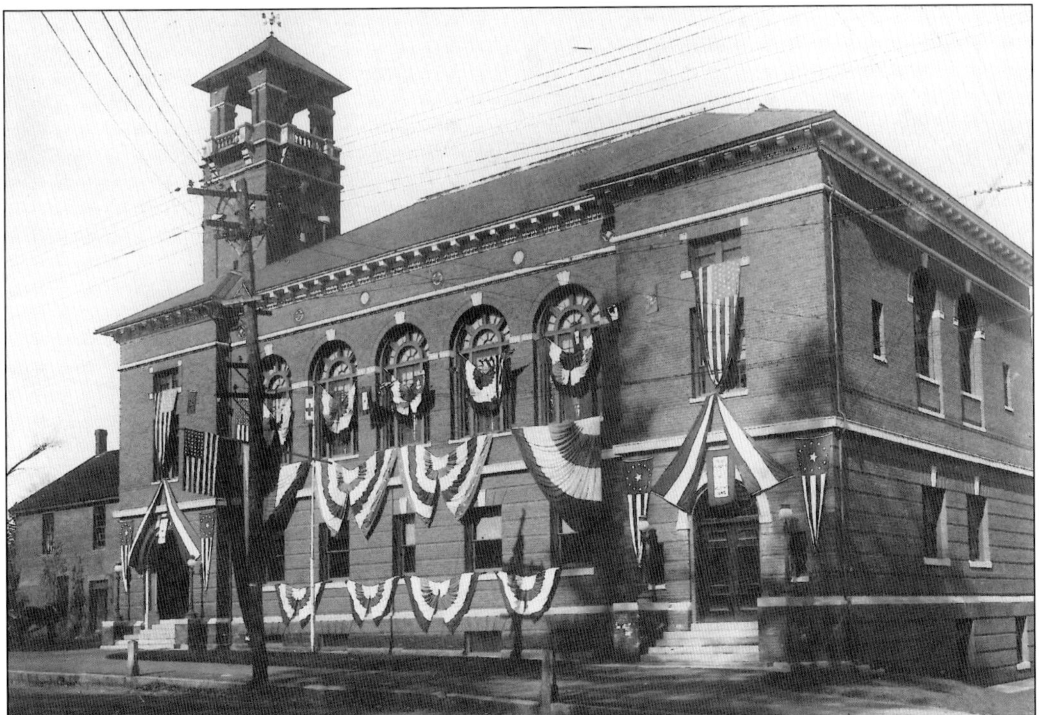

Town Hall, c. 1918. Replacing the former town hall, which burned in 1902, this structure was dedicated on May 7, 1904. This view with the town hall festooned with banners for a hero's welcome home from World War I shows, at left, the old schoolhouse, which housed the Merrick Public Library until 1884. (Courtesy of May-Boyce Collection.)

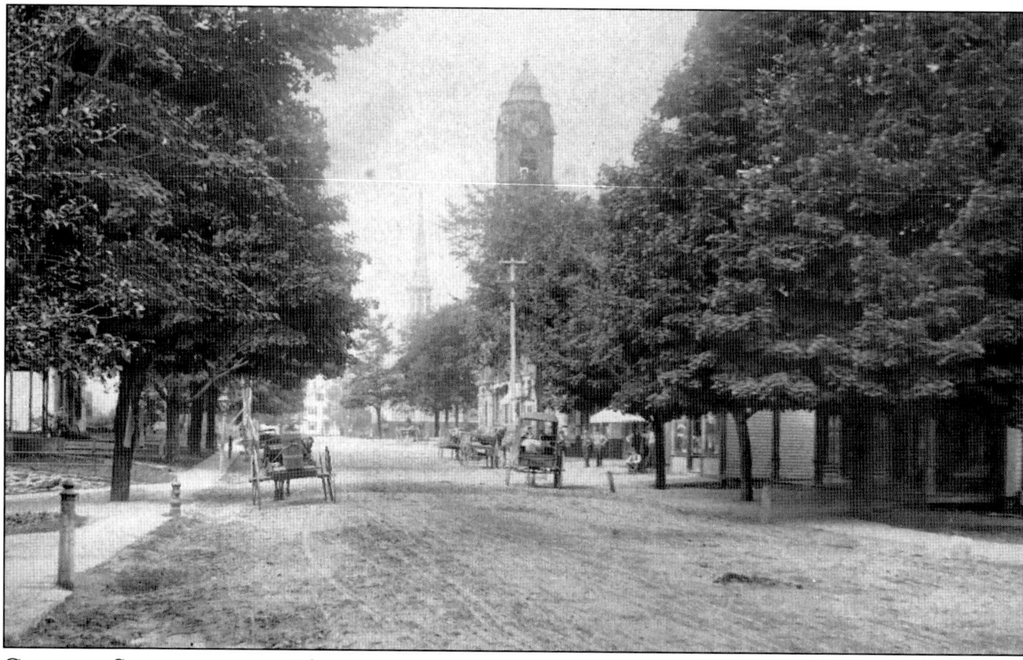

CENTRAL STREET, 1890S. The main throughway in town was lined with trees and with posts for the horses and buggies carting their owners to the shopping center of Brookfield. Note the telegraph pole aligned under the tower of the original town hall. (Courtesy of White's Landing on behalf of Winifred Broughton.)

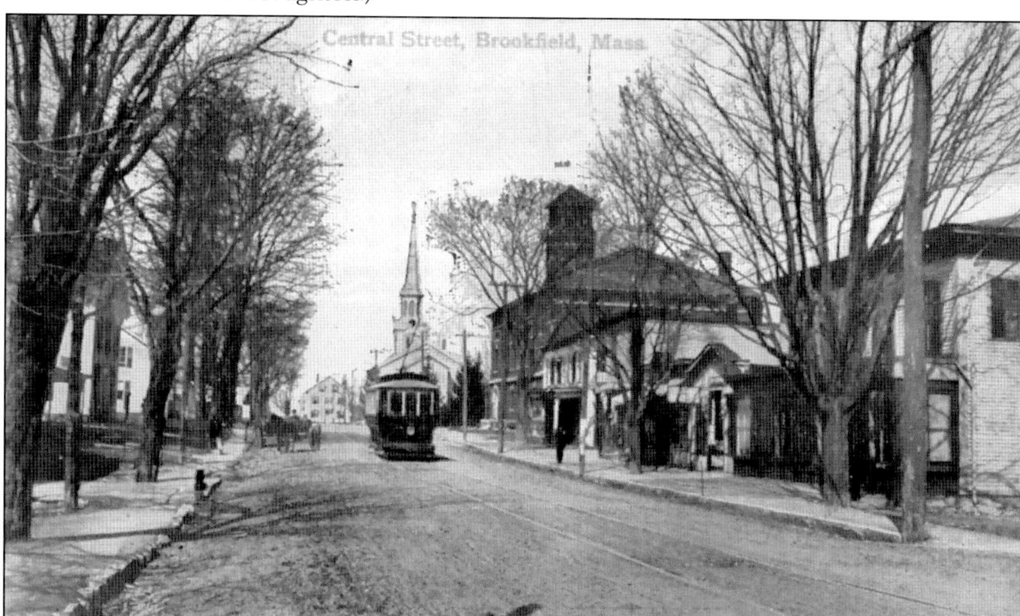

TROLLEY ON CENTRAL STREET, 1909. The Warren, Brookfield & Spencer Street Railway was organized in February 1896 during a meeting at the Hotel Metropole. The route was completed to West Warren by September 1897, with 10 single-truck 10-bench open cars built and seven single-truck closed cars built. Early riding exceeded expectations: several cars carried 100 passengers, although, a total of 50 was the seating capacity. (Courtesy of James Allen.)

Central Street Gentleman, c. 1890. The building commonly known as the Gerald Block (left) housed a clothing store, grocer, and dentist. John Winthrop Livermore dealt in furniture, pictures, coffins, and caskets at the Livermore Block (right). He married Mary Matilda Giffin, the only daughter of Charles Giffin, whose Civil War letters to and from his family are available at the library. (Photograph by Charles P. Blanchard; courtesy of Blanchard Means Foundation.)

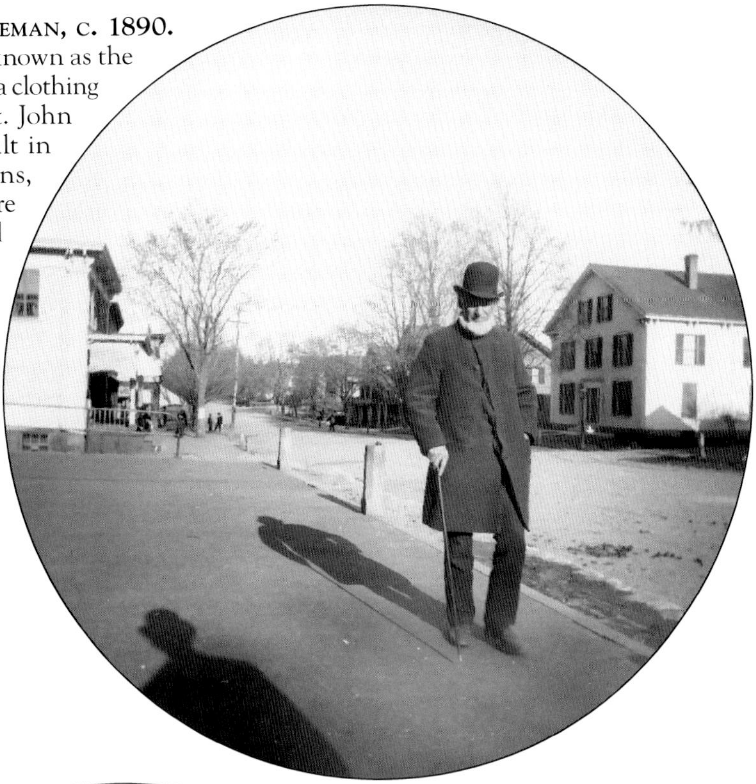

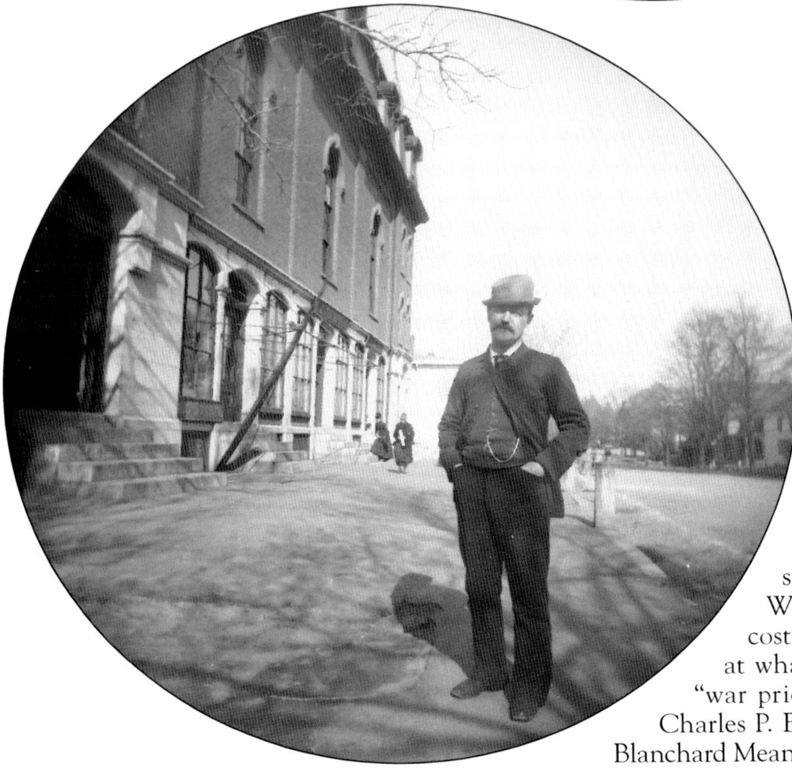

Original Town Hall, c. 1890. Built in 1866 and destroyed by fire on September 4–5, 1902, the first town hall housed municipal offices as well as businesses. Due to being constructed shortly after the Civil War, building materials cost an exorbitant $65,000 at what were referred to as "war prices." (Photograph by Charles P. Blanchard; courtesy of Blanchard Means Foundation.)

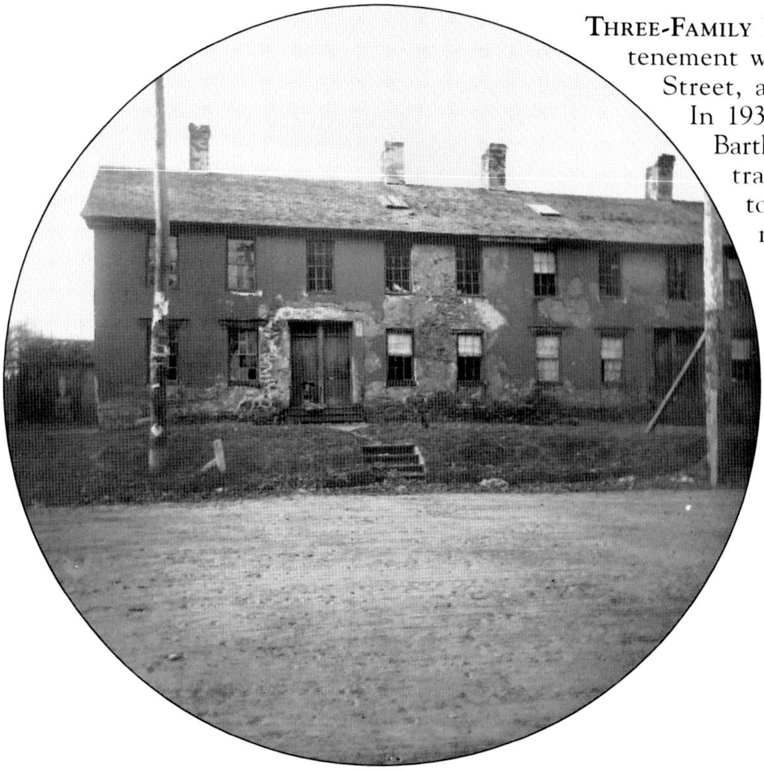

THREE-FAMILY HOUSE, C. 1890. This tenement was located on Central Street, across from town hall. In 1939, septuagenarian Ella Bartlett described Brookfield's transition from busy mill town to sleepy village, noting that because of job strikes in the 1880s "many people moved away . . . mill buildings just stood idle. After awhile, some of them was torn down, others just left to fall apart." (Photograph by Charles P. Blanchard; courtesy of Blanchard Means Foundation.)

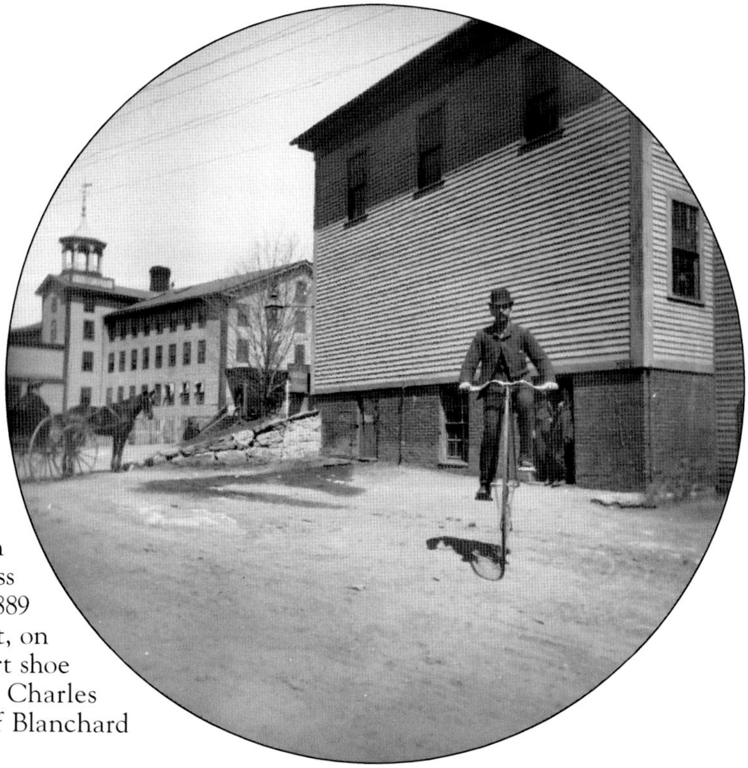

WARNER BLOCK, PLEASANT STREET, C. 1890. A man rides a penny-farthing in front of Oscar Bemis and Company, "dealers in meats of all kinds, vegetables in their season, lard, butter, canned goods, and all goods such as are found in a First Class Market," according to the 1889 business directory. At left, on Central Street, is the Burt shoe factory. (Photograph by Charles P. Blanchard; courtesy of Blanchard Means Foundation.)

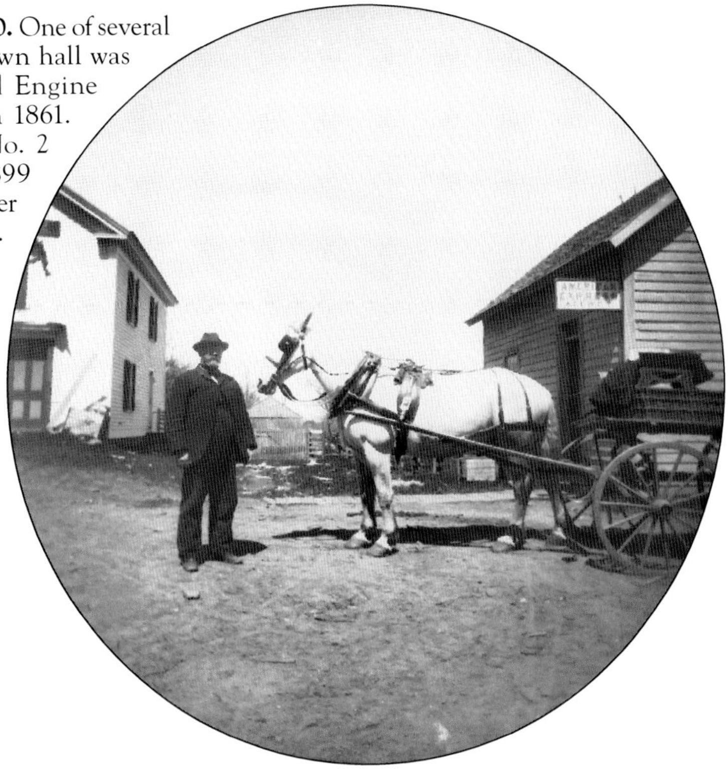

Behind Town Hall, c. 1890. One of several buildings behind the old town hall was the Cataract No. 2 Hand Engine Company (left), erected in 1861. The change to Steamer No. 2 Company occurred in 1899 with the purchase of a steamer engine for the fire department. The other building pictured is the town's American Express office. (Photograph by Charles P. Blanchard; courtesy of Blanchard Means Foundation.)

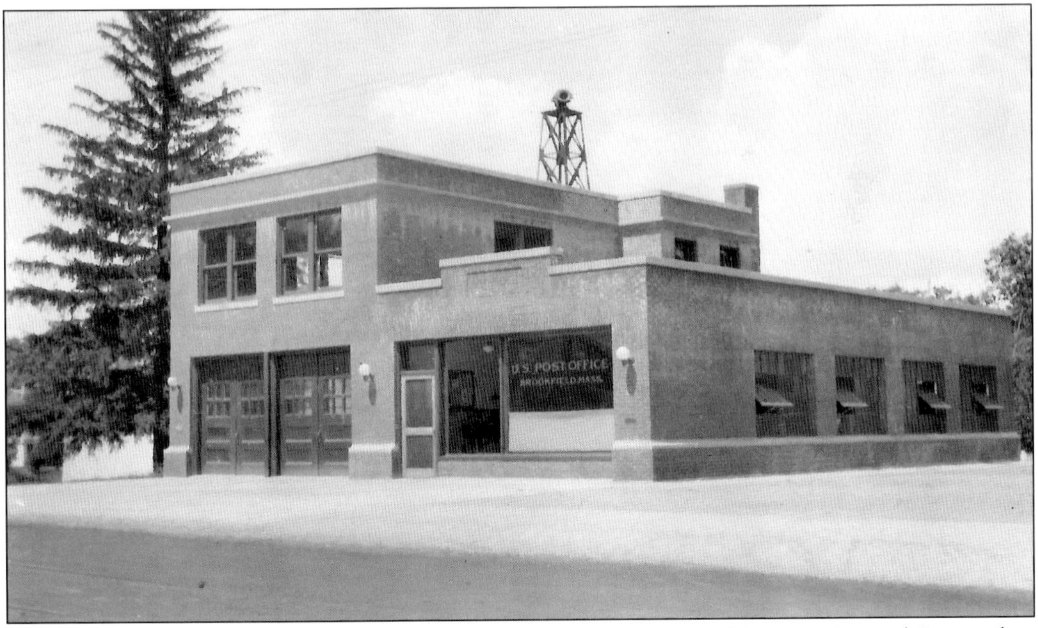

Fire Station and Post Office. This image of the new 1928 building on Central Street that housed both the fire department and post office was donated in memory of Velma Frazier to the Brookfield Fire Department. The donor wrote, "Velma appreciated the kindnesses shown her by the B.F.D. over the years . . . and she looked forward to enjoying your great Chicken Barbecues!" (Courtesy of Peter Martell.)

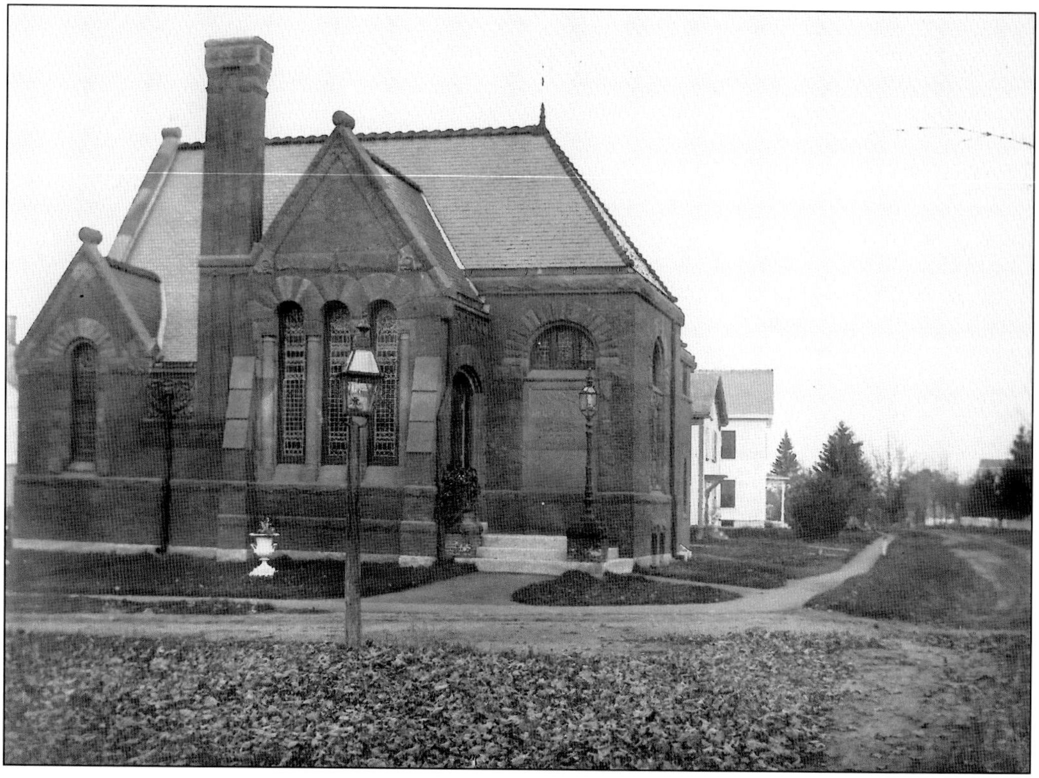

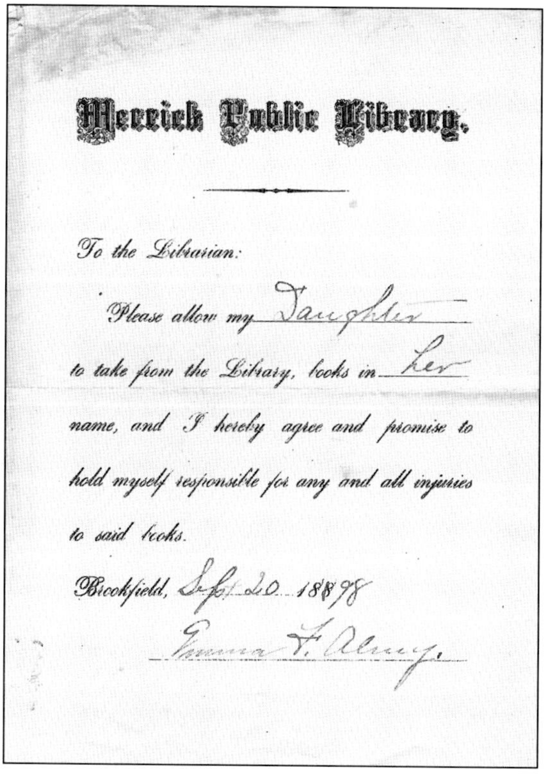

Merrick Public Library.

To the Librarian:

Please allow my Daughter to take from the Library, books in her name, and I hereby agree and promise to hold myself responsible for any and all injuries to said books.

Brookfield, Sept. 20. 1898

Emma F. Olney

BANISTER MEMORIAL HALL. Three generous donations made the town's library a reality. In 1867, Pliny Merrick, a Supreme Court justice, state representative, and senator, bequeathed the town $10,000 and his personal collection of books. In 1882, Nancy Felton donated the land on the corner of Common and Lincoln Streets as a tribute to her late husband, Oliver Felton. In 1883, William Banister of New York, a Brookfield native who had attended the Over-the-River schoolhouse in his youth, donated $10,000 to construct the building to house the library, to be known as Banister Memorial Hall, Merrick Public Library, in memory of his Brookfield ancestors. Above is an early view of the library; at left, a young reader is given permission to borrow books. (Both, courtesy of MPL.)

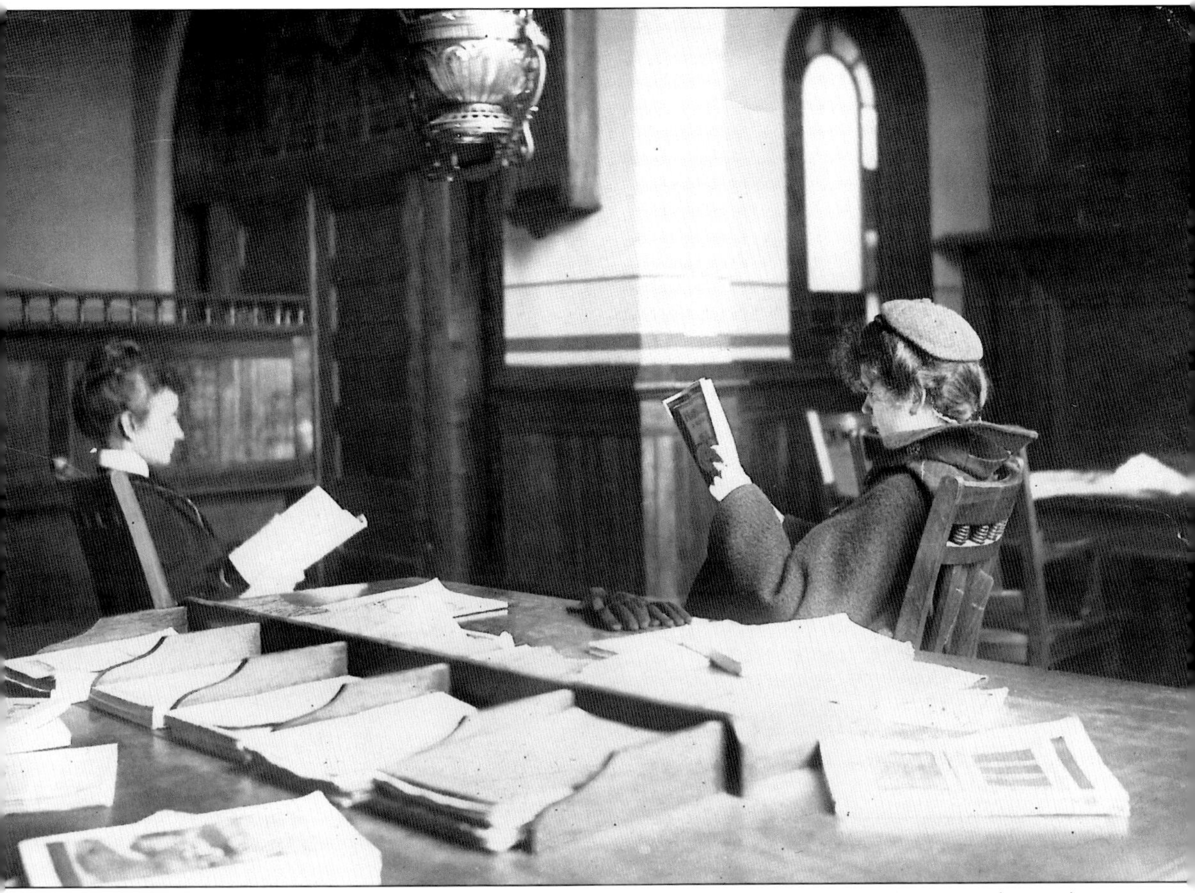

LIBRARY READING ROOM. The public library opened on January 31, 1884. This view shows the reading room as it looked at the end of the 19th century, furnished with cane chairs, tables, and the clock that is still used in the library today. The building's Queen Anne–style architecture, accented with urns, a gargoyle, arched windows, and arched interior doorways, was constructed with bricks manufactured in town, with a faced granite foundation, and trimmed with Longmeadow brownstone. The interior is finished in birch. Kerosene lamps, like the one hanging above the reading table, were at times lent to patrons, and two remain on display in the library today. The building has remained relatively unchanged for 125 years and is registered in the National Register of Historic Places. The money that Judge Pliny Merrick donated in 1867 is maintained as a perpetual fund to this day; he stated in his will that he had a "strong attachment to this town, in which I was born and spent my early years." (Courtesy of MPL.)

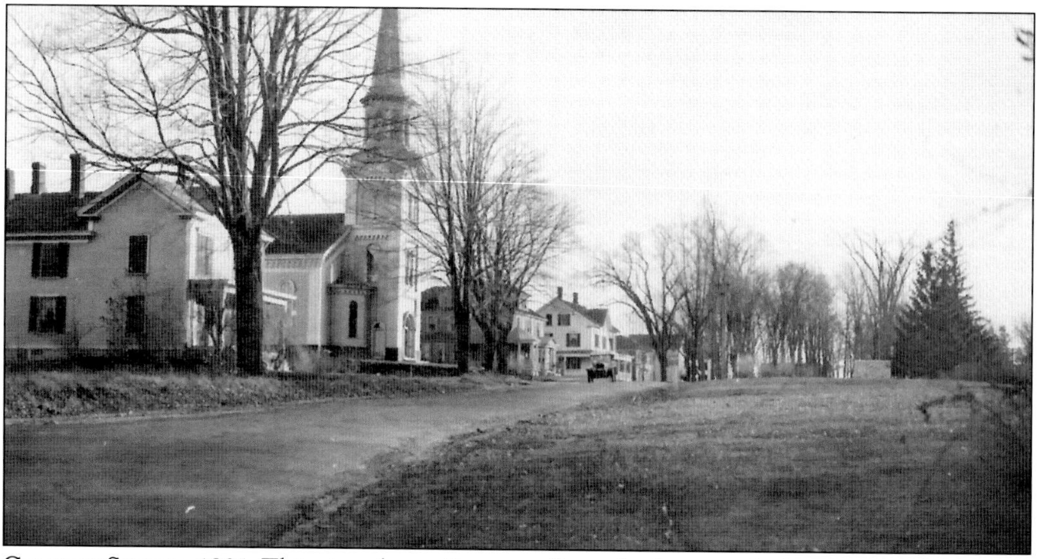

Common Street, 1921. This view shows Common Street looking south, "at a turn in the Boston Post Road, November 6, 1921." From left to right are the Clancy homestead, Congregational Church, Henry Crosby house, and Thomas Warner house. In 1898, the common was separated into two parcels, with the continuation of Central Street to River Street creating the northern section, known as the mall (foreground). (Courtesy of Barbara Clancy.)

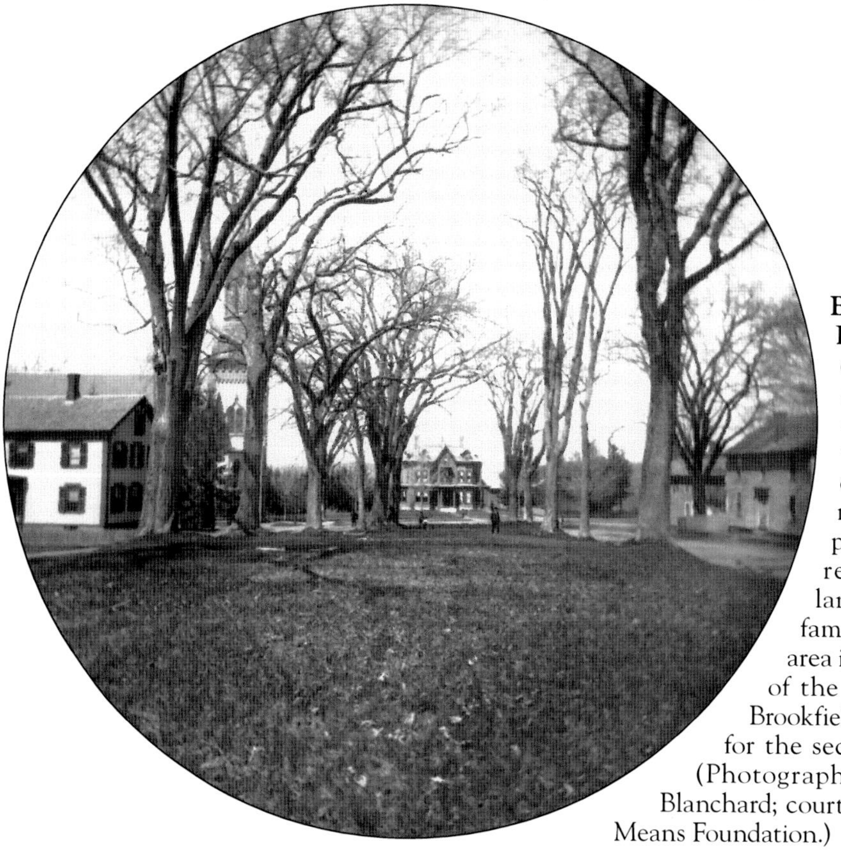

Banister Common, Looking North, c. 1890. In 1773, Solomon Banister donated a five-acre tract to the town of Brookfield for military training purposes to always remain as open land. The Banister family, for which the area is named, was one of the first families in Brookfield that came back for the second settlement. (Photograph by Charles P. Blanchard; courtesy of Blanchard Means Foundation.)

Blanchard Family. Abby Blanchard stands with a young boy, perhaps her cousin Joseph Blanchard, on the Congregational Church's sidewalk around 1890. Her father, Charles P. Blanchard, a worldwide traveler, dedicated his many resources and talents to the town. He resided at Elm Hill Farm, later home to Abby Blanchard and her husband, Oliver Means. (Photograph by Charles P. Blanchard; courtesy of Blanchard Means Foundation.)

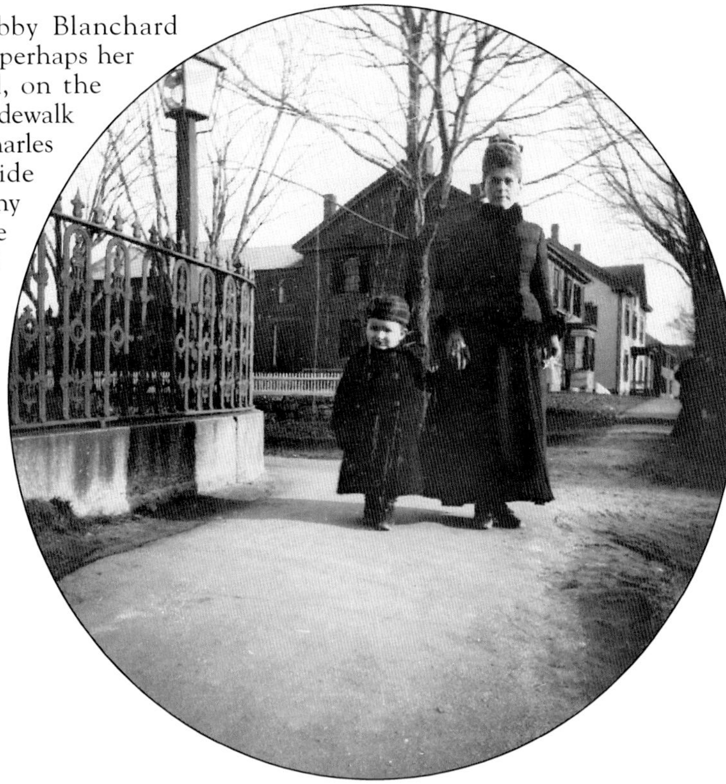

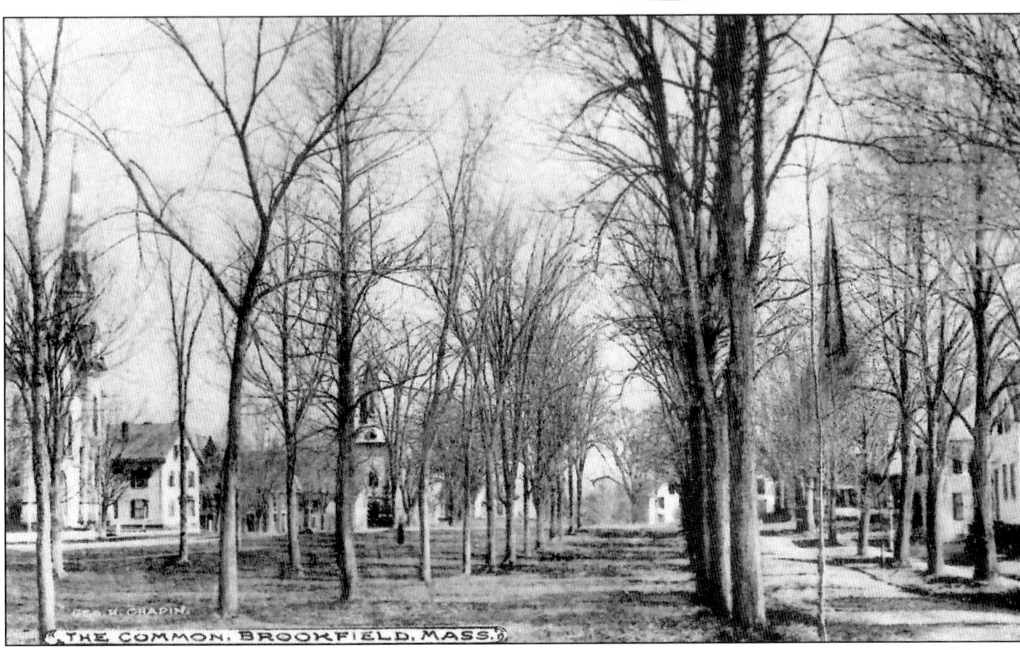

Common with Trees. In 1886, Charles Eddy wrote of the common that no one could quite remember when "the beautiful lines of shade trees were set out, but it was about sixty-five years ago, as some that are now living assisted in the work." Most of these trees were lost during the hurricane of 1938. (Courtesy of James Allen.)

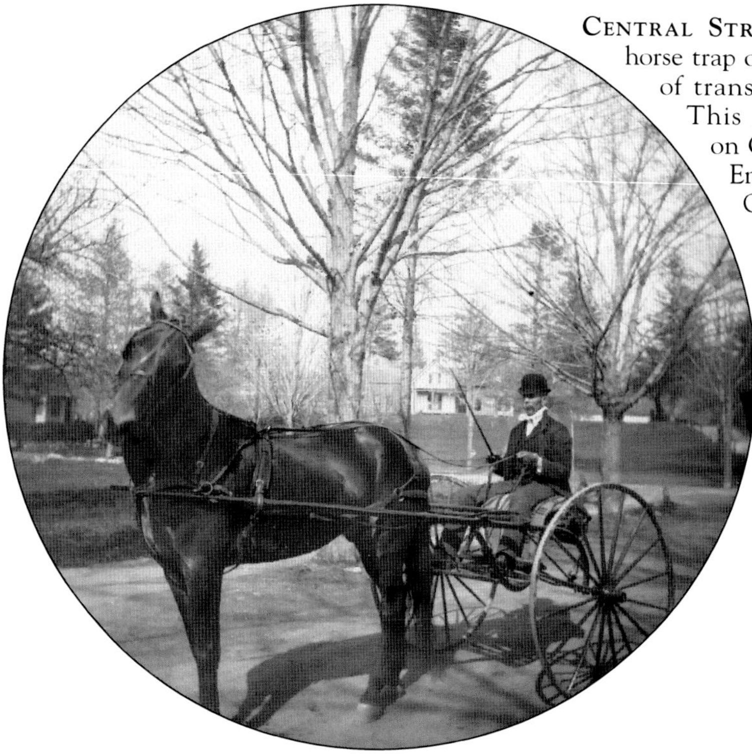

CENTRAL STREET. This two-wheeled horse trap or gig was a popular mode of transportation in the 1890s. This gentleman has stopped on Central Street in front of Emmons Twichell's property. Old Maple Street can be seen behind him, with the home of Walter Nichols in the center. (Photograph by Charles P. Blanchard; courtesy of Blanchard Means Foundation.)

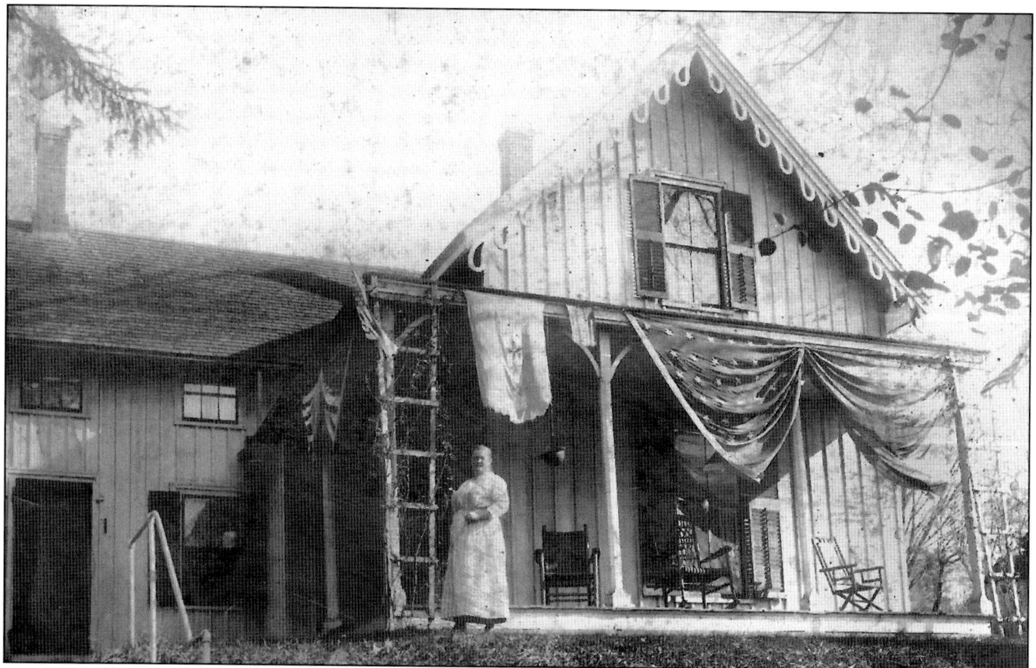

OLD MAPLE STREET. This home was built in the 1830s and purchased by the LaPointe family in 1945. This gentlewoman has bedecked her home for a 1909 event for which she has a clear view across Maple Street and down Central Street. The home siding is board and batten, popular in the 1800s. (Courtesy of Jean Paul LaPointe.)

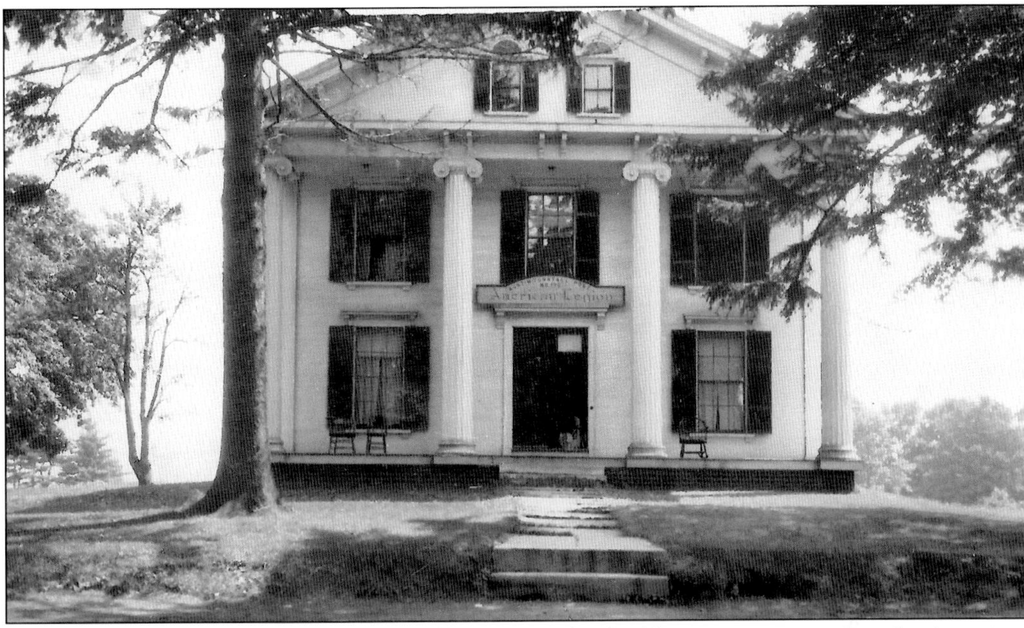

AMERICAN LEGION. Formerly the Twichell mansion, this building was converted to the American Legion, Austin-Tunstall Post No. 170. As became a common practice, the hall was named for the town's first two World War I veterans who died during service, W. Merrill Austin, who died July 3, 1918, at age 29, and William Robert Tunstall, who died August 14, 1918, at age 23, in an airplane crash. (Courtesy of James Allen.)

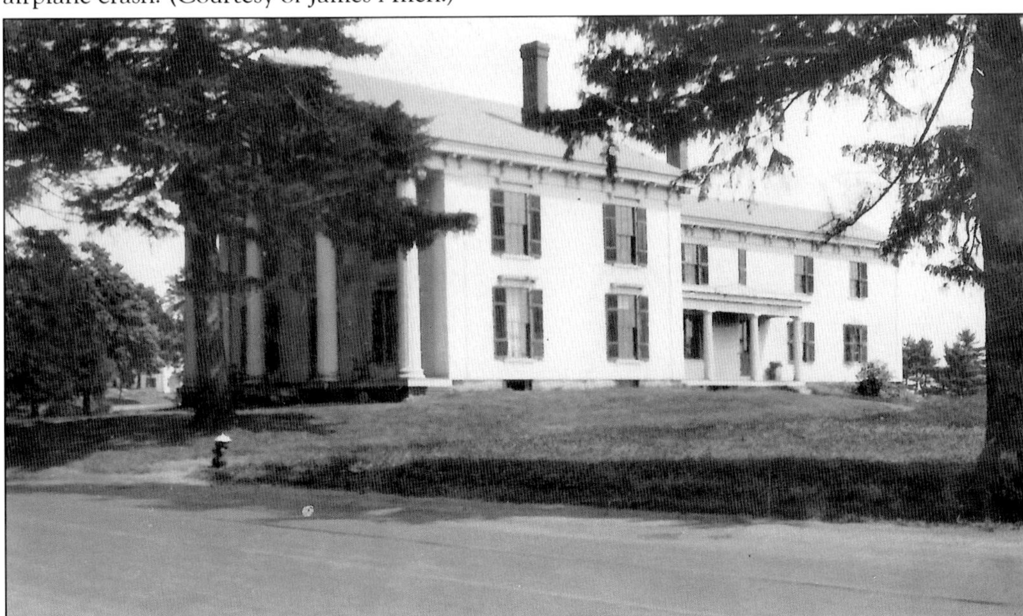

TWICHELL MANSION. Emmons Twichell was born in Brookfield in 1807 and later built a large boot and shoe factory in town. His son Emmons W. Twichell donated this Central Street property to the town in the early 1900s. As the American Legion, it was also a community center with Friday night dances, pool tables, and other activities. Brookfield Elementary School is now located on this property. (Courtesy of James Allen.)

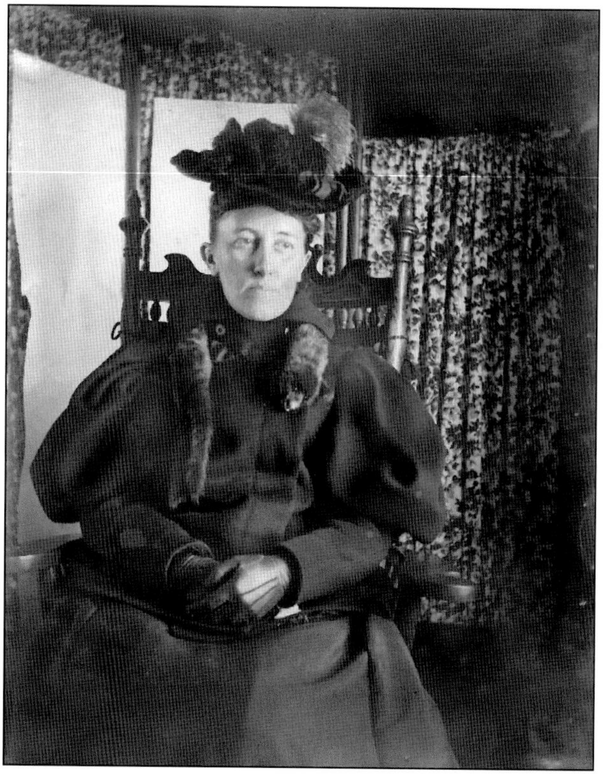

ALICE BLANCHARD. Born and raised in Brookfield, Alice Blanchard lived on Main Street. Noted in the *Unitarian Register*, she married Louis H.R. Gass in October 1910. Gass was a library trustee from 1886 to 1895. In 1902, he donated to the American Antiquarian Society 10 photographs of historic sites in Brookfield. (Courtesy of longtime resident.)

MAIN STREET, LOOKING NORTHEAST. This street view shows the business known as Joseph Guerin Horseshoeing and Jobbing (far right), which, in the 1889 business directory, promoted "Dr. Roberge's Patent Hoof Expander for the cure and prevention of Contraction, Quarter Cracks, Corns, etc." Horses were tended to in the downstairs barn, while carriages and wagons were hauled up the ramp and fixed upstairs. (Photograph by William Bullard; courtesy of Dennis LeBeau.)

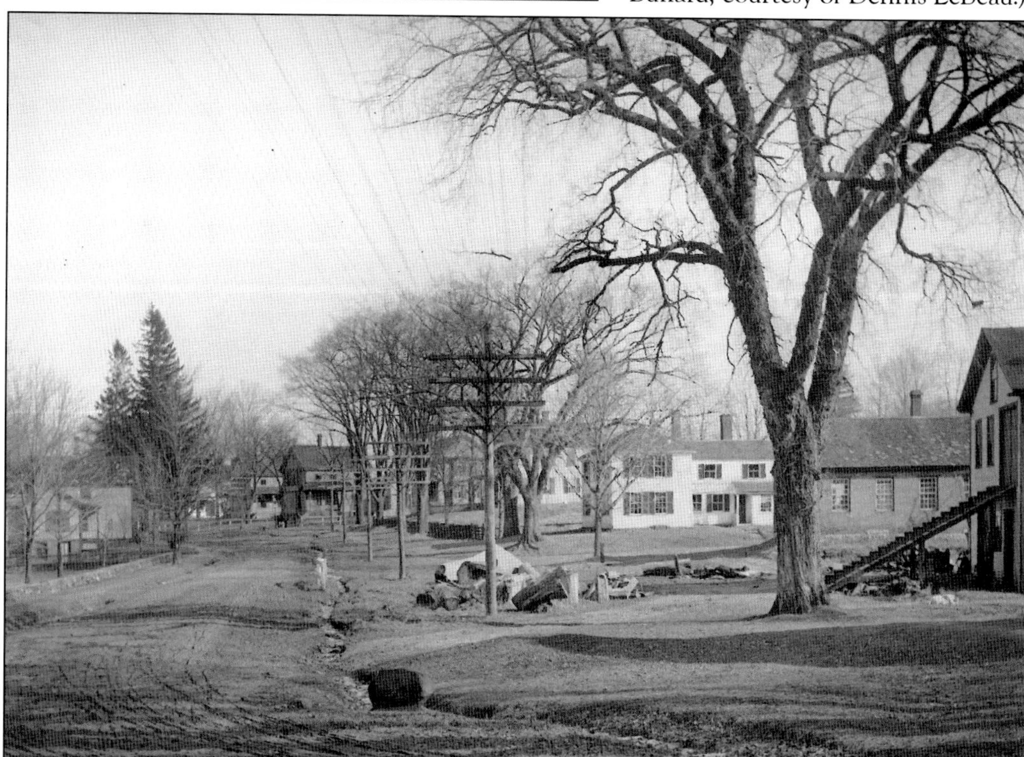

LEWIS MANSION. Built in 1804 as the Simeon Draper house, this Main Street mansion was host to famous visitors, including General Lafayette. It was also the summer home of four-year-old Charles Ross, who was kidnapped in Pennsylvania in 1874 in what became an infamous case. The building fell into disrepair, and the town purchased it in 1956–1957. It is now the site of Lewis Field. (Courtesy of William Jankins.)

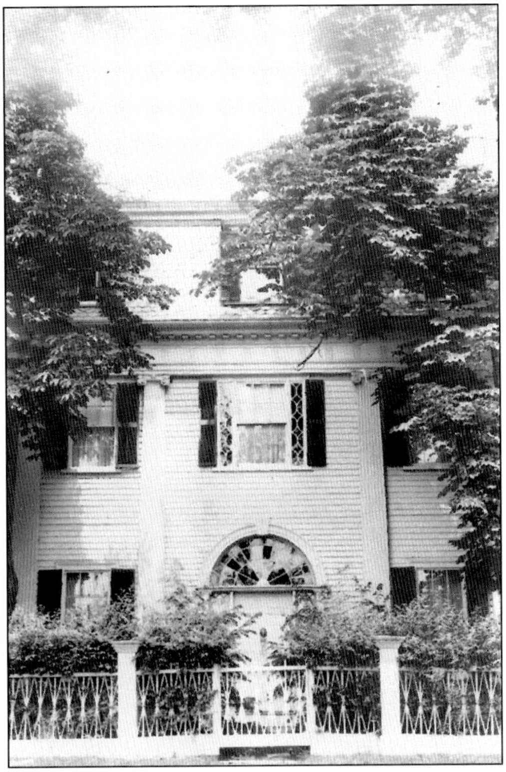

MAPLE AND MAIN STREETS. This view shows what was once a main intersection in town before the construction of Route 9. The road straight ahead leads past the Blanchard School to East Brookfield; the sign in the middle of the road points travelers left to North Brookfield and right to West Brookfield. Shown at right is the home of Louis H.R. and Alice Blanchard Gass. (Courtesy of longtime resident.)

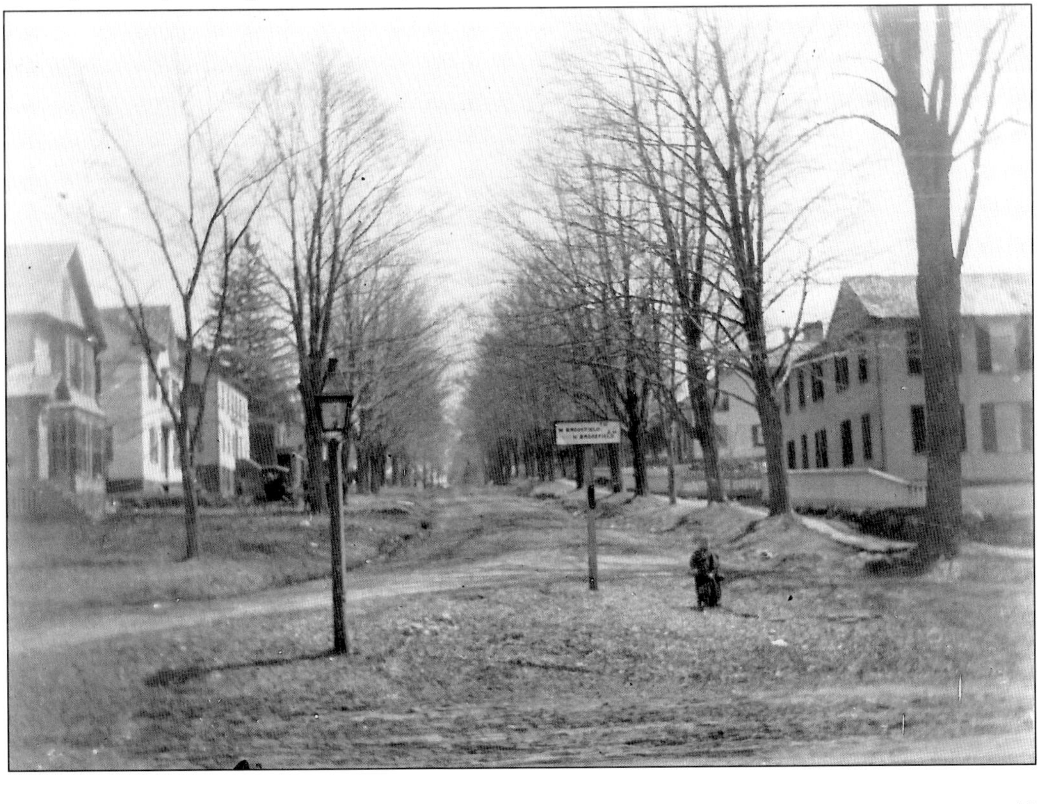

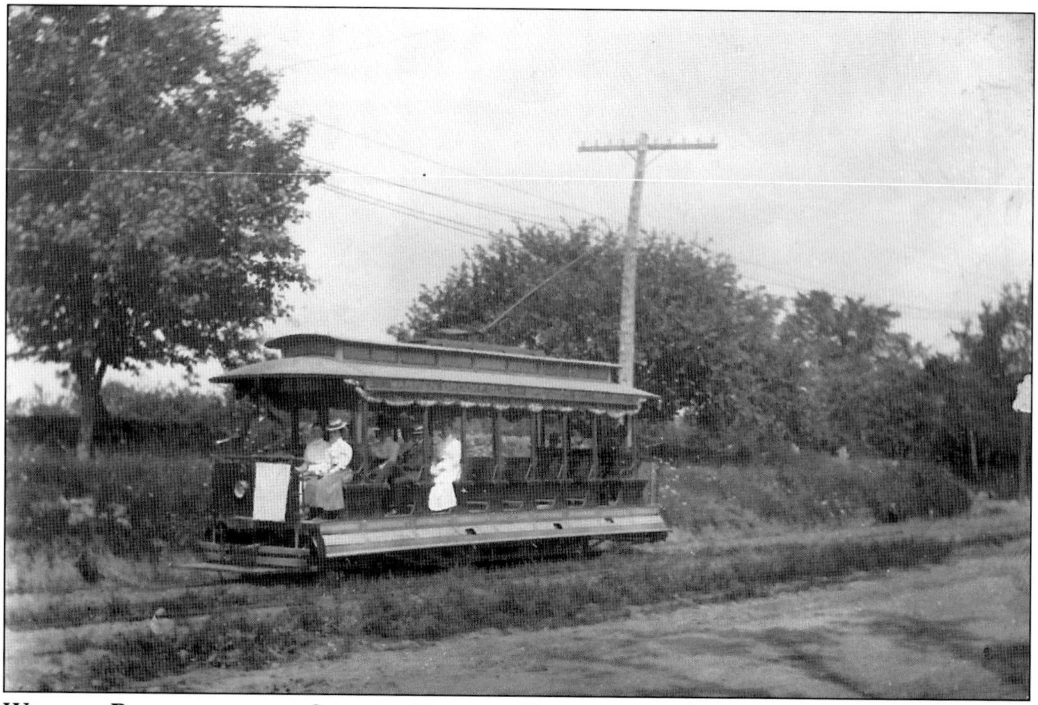

Warren, Brookfield, and Spencer Trolley. Shown is one of seven open cars on the trolley line nicknamed by locals the "Way-off, Bump, and See-Saw." The street railway included the Quaboag Junction, which was a carbarn and power station; the remains of the power station are located on the south side of Route 9, near the billboards and the parking lot for Carmella's Italian Kitchen. (Courtesy of longtime resident.)

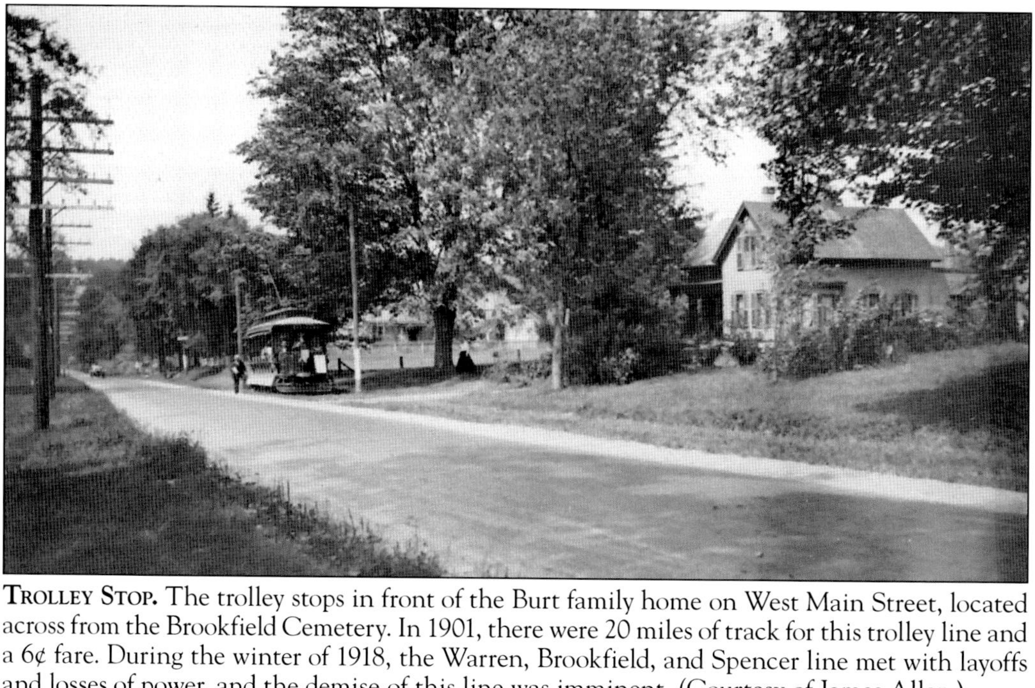

Trolley Stop. The trolley stops in front of the Burt family home on West Main Street, located across from the Brookfield Cemetery. In 1901, there were 20 miles of track for this trolley line and a 6¢ fare. During the winter of 1918, the Warren, Brookfield, and Spencer line met with layoffs and losses of power, and the demise of this line was imminent. (Courtesy of James Allen.)

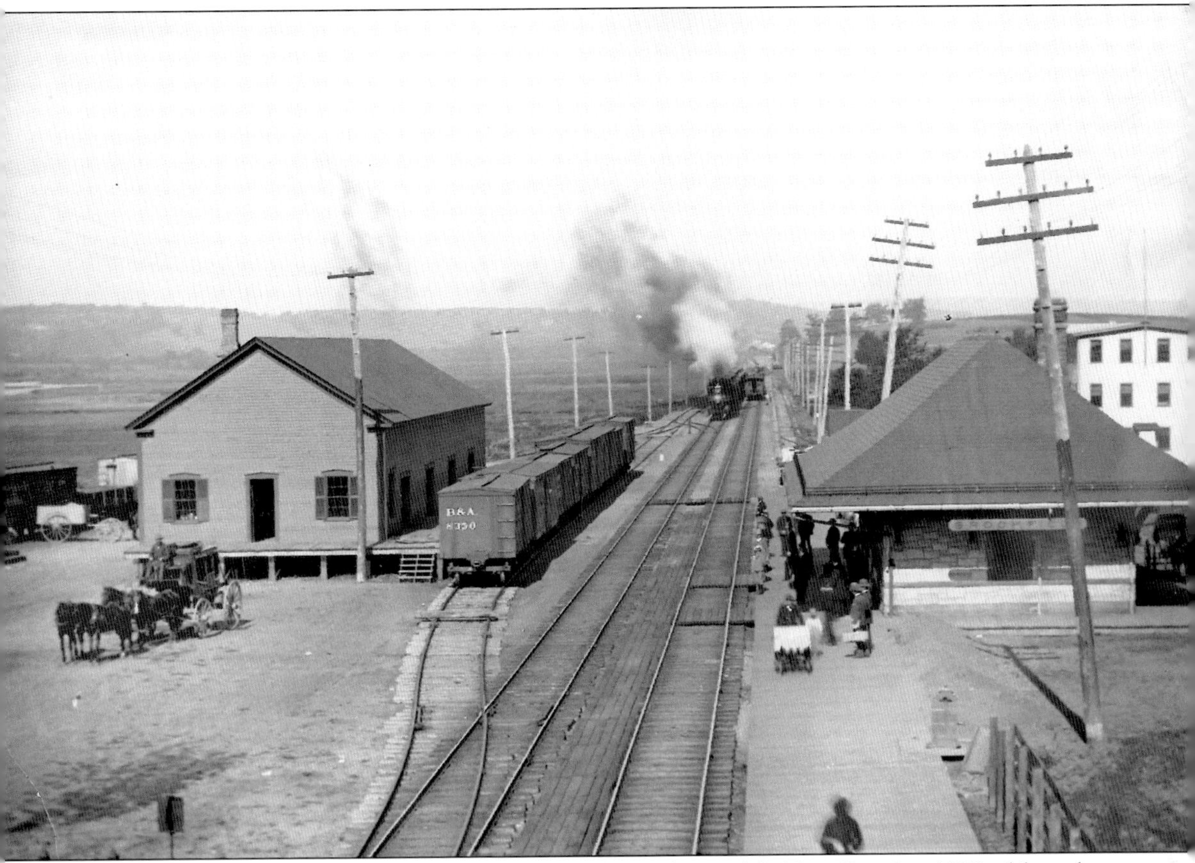

Brookfield Train Depot. The first train came through Brookfield in October 1839, although, this stone depot building (right) was not constructed until 1884, at which point seven passenger trains were stopping daily in town. The late 19th century was a time of great growth for Brookfield, as the trains enabled industries to thrive, and people could easily travel for business or pleasure to other towns along the Boston & Albany Railroad as well as to towns connected by stagecoach. Trains regularly delivered mail and newspapers, and there were two tracks as well as a siding for unloading freight, such as feed and coal for the Brookfield Grain Store, owned by Wirthmore Feeds, and lumber, shingles, and cement for the Rice and Gadaire Lumber Company freight house. The depot was full of diversions; Robert Wilder remembers families picnicking on the grass near McLaurin-Jones to watch troop trains pass through at the start of the Korean War. Although trains still pass through on the now-single track, they no longer stop and the depot is no longer standing. (Courtesy of Reta Priest Warman.)

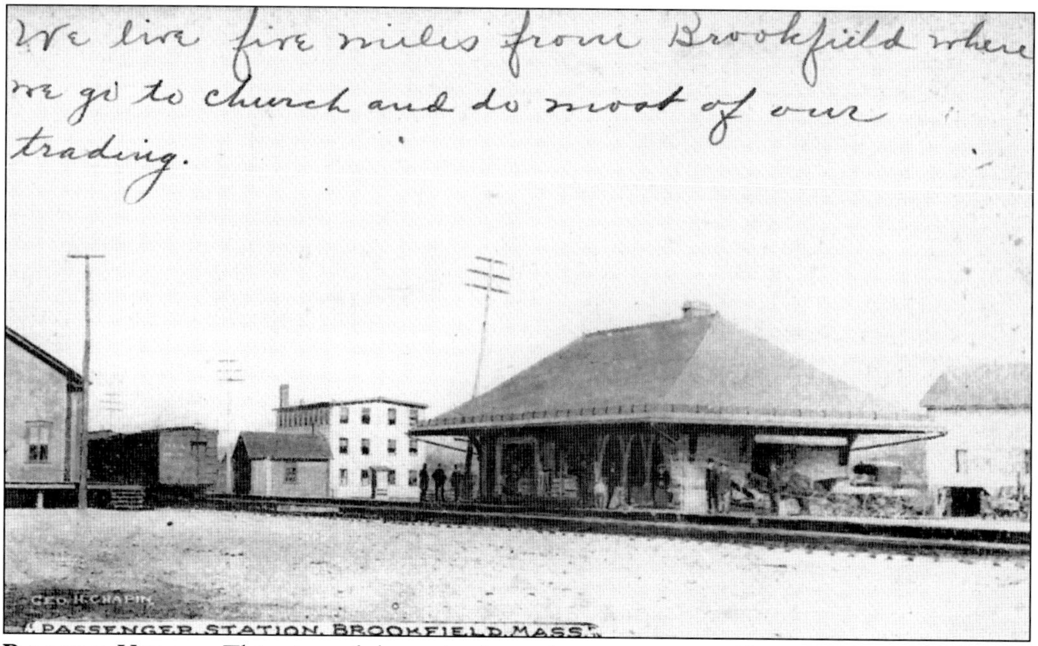

BUSTLING VILLAGE. This view of the train depot shows a variety of businessmen and travelers waiting for the train. The depot's first station agent was Washington Tufts, who held the position for 34 years. The building at left is A.L. Twichell and Company's factory, which, on a busy day in 1886, made 6,000 pairs of women's heels. (Courtesy of James Allen.)

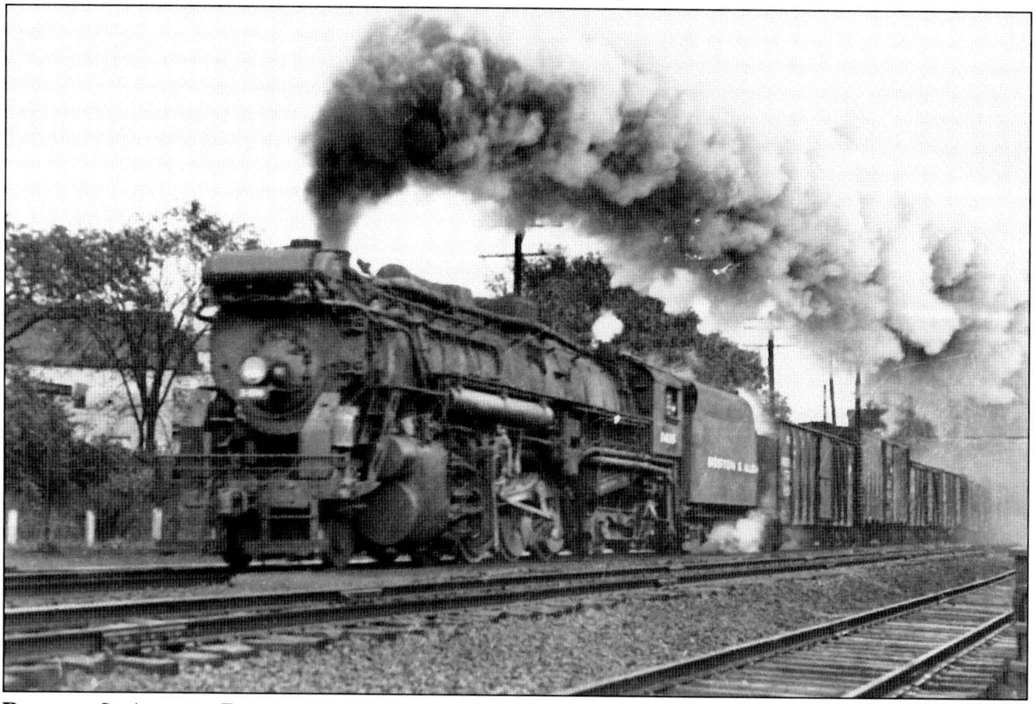

BOSTON & ALBANY RAILROAD. This Lima 1926 freight train barrels over the Brookfield tracks, leaving a giant cloud of smoke in its wake. The train was headed westward on October 17, 1945, traveling at 40 miles per hour and just recovering from a high-speed slip. (Courtesy of James Allen.)

Four

CHURCHES

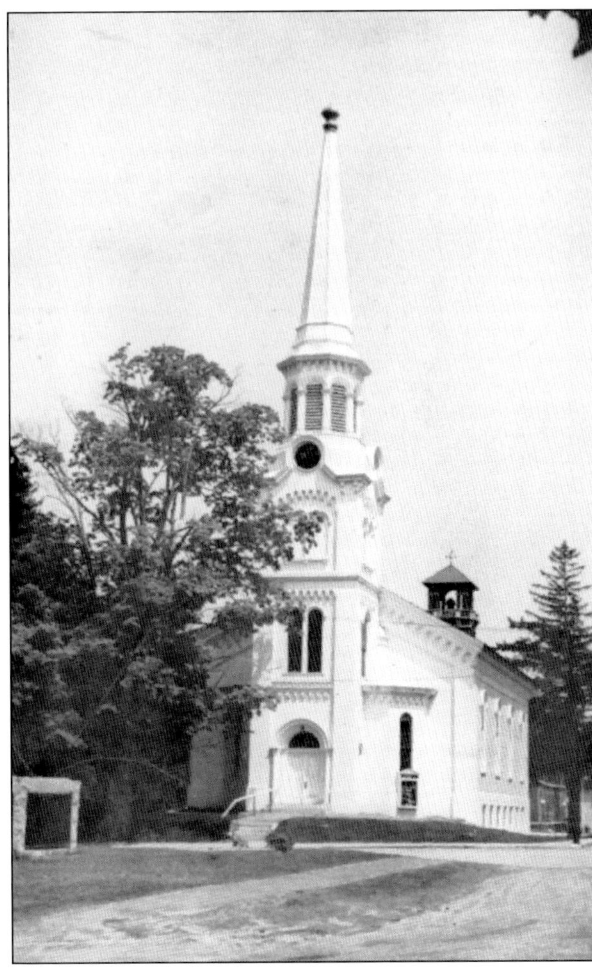

CONGREGATIONAL CHURCH. The town's first Congregational Church was built in 1754 with material from the 1717 church on Foster Hill. When the church divided into Congregationalists and Unitarians, the latter group kept the building while the former worshipped in private homes. The current building on the corner of Common and Central Streets was dedicated in 1857. (Courtesy of James Allen.)

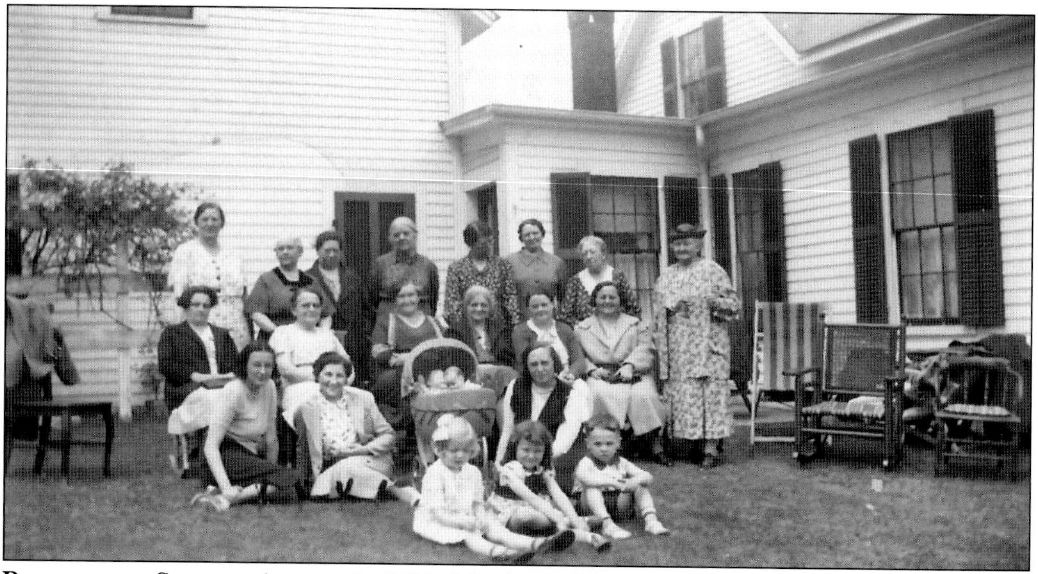

Benevolence Society, August 2, 1938. Members of the Congregational Church Benevolence Society gather for an outing. From left to right are (first row) Nancy Hunter, Barbara May, and Horace May; (second row) Laura Hazen, Becky Love, and Barbara Vivian May; (third row) unidentified, Mrs. McGowan, three unidentified people, and Anna Priest; (fourth row) Hildegard Hunter, unidentified, Sophronia Works (organist), unidentified, Nellie Sweet, and three unidentified people. (Courtesy of May-Boyce Collection.)

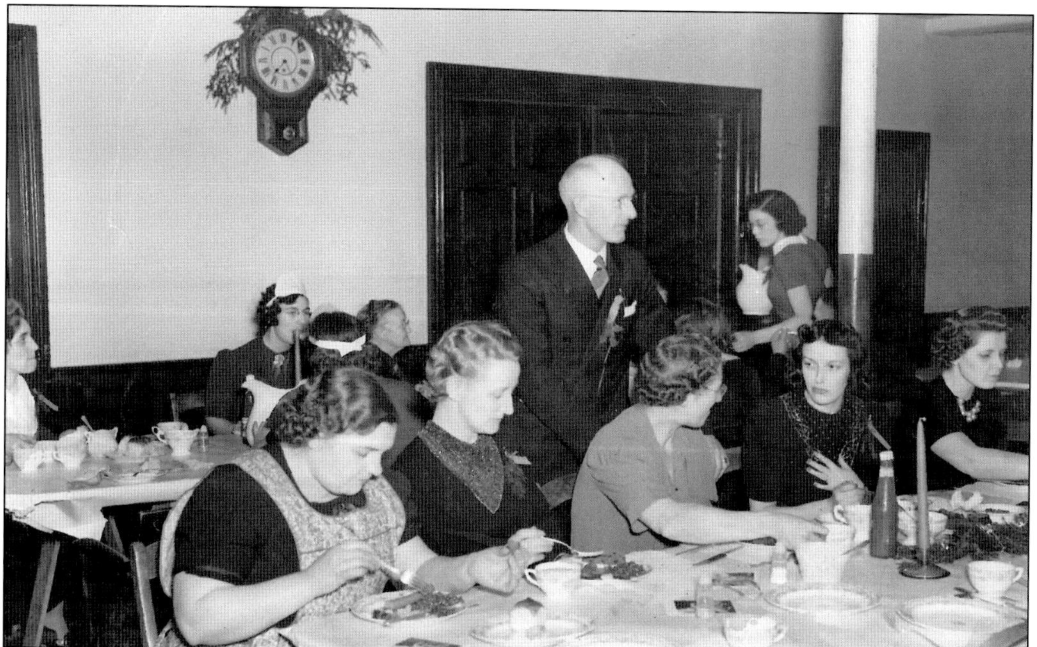

Congregational Church Supper, 1940. In conjunction with the welcome home party held in town hall for Elsie the Cow, the Orthodox Girls' Club of the Congregational Church hosted an old-fashioned New England supper of baked beans and brown bread. About 250 people were served, including Beatrice Steadman, Mrs. Amadon, Mrs. Woodard, Leona Finney, Laura Hazen, Mrs. Monroe, and Lee Boyce. Alvina Works holds the pitcher. (Courtesy of May-Boyce Collection.)

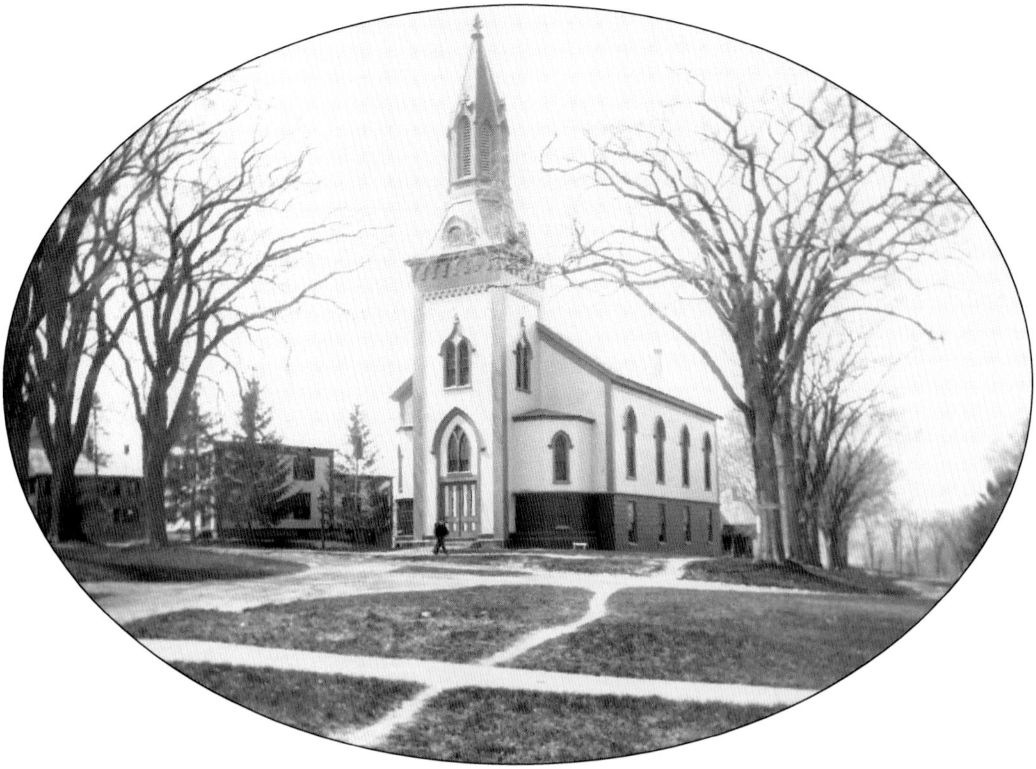

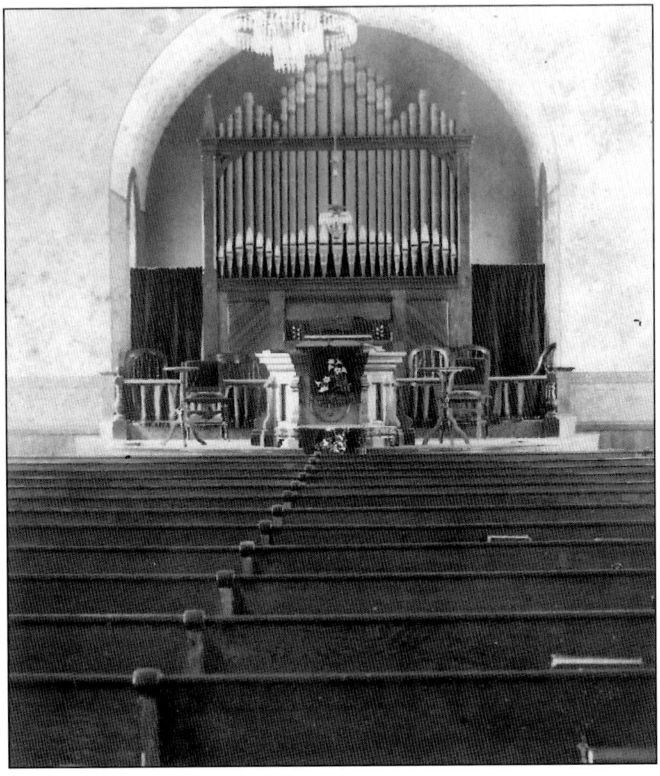

Methodist Church. Shown here in an exterior view from c. 1890, above, and an interior view from 1914, right, the Methodist Church was situated on the northwest corner of the common, on what is now the junction of River Street (Route 148) and West Main Street (Route 9). It was built in 1865 at a cost of about $8,000 and dedicated a year later. The building could seat about 400 people, and in 1885, the church had 100 members, with 140 people in the Sabbath School. That same year, the church was repaired and redone, and a new organ was put in. In the late 1930s, the church was torn down; the adjoining parsonage still stands. (Above, photograph by Charles P. Blanchard; courtesy of Blanchard Means Foundation; right, courtesy of MPL.)

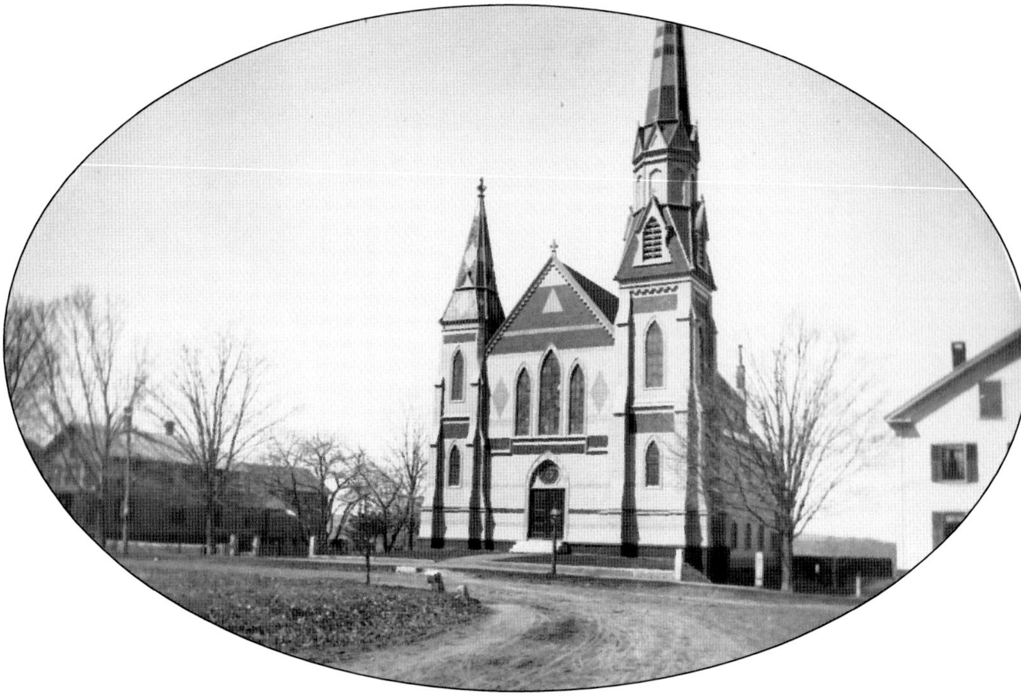

Unitarian Church. When the Unitarians grew too large for the 1754 church building they had owned since the 1827 division with the Congregationalists, they sold it to the Catholics and constructed the white church, shown above, in 1868. In 1911, the church spire was struck by lightning and the building burned to the ground. The Reverend William L. Walsh, with the help of a small group of men, was able to save the piano (but not the organ), vestry fixtures, pewter communion service, and several portraits. The building was replaced in 1912 with the current stone structure, shown below at the same location on River Street, and is now known as the Brookfield Unitarian Universalist Church. (Above, photograph by Charles P. Blanchard; courtesy of Blanchard Means Foundation; below, courtesy of longtime resident.)

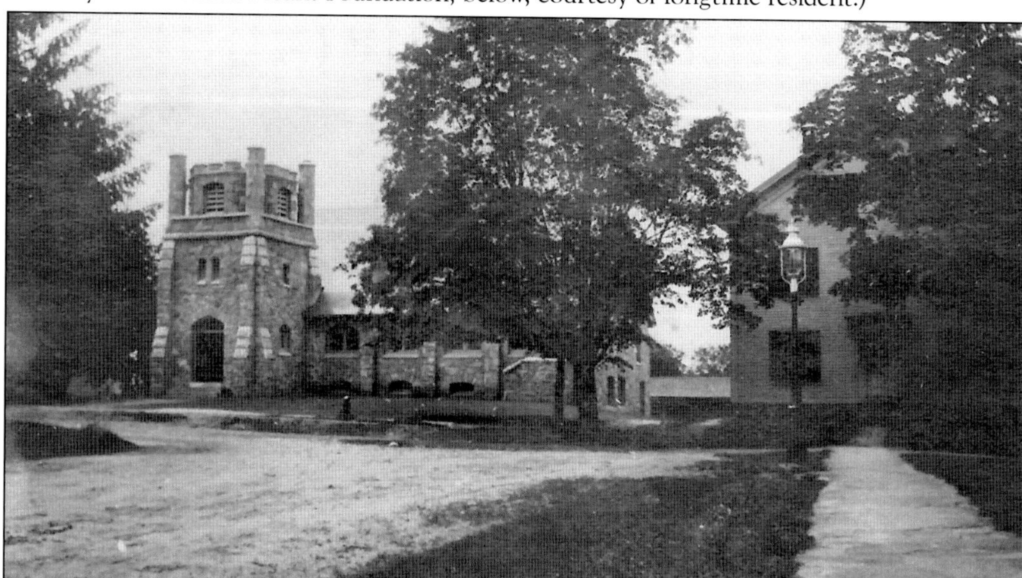

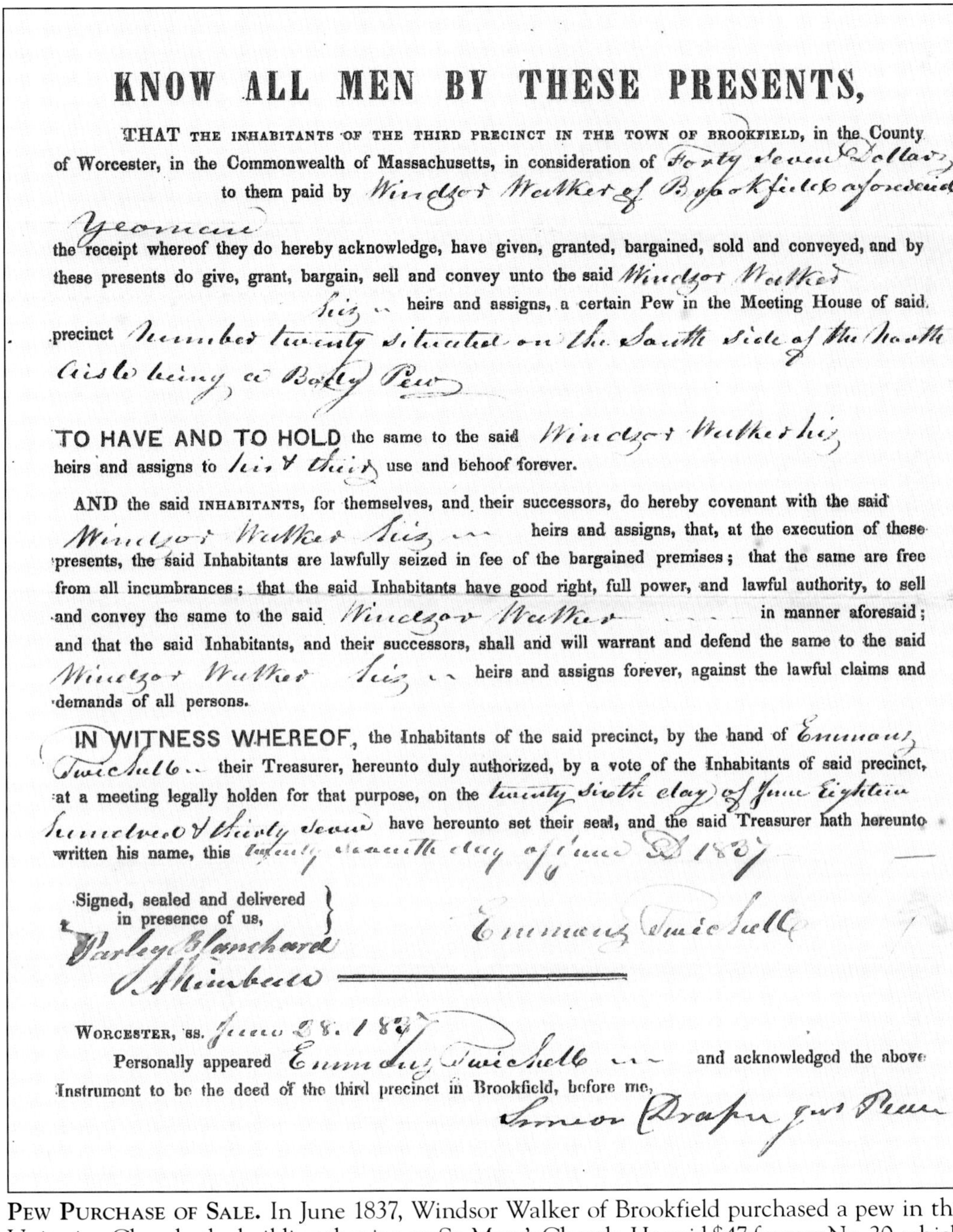

KNOW ALL MEN BY THESE PRESENTS,

THAT THE INHABITANTS OF THE THIRD PRECINCT IN THE TOWN OF BROOKFIELD, in the County of Worcester, in the Commonwealth of Massachusetts, in consideration of Forty seven Dollars to them paid by Windsor Walker of Brookfield aforesaid Yeoman the receipt whereof they do hereby acknowledge, have given, granted, bargained, sold and conveyed, and by these presents do give, grant, bargain, sell and convey unto the said Windsor Walker his heirs and assigns, a certain Pew in the Meeting House of said precinct number twenty situated on the South side of the North Aisle being a Body Pew

TO HAVE AND TO HOLD the same to the said Windsor Walker his heirs and assigns to his & their use and behoof forever.

AND the said INHABITANTS, for themselves, and their successors, do hereby covenant with the said Windsor Walker his heirs and assigns, that, at the execution of these presents, the said Inhabitants are lawfully seized in fee of the bargained premises; that the same are free from all incumbrances; that the said Inhabitants have good right, full power, and lawful authority, to sell and convey the same to the said Windsor Walker in manner aforesaid; and that the said Inhabitants, and their successors, shall and will warrant and defend the same to the said Windsor Walker his heirs and assigns forever, against the lawful claims and demands of all persons.

IN WITNESS WHEREOF, the Inhabitants of the said precinct, by the hand of Emmons Twichell their Treasurer, hereunto duly authorized, by a vote of the Inhabitants of said precinct, at a meeting legally holden for that purpose, on the twenty sixth day of June Eighteen hundred & thirty seven have hereunto set their seal, and the said Treasurer hath hereunto written his name, this twenty seventh day of June AD 1837

Signed, sealed and delivered in presence of us,

Parley Blanchard

J. Kimball

Emmons Twichell

WORCESTER, ss. June 28. 1837

Personally appeared Emmons Twichell and acknowledged the above Instrument to be the deed of the third precinct in Brookfield, before me,

Simeon Draper Just Peace

PEW PURCHASE OF SALE. In June 1837, Windsor Walker of Brookfield purchased a pew in the Unitarian Church, the building that is now St. Mary's Church. He paid $47 for pew No. 20, which was "situated on the South side of the North Aisle being a Body Pew," meaning it was enclosed by a door. The amount he paid was the equivalent of six full weeks' worth of wages for an average man working seven days per week. Once purchased, the pew became Walker's property and could legally be passed down to his heirs upon his death. Walker is noted as a "yeoman," meaning he attended church but had not yet had a vision or experience with God that would make him a "freeman." The document was signed by Emmons Twichell, Parley Blanchard, and Simeon Draper. (Courtesy of William Jankins.)

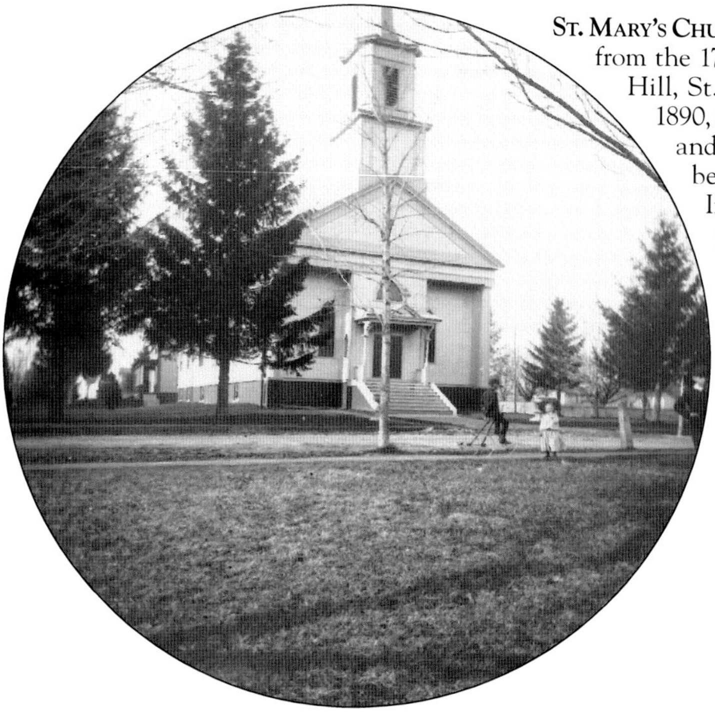

St. Mary's Church. Built in 1754 with timbers from the 1717 meetinghouse atop Foster Hill, St. Mary's, shown here around 1890, served the Congregationalists and then the Unitarians before becoming a Catholic Church. In 1867, Father Moran of Ware purchased the building from the Unitarians and moved it from the common to its present location on Lincoln Street. (Photograph by Charles P. Blanchard; courtesy of Blanchard Means Foundation.)

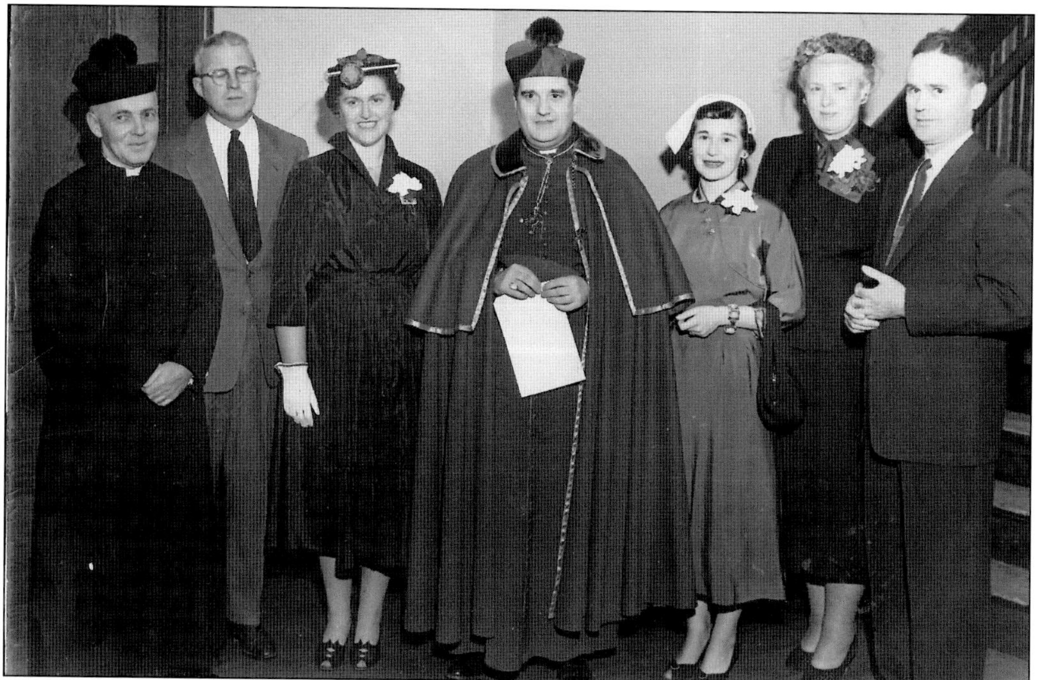

Bishop Wright's Visit. John Wright (center), auxiliary bishop of Boston, was installed on March 7, 1950, as the first bishop of the new Worcester Diocese and is shown here during a visit to St. Mary's Church. Pictured are, from left to right, Rev. Paul Shaughnessy, John McKelligott, Mary Leach, Bishop Wright, Irene Glass, Margaret Bonner, and Robert Kelly. (Courtesy of Docwra family and *Worcester Telegram & Gazette*.)

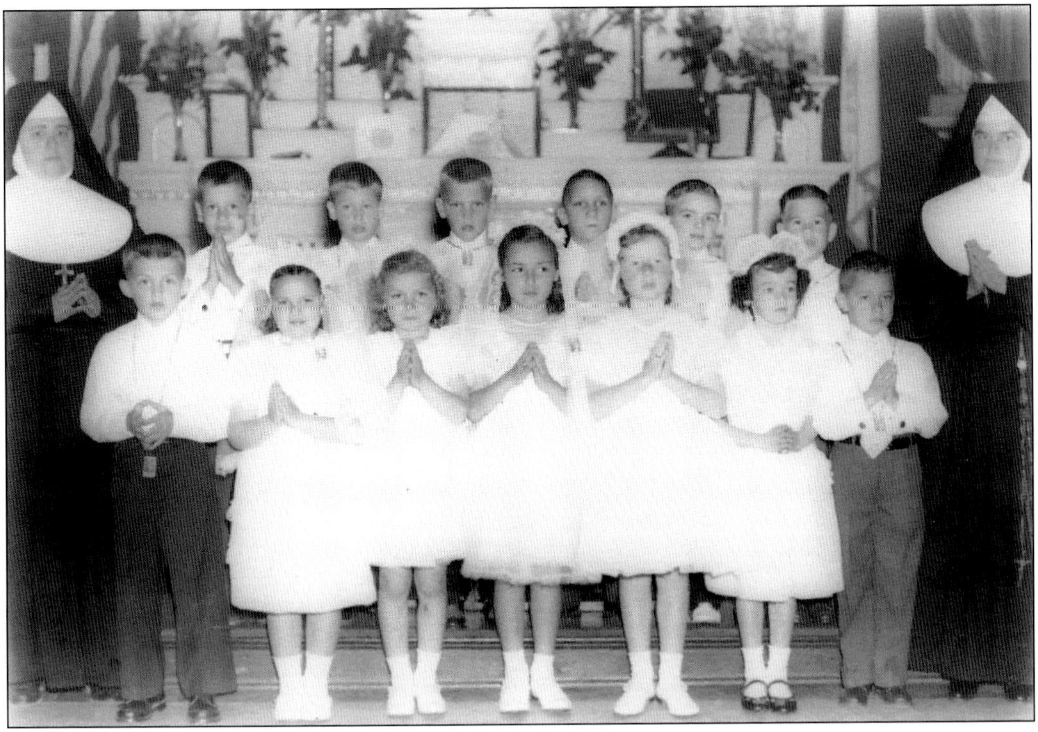

FIRST COMMUNION, 1956. The children posing for their First Communion portrait are, from left to right, (first row) Eugene Toto, Linda Prizio, Marcia Yaskoski, Irene Pena, Mary Beth Learnard, Sandra Porter, and Raymond Stearns; (second row) Horace Squire, Alan Glass, Steven Warner, James Paradise, Richard Woodis, and Mark Kelly. (Courtesy of Linda Prizio Lincoln.)

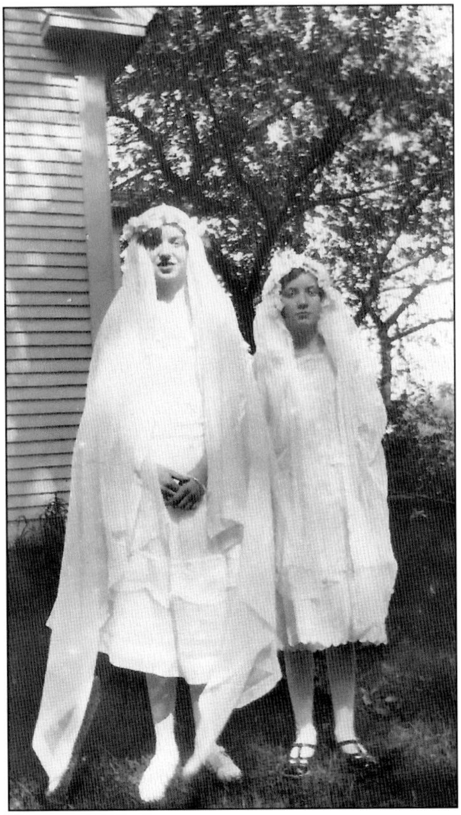

CONFIRMATION, 1920S. Lillian (left) and Louise Menard of Hayden Avenue pose in their white dresses for Confirmation. The girls attended St. Mary's Church. The parish was founded in May 1885, and at the time of its 100th anniversary in 1985, there were 175 practicing families. The rectory adjacent to the church on Howard Street was torn down in the last decade. (Courtesy of Sheila Pronto McCarthy.)

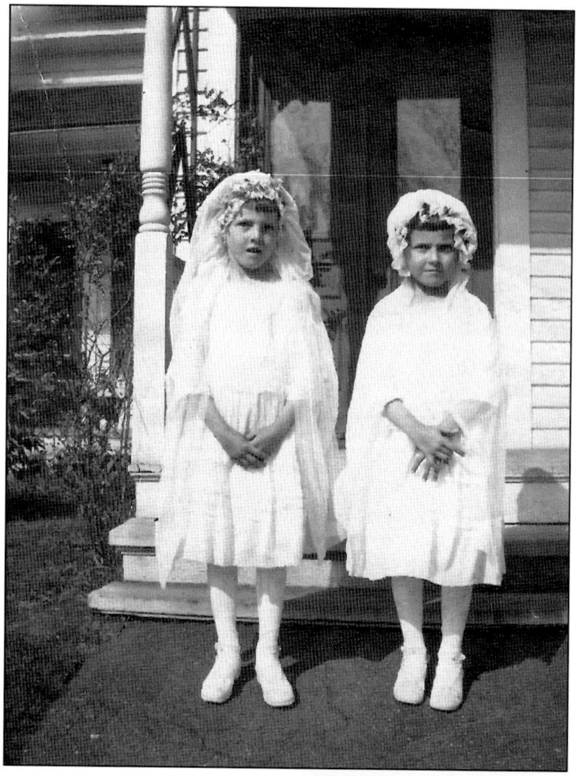

First Communion, 1920. Twins Margaret (left) and Madelyn Leach pose in front of their Kimball Street home on the day of their First Communion at St. Mary's Church. Margaret became a nurse and died young of pneumonia. Madelyn lived all her life in Brookfield, working at the post office and as a reporter; she and her husband, John Docwra, raised two daughters, Margaret and Katherine. (Courtesy of Docwra family.)

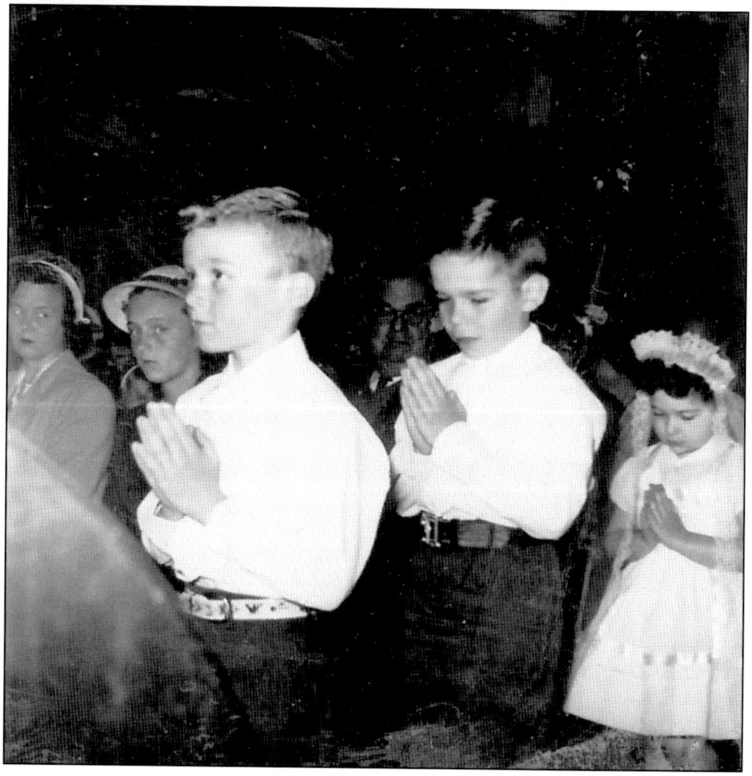

First Communion, c. 1953. Clement Porter (left) and David Nolan (center) proceed down the aisle at St. Mary's Church during their First Communion. The early 1950s were a time of change for St. Mary's, as the church was shifted from the Springfield Diocese to the new Diocese of Worcester and both East Brookfield and West Brookfield were designated as separate parishes. (Courtesy of Clement Porter.)

Five

EDUCATION

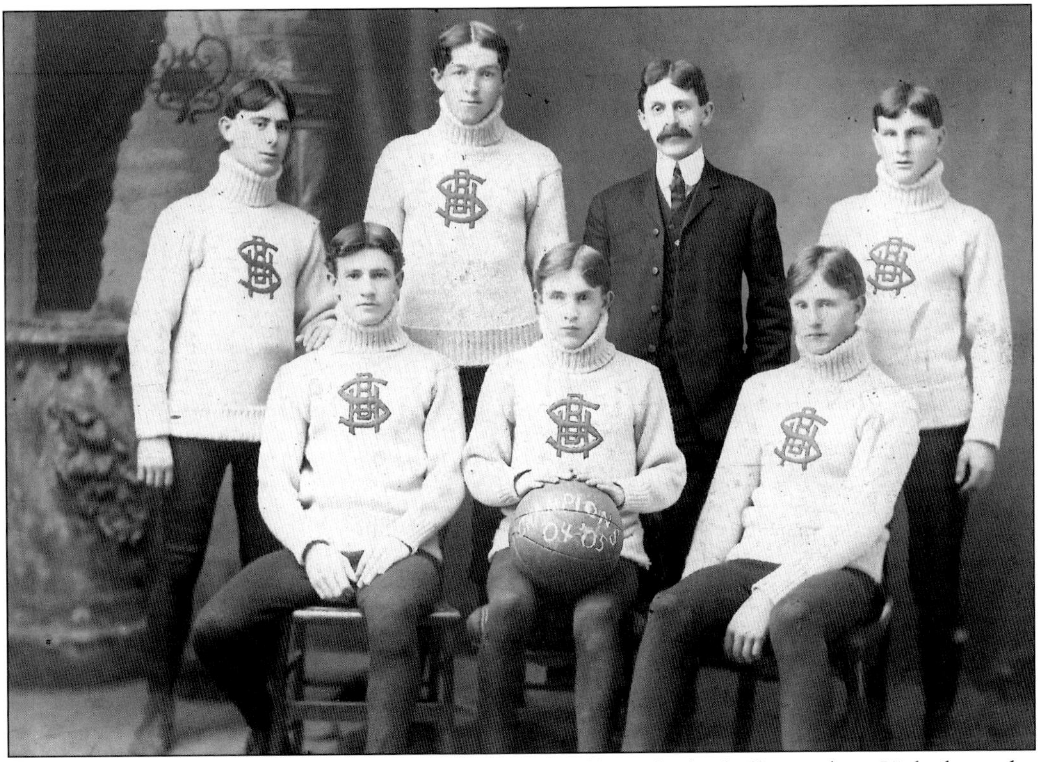

BASKETBALL CHAMPIONS. The Brookfield High School boys' basketball team beat Holyoke at the Springfield Auditorium to win the 1904–1905 state championship. Pictured here are, from left to right, (first row) George McDonald, team captain William Clancy, and Thomas Durkin; (second row) team manager Albert "Chalky" Balcom, William "Chuck" O'Brien, school principal Guy Howard, and Raymond Gerald. (Courtesy of MPL.)

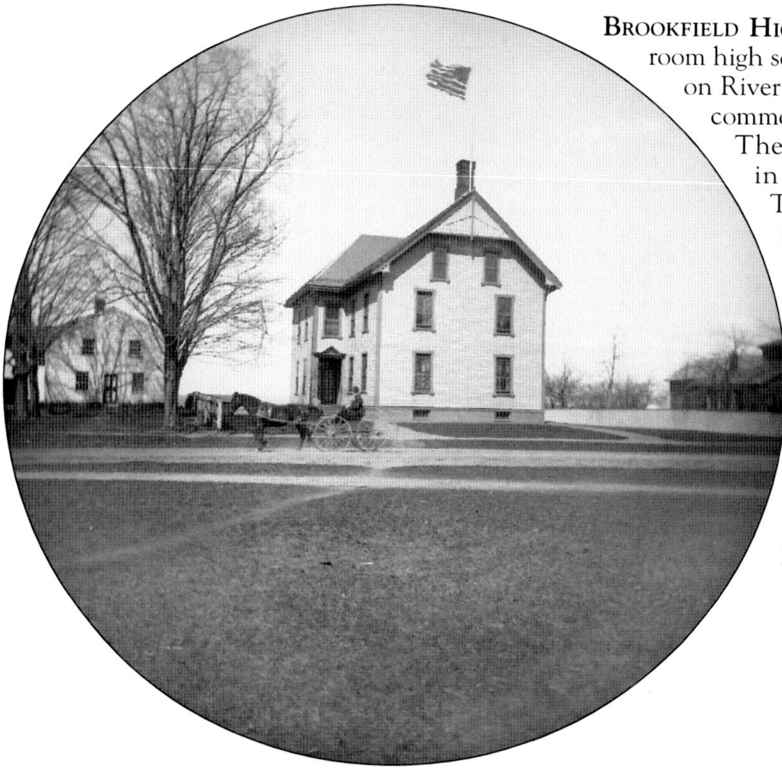

Brookfield High School. The four-room high school was built in 1884 on River Street across from the common at the cost of $8,500. The last class graduated in 1954, and while the Tantasqua Regional School in Fiskdale was completed, students attended classes at the town library and churches as well as area elementary schools. The high school was razed in 1957. (Photograph by Charles P. Blanchard; courtesy of Blanchard Means Foundation.)

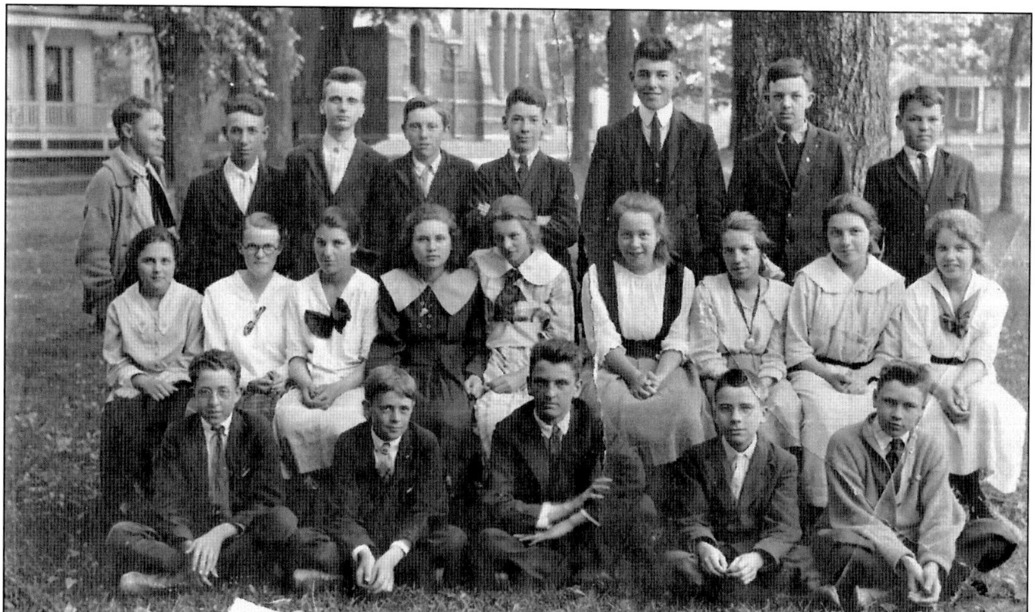

Class Photograph on Common, c. 1920. From left to right are (first row) Robert Harwood, Veron Love, John Finney, Frank Locke, and Robert Pouley; (second row) Marion Hanson, Ethel Johnson, Lillian Longway, two unidentified people, Gertrude Blemer, Fannie Hall, Millie Wright, and Clara Pratt; (third row) Richard Pouley, unidentified, Merville Locke, Richard Worthington, Leon Pratt, Ferdinand Longway, Howard Drake, and Horace May. (Courtesy of May-Boyce Collection.)

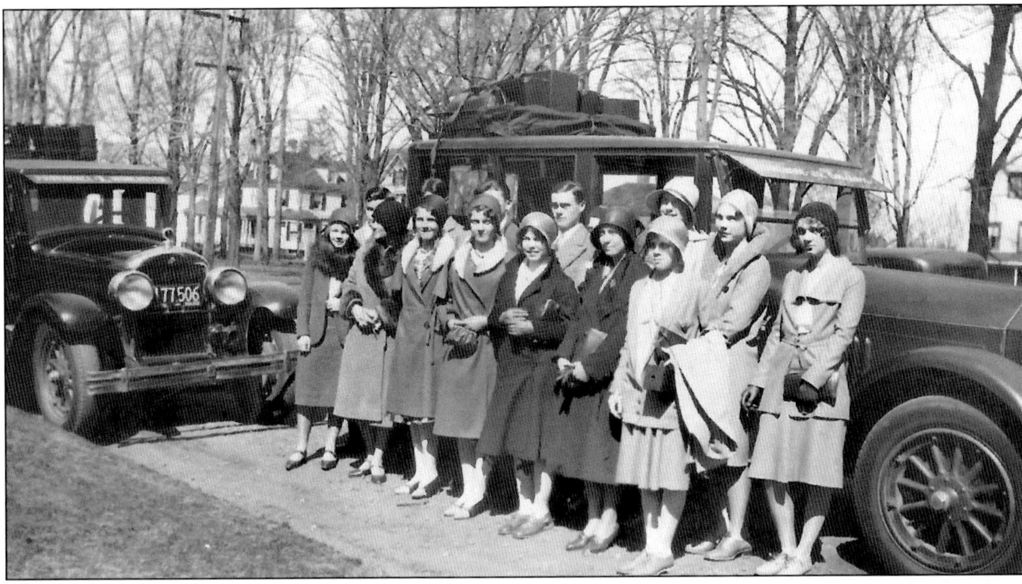

High School Class Trip, c. 1930. Seniors line up on the common in front of the high school before departing for their class trip to New York City. Identified students include Barbara Vivian Boyce May (first row, second from right); Evelyn Turner Gregory (first row, far right), with her Brownie camera; Faith Sensible (second row, second from right); and Elizabeth Reed (second row, far right). (Courtesy of May-Boyce Collection.)

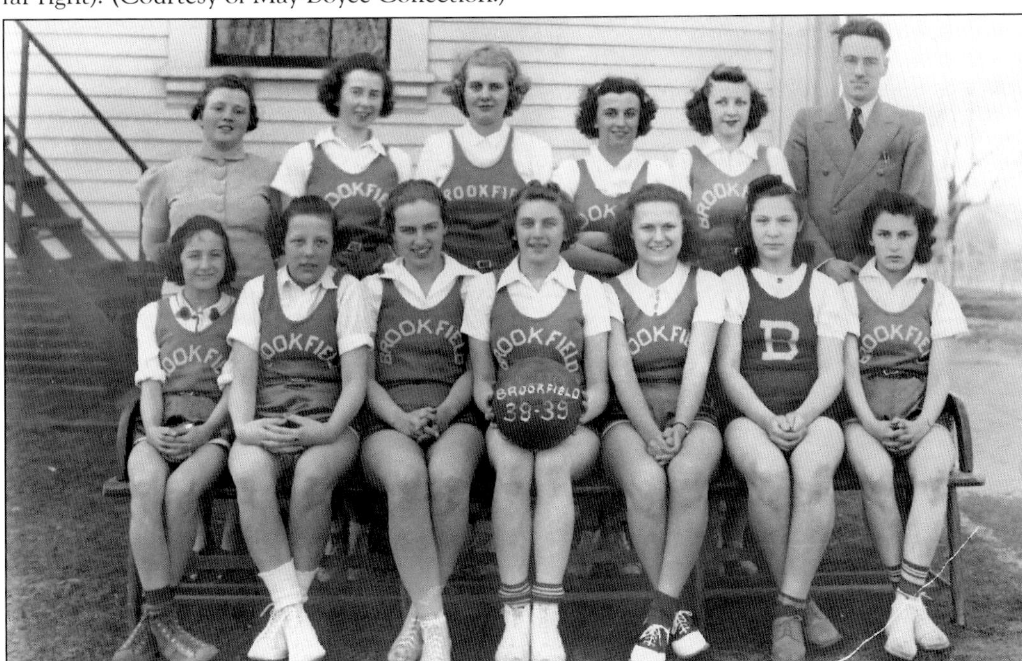

Girls' Basketball Team, 1938–1939. Members of the girls' basketball team pose behind the high school. Pictured here are, from left to right, (first row) Margaret Seery, Ruth Chickering, Edna McNamara, Frances Herbert, Sally Toppin, Myrtle O'Day, and Beatrice Miller; (second row) Christine Gorman, Sally Boyce Powell, Elizabeth Lynd, Julie Charron, Mildred Watson, and principal Seavy Morse. (Courtesy of May-Boyce Collection.)

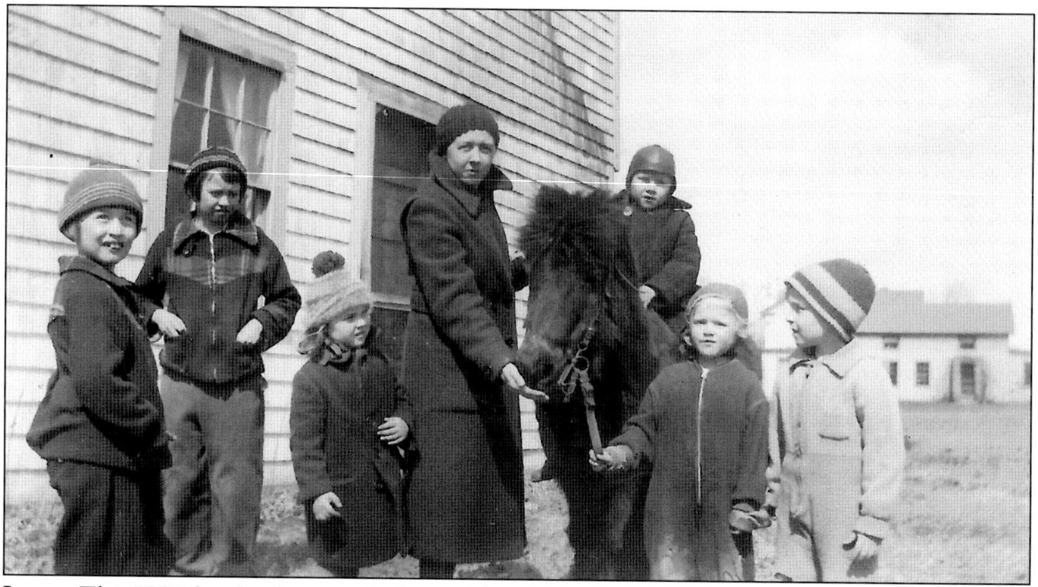

Jimmy. This 1938 family photograph shows Alice Wilson Achilles (center) with her children and her pony, Jimmy, whom she rode to Brookfield High School when she was in seventh grade in 1919. She rode the pony from Sibley farm, now the Jeppson's Oakholm Farm, and kept him in Dr. Mary Sherman's barn next door (later known as Dr. Pease's) while she was in school. (Courtesy of Gloria Achilles Faugno.)

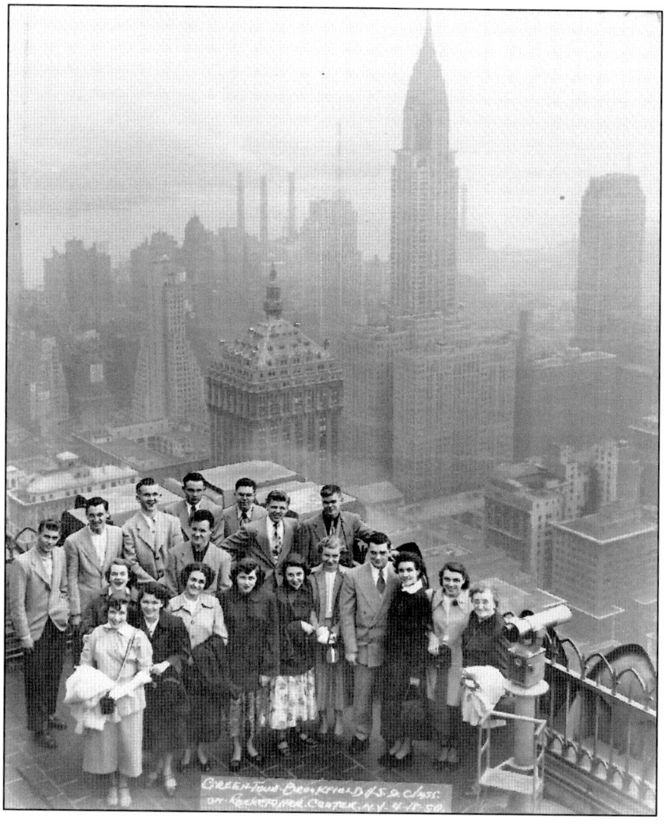

Senior Trip, 1950. Atop Rockefeller Center are, from left to right, (first row) Patricia Hastings Medeiro, Sylvia Hebert Plimpton, Elaine Robidoux Betchley, Audrey Mues Griffin, Gloria Mundell Justo, Nancy Jacobson Rikert, George Crooks, Joanne Jeffreys Dirlam, Barbara Delisle Turner, and advisor Mary Derrick; (second row) Norma Grimes, Paul Byrne, James Flannery, and James Barr; (third row) William Woodard, Richard Allen, George Reed, James Wilson, and Robert Pierce. (Courtesy of Barbara Delisle Turner.)

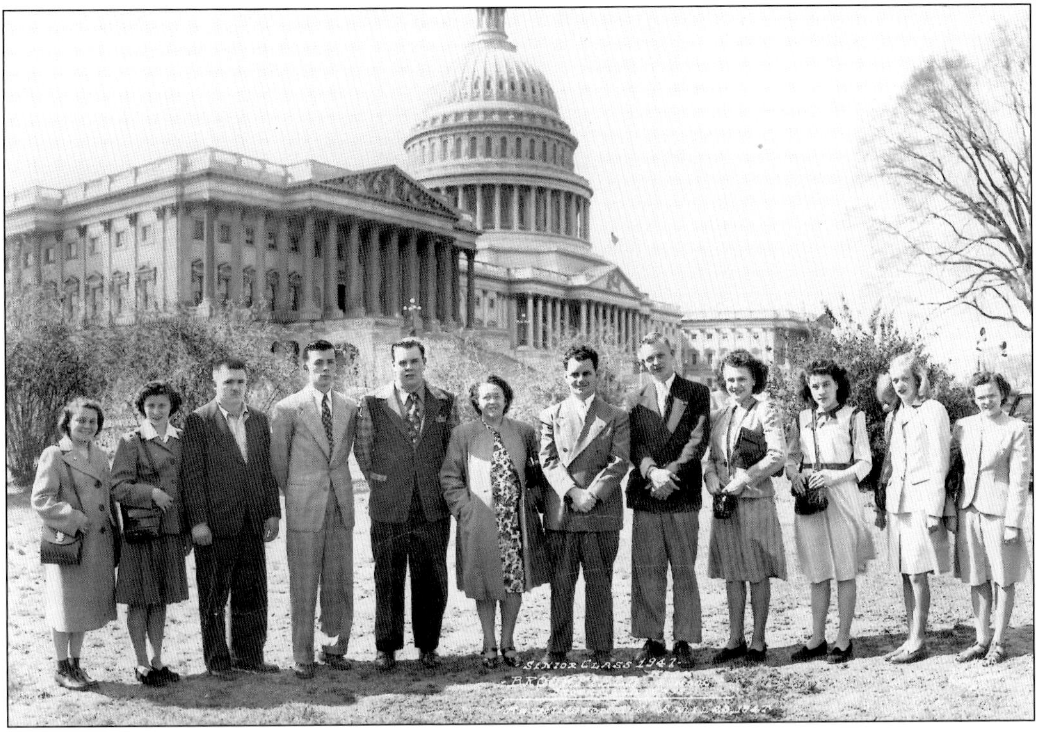

SENIOR CLASS TRIP, 1947. Visiting the nation's Capitol are, from left to right, Edith Pierce Messer, Marian Steadman Ruggles, Gilson Merriam, Roland Wilson, Charles Hickman, chaperone Alice Sheldon, teacher Francis Bansfield, Wilfred Steadman, Ruth Robidoux Garrepy, Edith Evans Anderson, Norma Crooks Coughlin, and Barbara Sheldon Steadman. Roland Wilson was later Tantasqua district superintendent for 23 years; the Steadmans have been longtime library trustees. (Courtesy of Wilfred and Barbara Sheldon Steadman.)

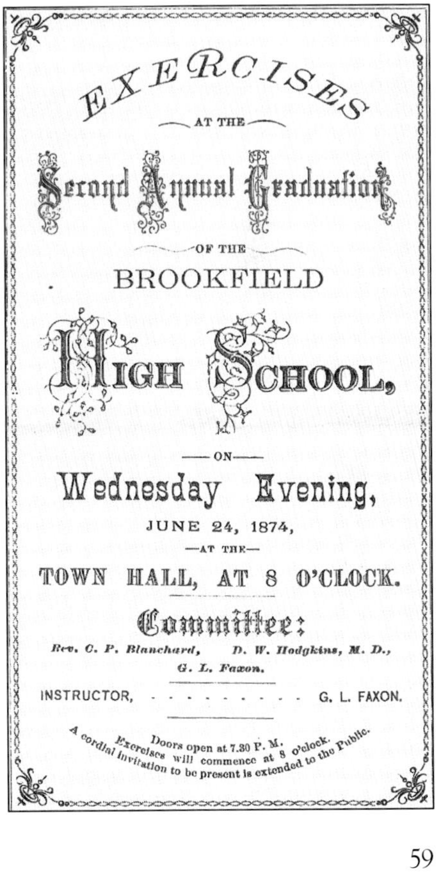

EXERCISES

AT THE

Second Annual Graduation

OF THE

BROOKFIELD

HIGH SCHOOL,

ON

Wednesday Evening,

JUNE 24, 1874,

AT THE

TOWN HALL, AT 8 O'CLOCK.

Committee:

Rev. C. P. Blanchard, D. W. Hodgkins, M. D., G. L. Faxon.

INSTRUCTOR, ... G. L. FAXON.

Doors open at 7.30 P. M.
Exercises will commence at 8 o'clock.
A cordial invitation to be present is extended to the Public.

HIGH SCHOOL GRADUATION EXERCISES, 1874. A class of six received diplomas at the town hall on June 24, 1874. At the previous graduation, according to the 1873–1874 school committee report, one pupil, Myrtilla Sherman, "completed the prescribed four years' course of study, and received the diploma of graduation, the first to attain this honor in the eight years' existence of the school." (Courtesy of Reta Priest Warman.)

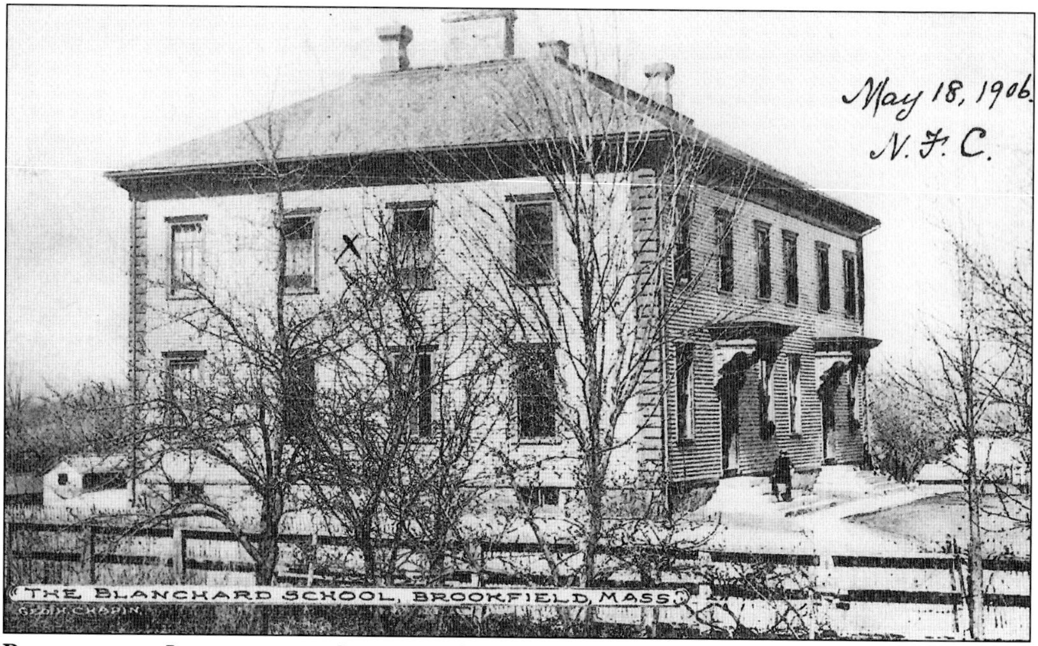

PRIMARY AND INTERMEDIATE SCHOOL. The Blanchard School was built on Maple Street in 1862 and housed younger students until 1958, when the current elementary school was opened. Its one-acre schoolyard was substantially diminished when Route 9 was constructed around 1925. Former student Andrea Campbell Faugno remembers that clean fingernails and a clean handkerchief earned a student a ride down the slide in the second-grade classroom. (Courtesy of Carolyn Potter Murray.)

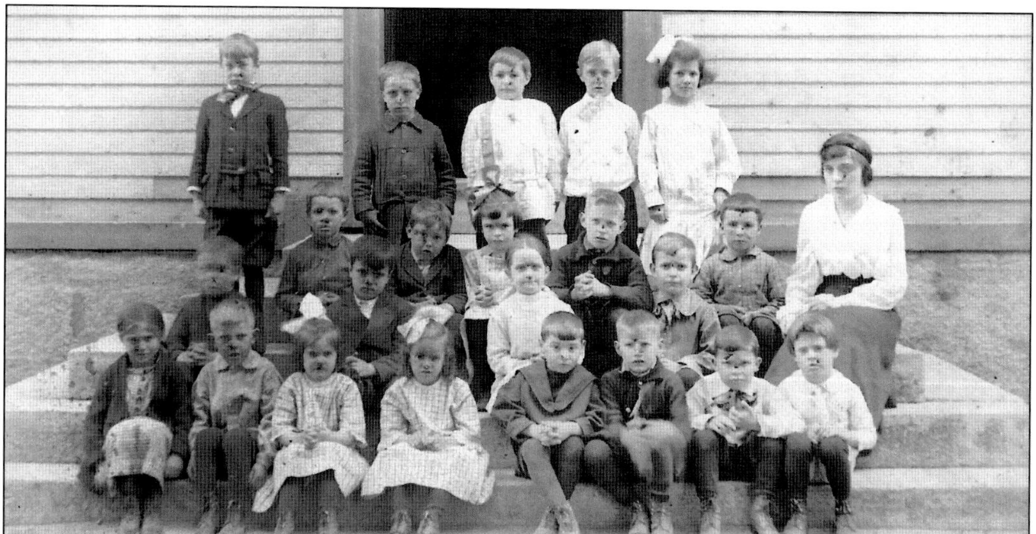

BLANCHARD SCHOOL, 1914–1915. From left to right are (first row) Josephine Faugno, Martin Leach, Julia Boynton, Grace Boynton, Fred Charron, unidentified, Clifford Sweet, and Harold Wright; (second row) Thomas Kelly, Arthur Ritchie, Sophie Mahoney, and two unidentified; (third row) Philip Young, Thomas Roberts, Emily Foster, Ralph Young, and unidentified; (fourth row) unidentified, William Prizio, Ted Prizio, Julius Nichols, and Loana Nichols. (Courtesy of Loana Nichols Gadaire and Paula Gadaire Woodard.)

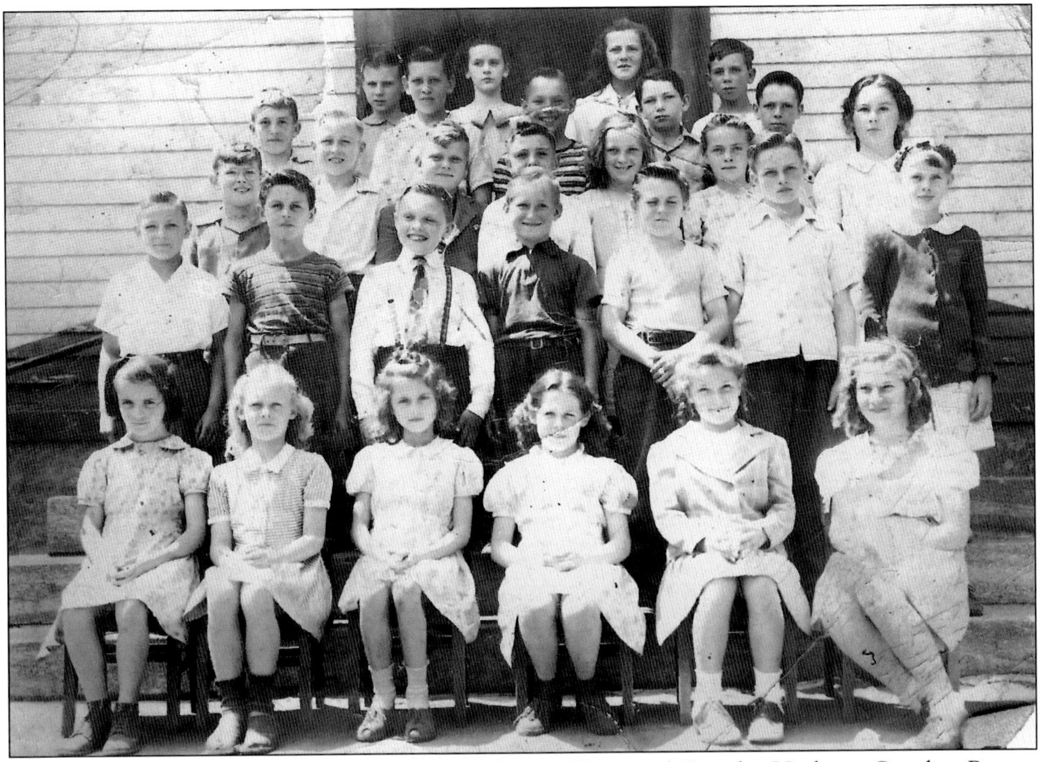

BLANCHARD SCHOOL, 1945. From left to right are (first row) Rosalie Herbert, Carolyn Potter, Patricia Purcell, Norma Burdett, Sandra Love, and Ida Jacobs; (second row) George Gallaway, William Morin, Richard Terry, Harvey Smith, Ralph Nichols, William Prizio, and Ruth Gensler; (third row) John Morrill, Ralph Achilles, Raymond Ruggles, Michael Seery, Mildred Allen, June Fairbanks, and Caroline Gustafson; (fourth row) Kenneth Grimes, Gilbert Evans, Paul Johnson, Ralph Holbrook, and Joel Bolshaw; (fifth row) Eleanor Robideaux, Loretta Knight, Ann Smith, and Walter Ambach. (Courtesy of Lori Dorney Britch.)

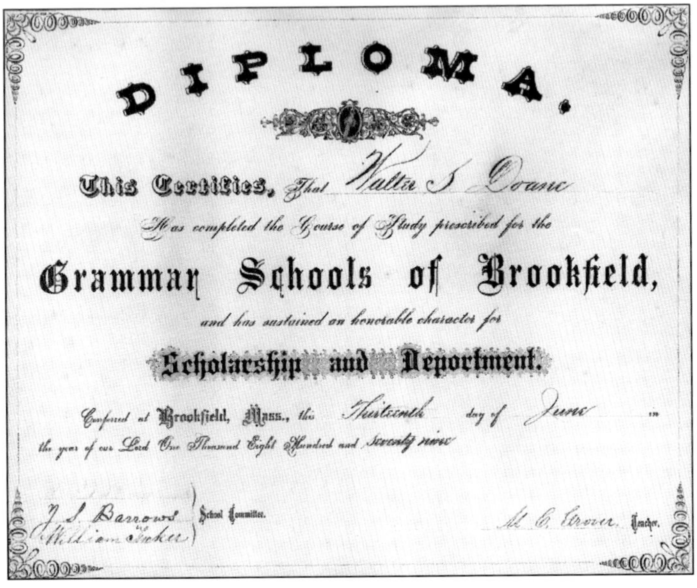

DIPLOMA.

This Certifies, That Walter S Doane

Has completed the Course of Study prescribed for the

Grammar Schools of Brookfield,

and has sustained an honorable character for

Scholarship and Deportment.

Conferred at Brookfield, Mass., this Thirteenth day of June in the year of our Lord One Thousand Eight Hundred and seventy nine

J. S. Barrows / William Tucker — School Committee.

M. E. Grover, Teacher.

GRAMMAR SCHOOL DIPLOMA, 1879. Walter S. Doane's diploma for completing the course of grammar school study, conferred on June 13, 1879, was signed by his teacher M.E. Grover and by school committee members Charles P. Blanchard, J.S. Barrows, and William Tucker. In 1879, there were 577 students enrolled in 14 Brookfield schoolhouses, at an average cost to the town of $12.51 per scholar. (Courtesy of MPL.)

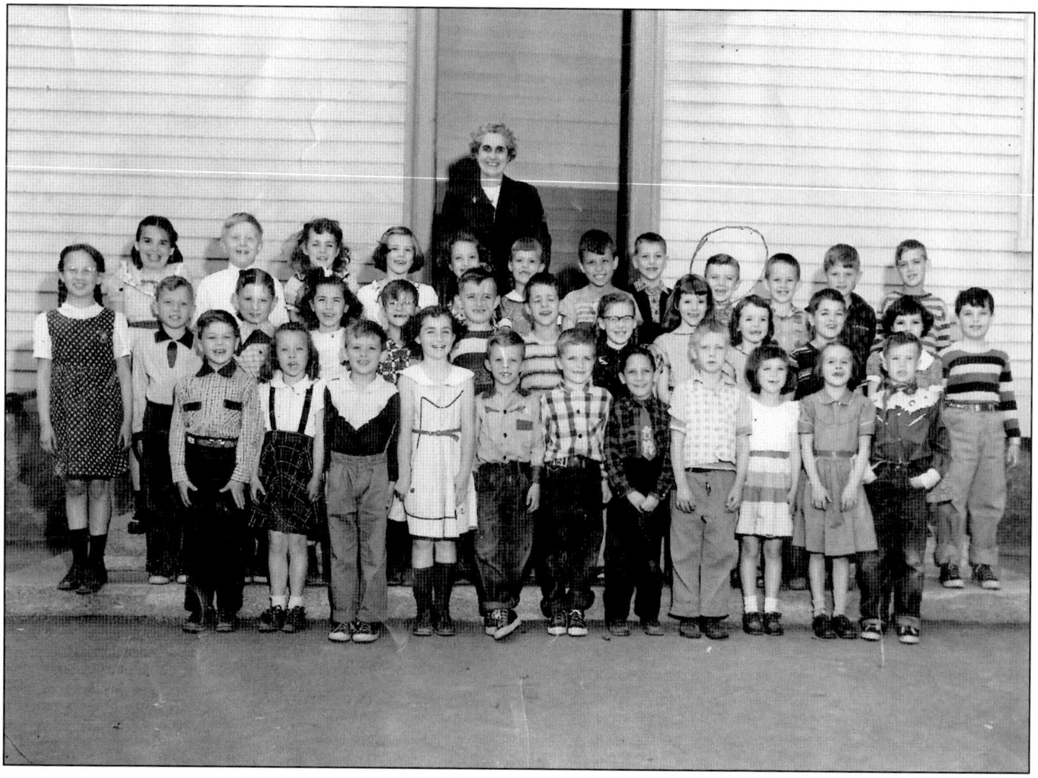

Blanchard School, 1953. Mary O'Donnell's second-grade class included, from left to right, (first row) unidentified, Muriel Cantell, Donald Faugno, unidentified, Carl Barnes, Robert Labreque, James Paradis, Lawrence Huckins, unidentified, Ellen Robinson, and Michael Pecha; (second row) Sylvia Brown, Robert Pratt, two unidentified, Neil Shailer, Peter Terry, two unidentified, Rita Laflamme, Jean Laflamme, Arthur Robbins, and unidentified; (third row) Barbara Violetta, Fred Gross, Peggy Gardner, three unidentified, William Martin, John Woodard, Clement Porter, David Broughton, Douglas Gadaire, and unidentified. (Courtesy of Clement Porter.)

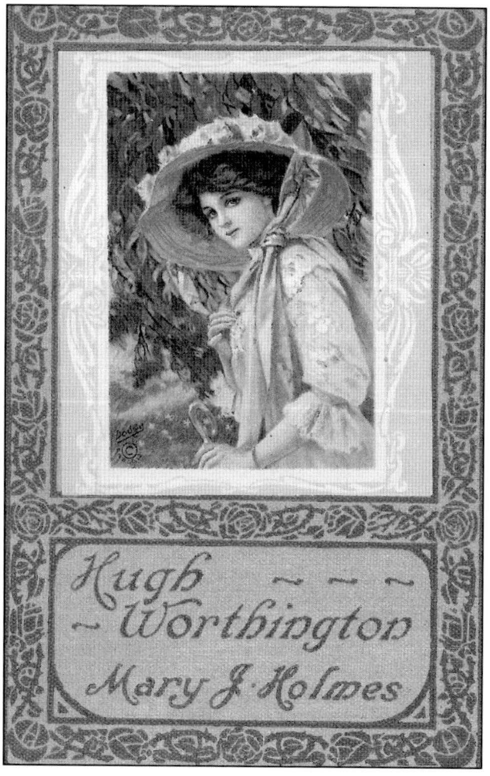

Mary Jane Holmes's Book Cover. Born in 1825 in the Rice Corner district, Mary Jane Hawes attended the Rice Corner schoolhouse and later taught there. After marrying Daniel Holmes, she moved to New York and became a bestselling novelist, selling over two million copies of her 39 novels before her death in 1907. Her novels focused on stories of everyday people, often based on Brookfield folks. (Courtesy of MPL.)

ELEMENTARY SCHOOL, OCTOBER 1973. School nurse Barbara Clancy measures the height and weight of fourth-grader John Nelson. In celebration of Brookfield's 300th anniversary, Clancy, school nurse from 1968 to 2001, wears an original uniform, including a cap in the shape of the school's Ether Dome, from her nursing school, Massachusetts General Hospital where ether was first successfully used. (Courtesy of MPL and *Worcester Telegram & Gazette*.)

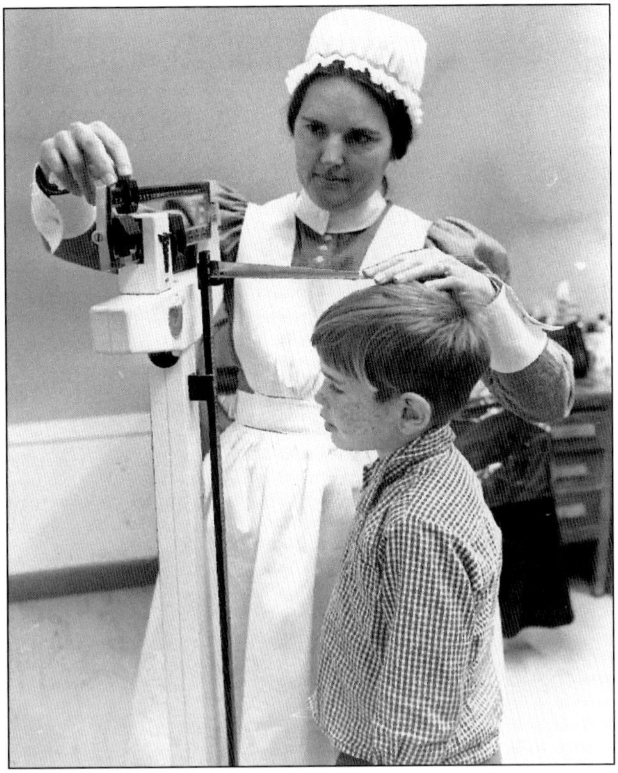

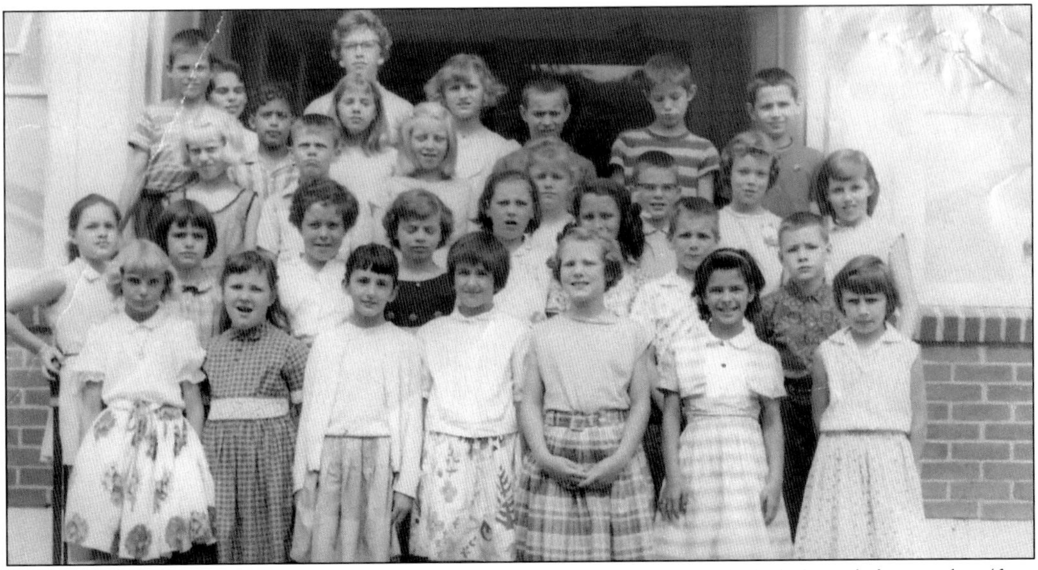

ELEMENTARY SCHOOL, 1961. Nancy Comeau's fourth-grade class included, from left to right, (first row) Betty Walker, Christine LaBarge, unidentified, Kerry Campbell, Colleen Dorney, Sheila Pronto, and Jean Bozyk; (second row) Barbara Turner, Janice Terry, Francis Ann Chaffee, Christine Bussiere, Ruth Spence, Lisa Pion, unidentified, and David Bourdeau; (third row) Christine Corrow, Dennis Faugno, Linda Cote, Sarah Whitcomb, Donald Powell, Laurel Glass, and Katherine Docwra; (fourth row) Ken J., Nancy Mundell, Ronald Laviera, Nancy Comeau (teacher) Anne Squire, Bonnie Williams, Ernest B., Randall Bennett, and Raymond L. (Courtesy of Docwra family.)

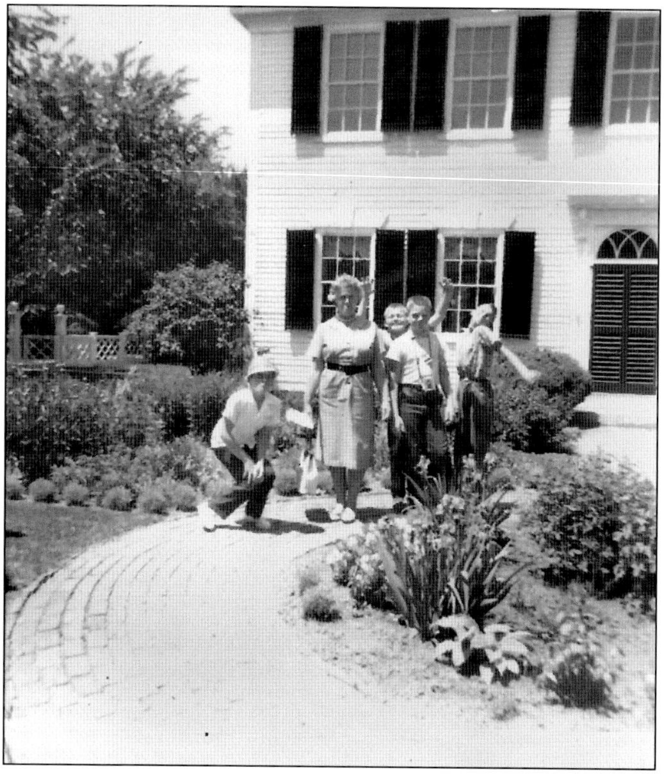

Elementary School Field Trip, 1962. Sixth graders ham it up for the camera on the annual class trip to Old Sturbridge Village. Shown here in front of the Salem Towne House are, from left to right, James Porter, teacher/ principal Mary Leach, Thomas Green, Wayne Banwell, and Harvey Beeman. (Photograph by and courtesy of Andrea Campbell Faugno.)

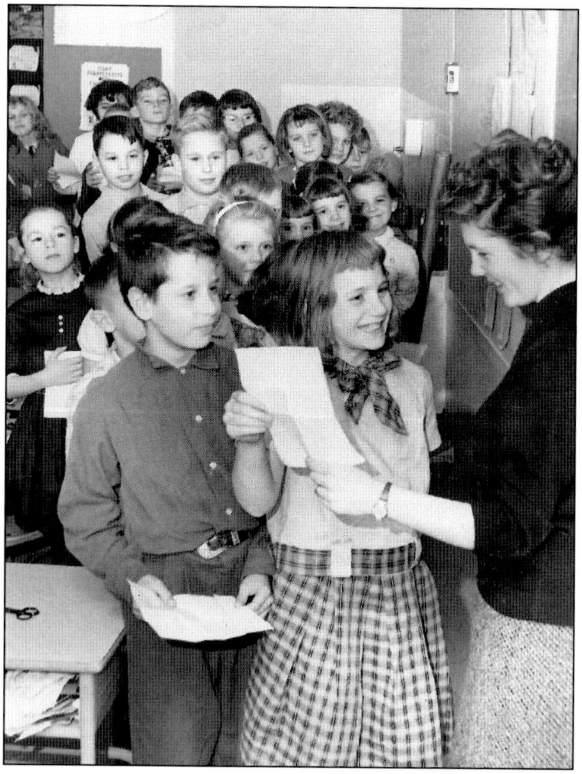

Elementary School, February 1960. Janet Cohen's fourth-grade students present goodbye notes before she departs on maternity leave. In the front are Horace Squire (left) and Susan Johnson. Other students include Nancy Krock, Debra Schneider, Janice Robinson, Ellen Nelson, Charlene Fredette, James Valley, Alan Glass, Sally Noyes, Andrea Campbell, Donna Willett, Robert Ruggles III, Marcia Yaskoski, Timothy Nolan, and Linda Zadroga. (Courtesy of Andrea Campbell Faugno and *Worcester Telegram & Gazette*.)

Six

BUSINESSES

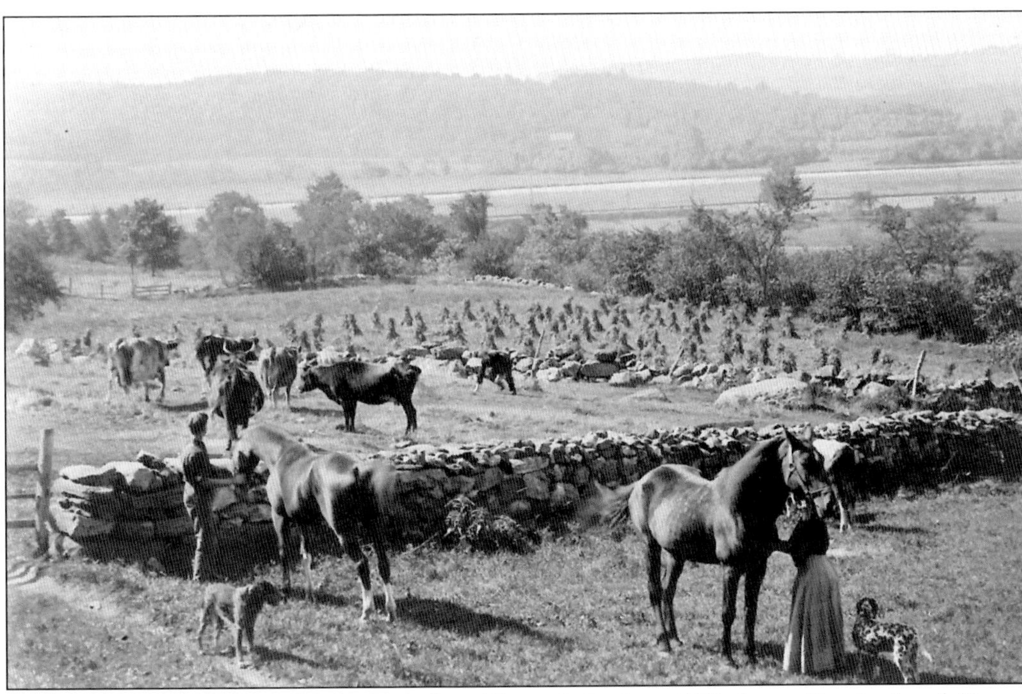

BROOKFIELD INN FARM. Before Jane Meehan Chapin's death in 1925, she and her husband, George H. Chapin, and her sister Mary Ann Meehan lived in the Oliver Crosby mansion along with their brother Henry, who ran this farm on West Main Street. The farm was run in conjunction with the Chapins' Brookfield Inn up the road, where Mary Anne Meehan was a cook. (Courtesy of Harris M. Gray.)

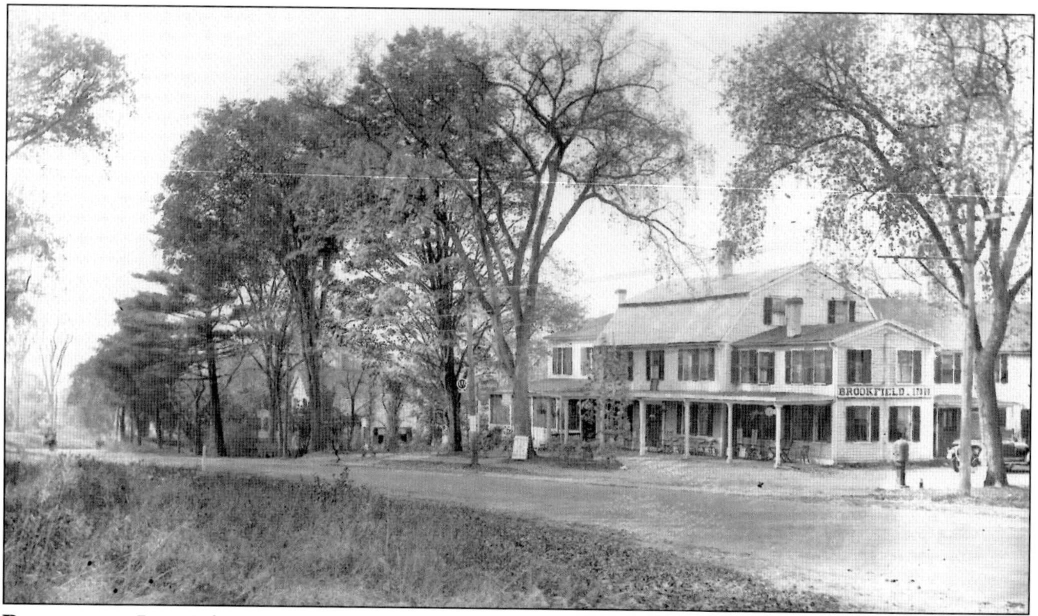

BROOKFIELD INN. The inn was an important rest stop along the old Boston Post Road (now West Main Street, Route 9). Also known as the Brookfield House and the 1771 House, early-20th-century owner Jane Chapin fixed upon the year 1771 seemingly arbitrarily. The inn has been visited by such notables as Franklin D. Roosevelt during his 1932 presidential campaign. (Photograph by William Bullard; courtesy of Dennis LeBeau.)

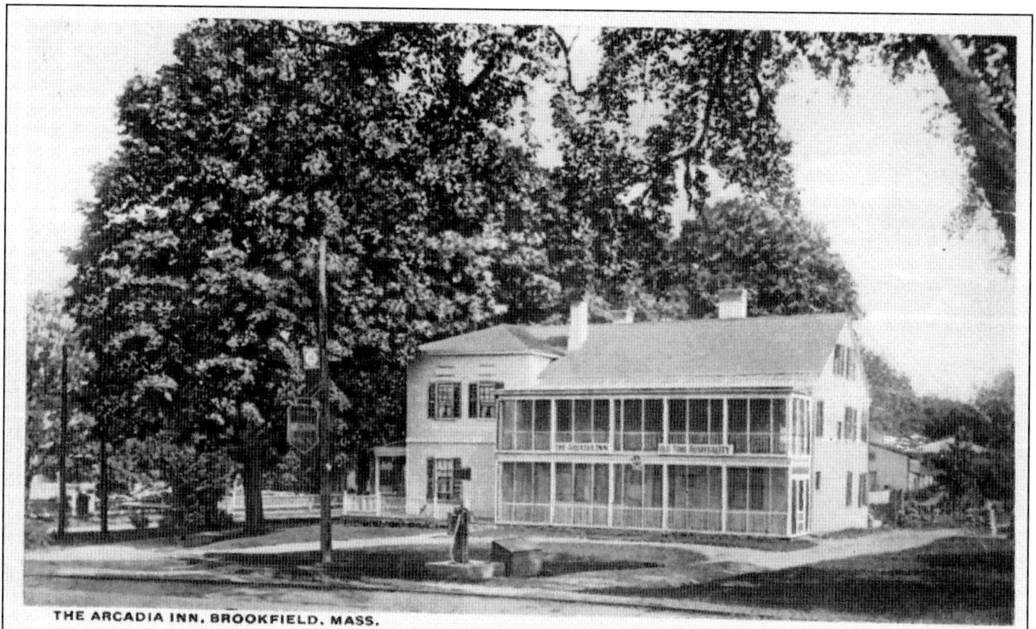

ARCADIA INN. In 1810, Francis Howe constructed this property and a separate building that housed the town's first post office, destroyed by fire in 1863. Converted in 1898 to serve as an annex to the Brookfield Inn, the Arcadia Inn was located at the corner of Post Road and Common Street. The many travelers who passed through town had a variety of choices for overnight accommodations. (Courtesy of William Jankins.)

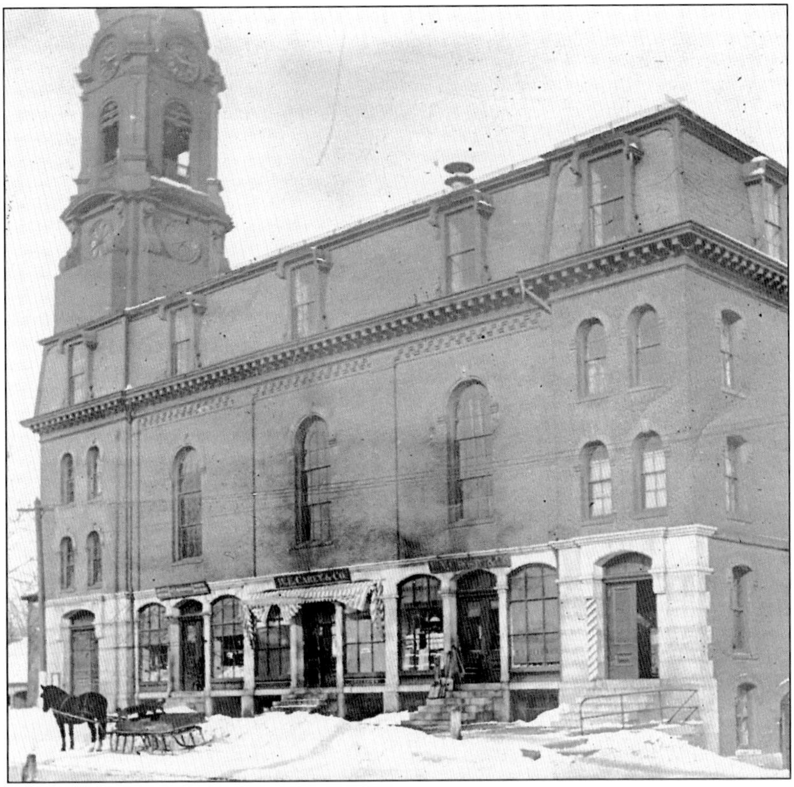

Town Hall Block, 1901. The first floor of the 1866 town hall housed the offices of the selectmen and town clerk as well as the storefronts of Henry W. Irwin Men's Furnishing, A. Hooker Barbershop, and Henry Crosby Dry Goods. The second floor housed the main stage and Dr. Newhall's office, while third-level occupants included the Dexter Post of the Grand Army of the Republic. (Courtesy of longtime resident.)

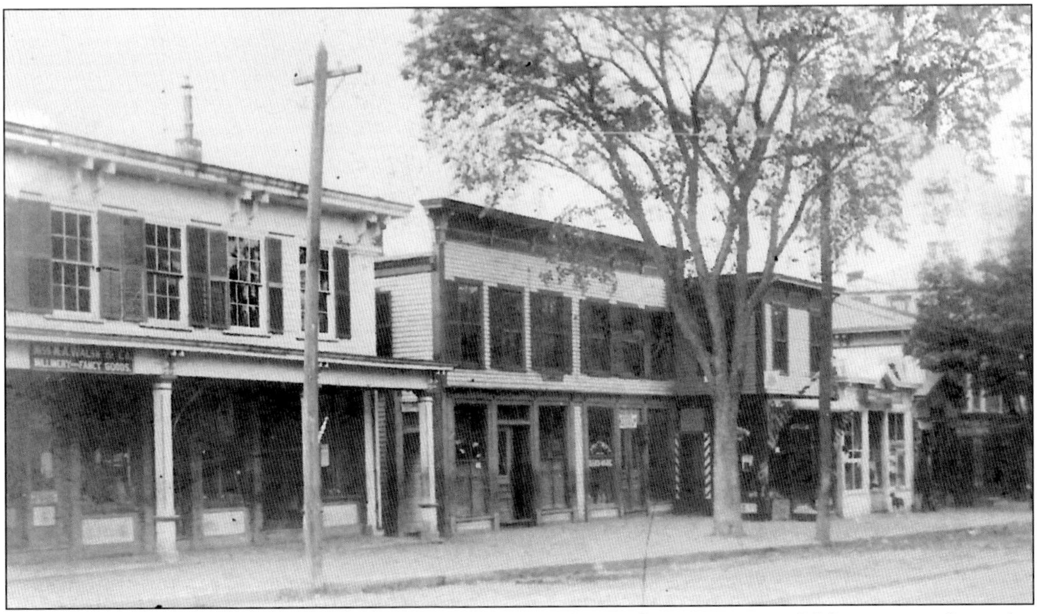

Gerald and Crosby Blocks, 1902. Central Street housed many successful businesses from the mid-1850s to the early 1900s. The shops were sectioned off into blocks named for the owner of the property; block names included Town House, Gerald, Crosby, Warner, Tyler, and Post Office. Businesses ranged from a haberdasher, milliner, barber, dentist, lawyer, and jeweler to three grocery stores and a roller rink. (Courtesy of Harris M. Gray.)

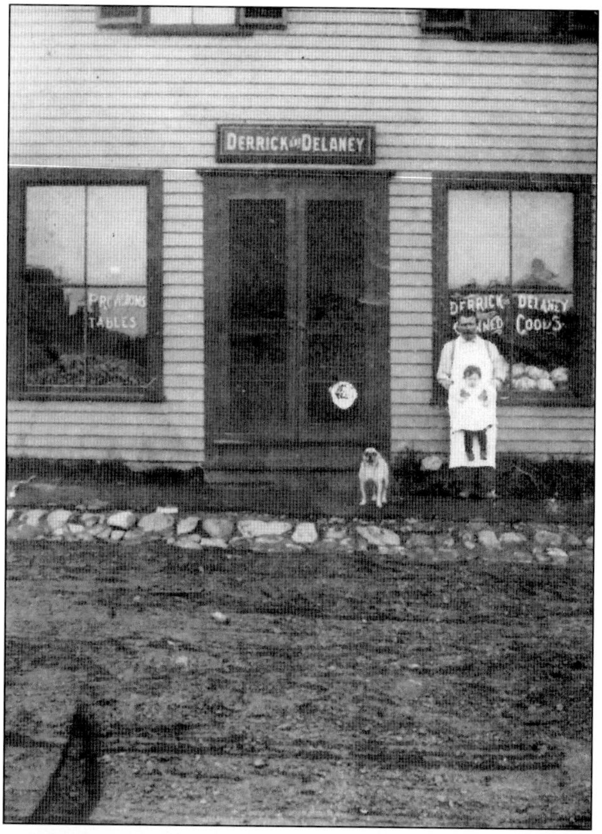

DERRICK AND DELANEY, 1901. The original Derrick and Delaney Meats and Produce Building, which stood on Prouty Street, is shown here in both an exterior view, left, and an interior view, below. This building was destroyed by fire in January 1902, and the business relocated to the basement of the town hall, which burned to the ground later that year in September. The business then relocated briefly to the basement of the Gerald Block, the current-day Tip-Top Country Store on Central Street. Proprietor Edward Francis Delaney, shown below at right, and his wife, Nellie Derrick, lived on Sherman Street. (Both, courtesy of Mary Remillard, great-granddaughter of Edward Francis Delaney.)

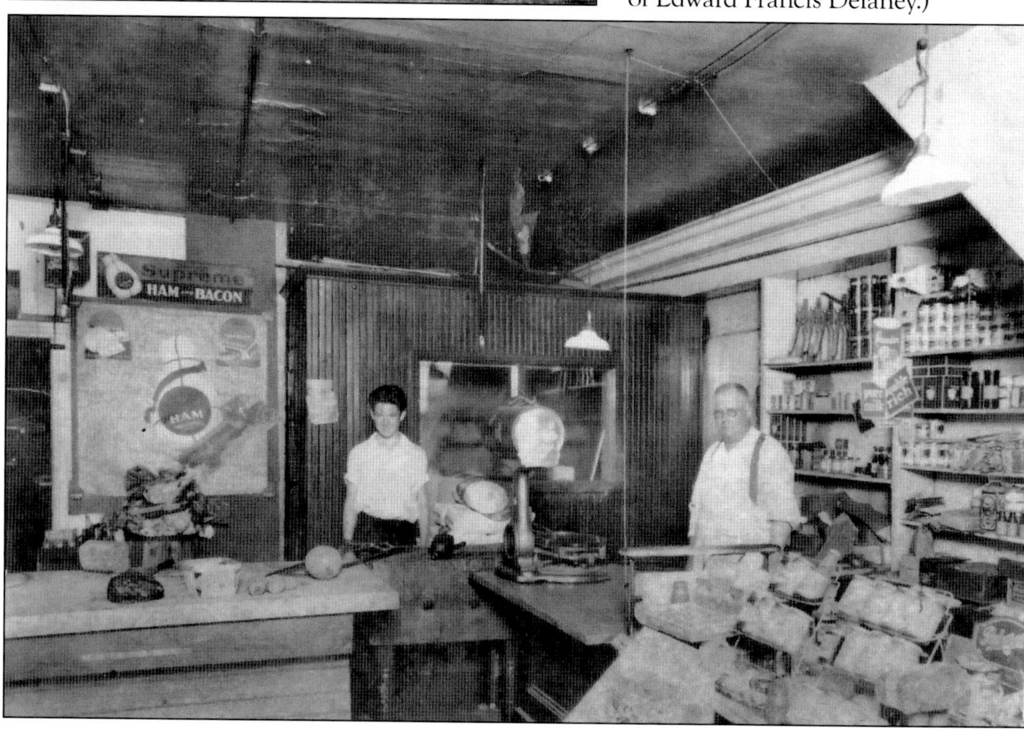

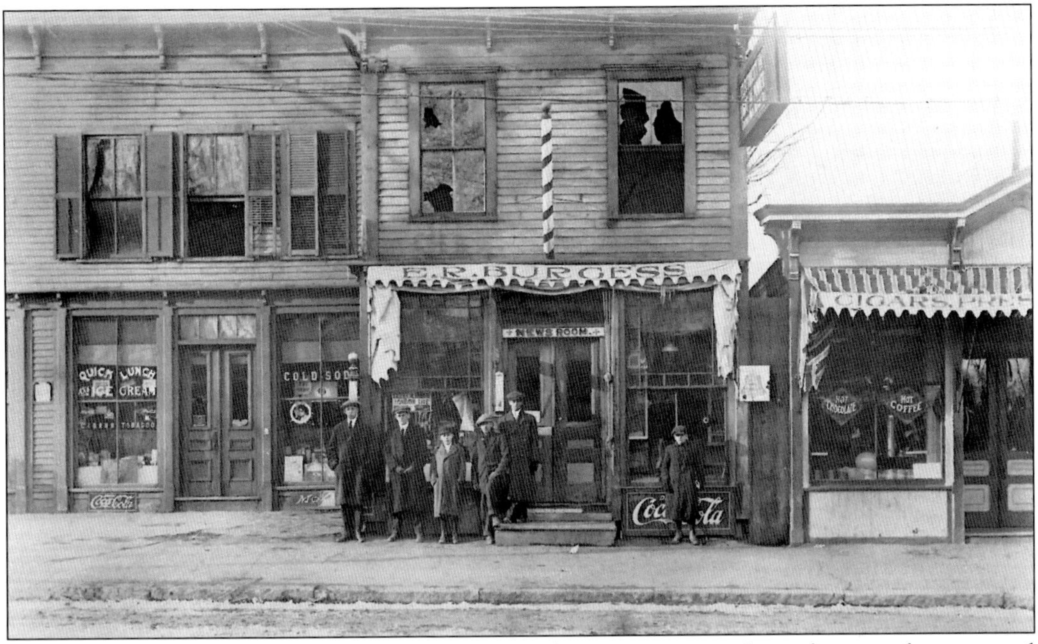

E.R. Burgess, 1902. These Central Street buildings were just a short distance from several structures that burned in 1902. Perhaps a precursor to the gentle demise of bustling commerce in town, the Warren, Brookfield & Spencer Street Railway ceased operations in 1918, and in 1925, the new state road (Route 9) rerouted automobile traffic to the north. This site is now an empty lot. (Courtesy of Sheila Pronto McCarthy.)

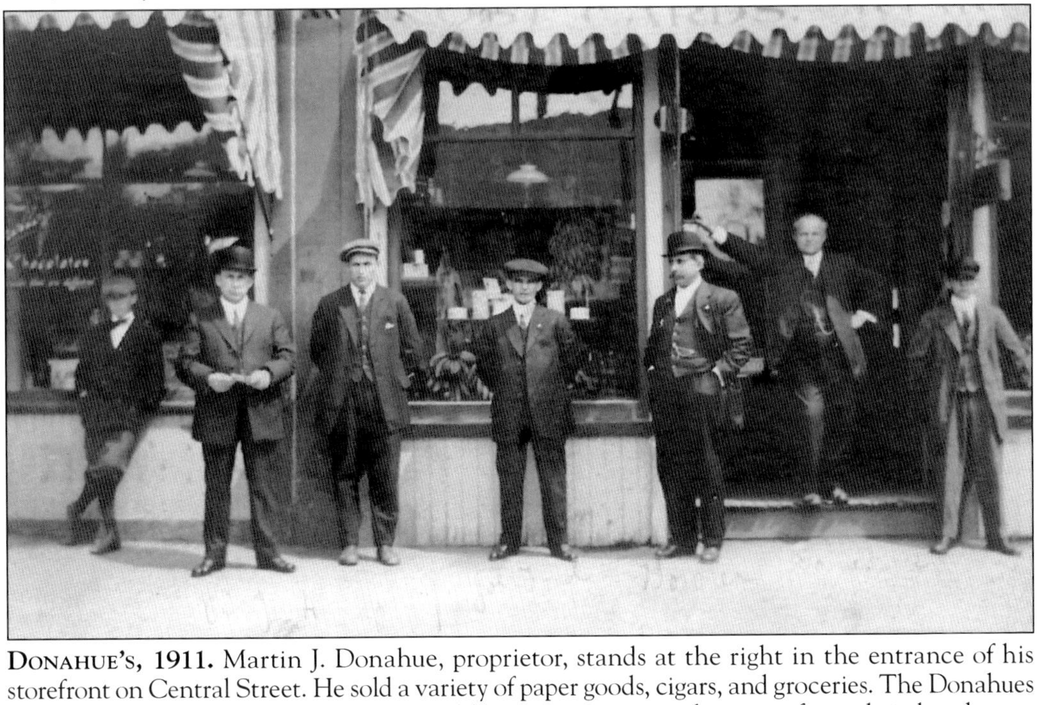

Donahue's, 1911. Martin J. Donahue, proprietor, stands at the right in the entrance of his storefront on Central Street. He sold a variety of paper goods, cigars, and groceries. The Donahues also owned the Gerald Block and rented boats to citizens and visitors from their boathouse, Donahue's Landing on the Quaboag River. (Courtesy of Barbara Clancy.)

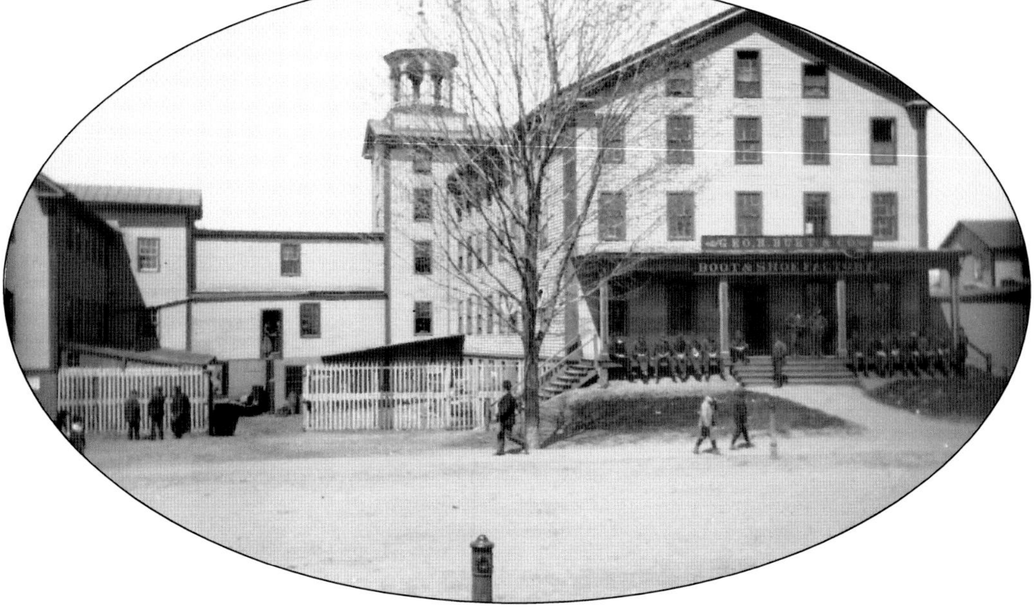

BOOT AND SHOE FACTORY. Aaron Kimball and John Parmelee Robinson built this Central Street factory in 1828 and referred to it as "The Big Shop." In 1861, Aaron Kimball retired and sold the property to Henry Twichell, his bookkeeper, who in turn sold the property in 1864 to his brother Emmons Twichell. The town's major employer went bankrupt during the 1879–1880 depression. Soon thereafter, the building was purchased by George H. Burt and Company, who hired 500 employees and manufactured an average of 300 cases of shoes per day. When Foster and Moulton purchased the factory in 1906, they tore down two-thirds of the structure, leaving what is present-day Gavitt Wire Company, based in the building since 1928. (Above, photograph by Charles P. Blanchard; courtesy of Blanchard Means Foundation; below, courtesy of Carolyn Potter Murray.)

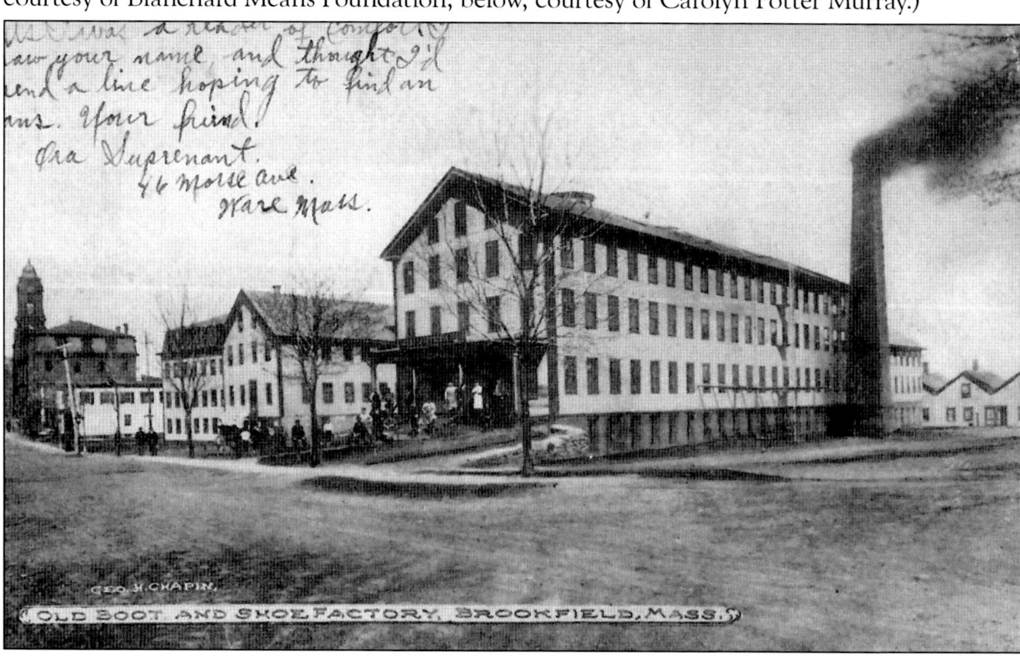

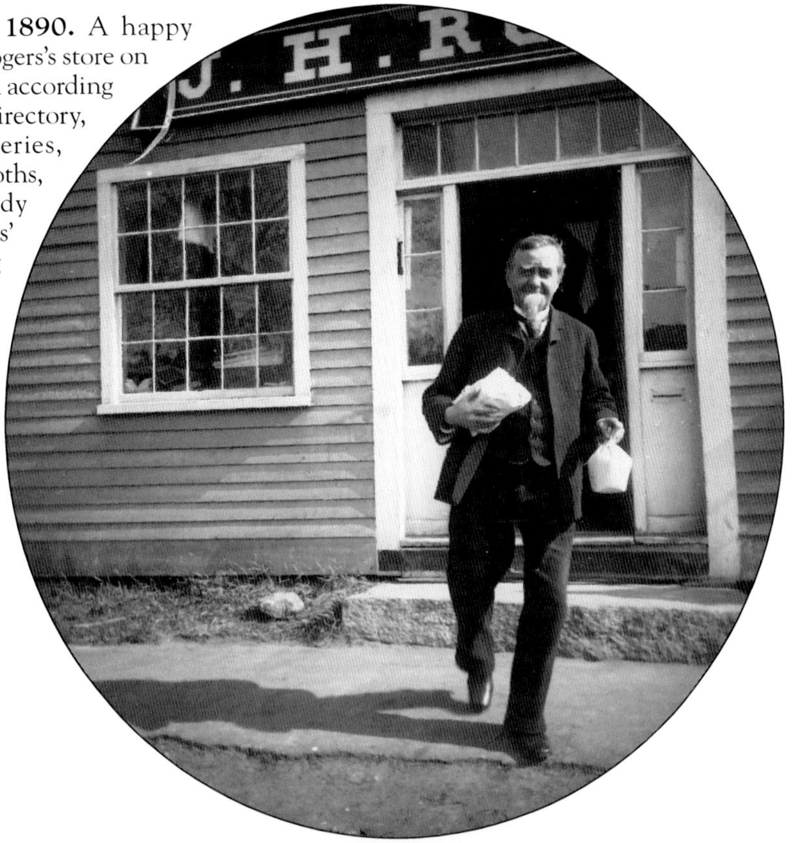

ROGERS'S STORE, C. 1890. A happy customer leaves J.H. Rogers's store on Common Street, which according to the 1889 business directory, sold dry goods, groceries, flour, and "Floor Oil Cloths, Hemp Carpets, Ready Made Clothing, Ladies' and Gents' Furnishing Goods, Hats, Caps, Furs in their season, Boots, Shoes and Rubbers, Crockery, [and] Glass ware." (Photograph by Charles P. Blanchard; courtesy of Blanchard Means Foundation.)

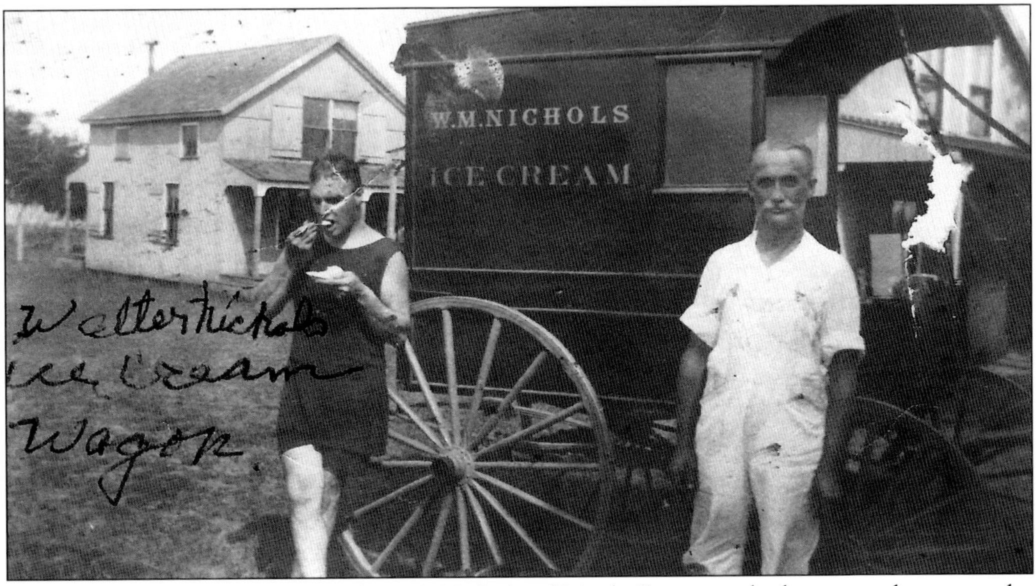

ICE CREAM WAGON, 1920S. Walter M. Nichols of Maple Street worked as a conductor on the Warren, Brookfield & Spencer Street Railway before beginning his ice cream business. At the turn of the century, the treat could be had, among other places, at the ice cream room in the old library building next to town hall. (Courtesy of Loana Nichols Gadaire and Paula Gadaire Woodard.)

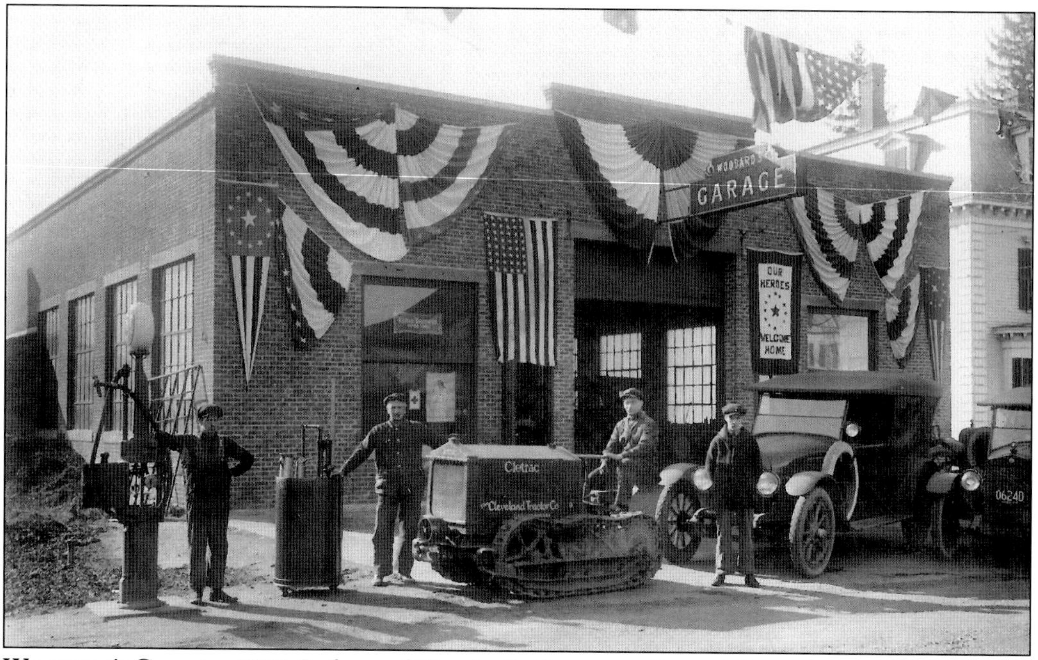

Woodard's Garage, 1918. In front of Woodard's Garage on Central Street are, from left to right, Robert Woodard, George Woodard Sr., Elmer Fisher, and George Woodard Jr. Built in 1917, the business has been run by John Woodard ever since he returned home from the Air Force in 1970. Woodard Sr. held the first steam engine engineer's license, and Fisher patented the hydraulic lifter. (Courtesy of Woodard family.)

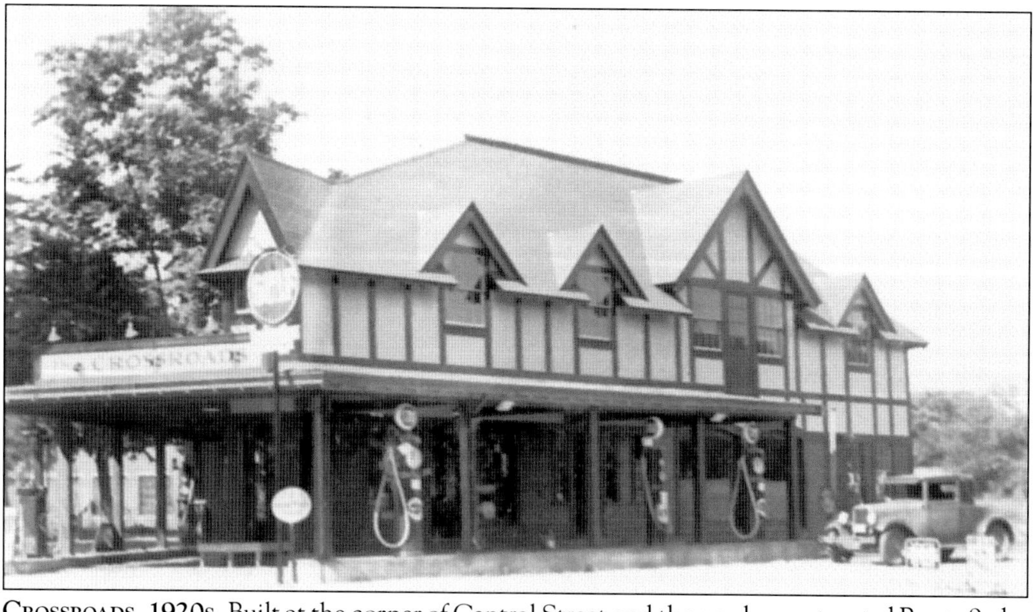

Crossroads, 1920s. Built at the corner of Central Street and the newly constructed Route 9, the Crossroads was a diner and gas station. Early Gulf pumps are shown here; Woodard's Garage on Central Street boasted the one-time oldest Gulf station in New England. Both businesses were built by George Woodard Sr. The Crossroads was later known as the Post Road Restaurant and the Gables. (Courtesy of Woodard family.)

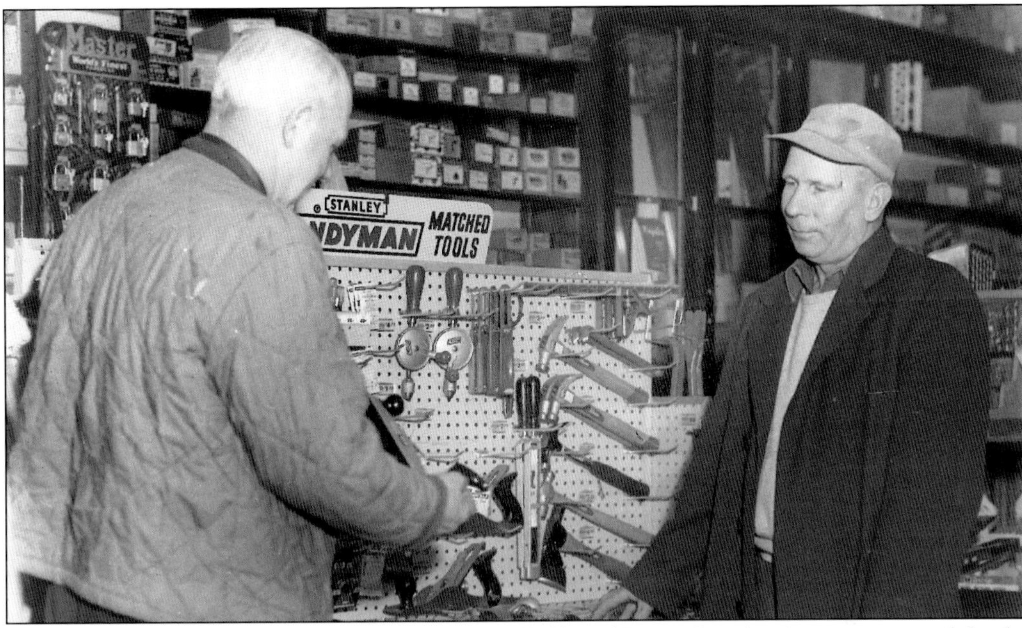

RICE AND GADAIRE, LATE 1960S. Paul Gadaire (left) and Roger Swetland examine a tool display inside the Rice and Gadaire Lumber Company store on Central Street, located across from the town hall. Charles F. Rice started the business after he retired from a successful mill and grain business in 1905, and it continued into the 1980s. (Photograph by L. Roger Parquette; courtesy of Loana Nichols Gadaire and Paula Woodard Gadaire.)

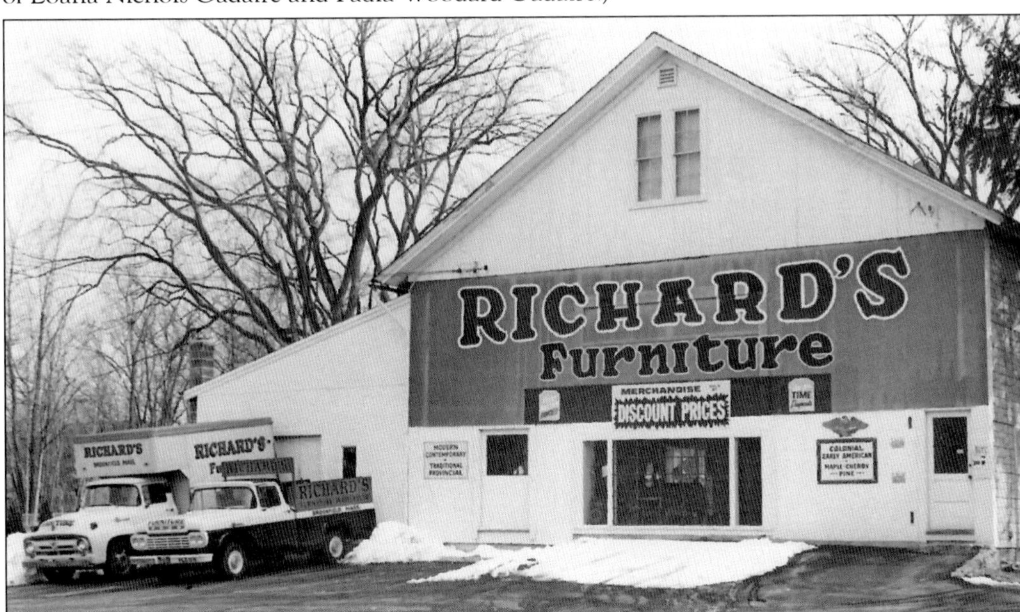

RICHARD'S FURNITURE, 1950S. Richard Bourdeau, inspired by an uncle in the furniture business, started Richard's Furniture in 1953. His son David earned a business degree at Providence College, became manager of the store in 1974, and purchased it in 1980, soon doubling the business and expanding to western Massachusetts with three more stores. Today, the store is Tombstone Trading, his "retirement hobby," opened in 2006. (Courtesy of Bourdeau family.)

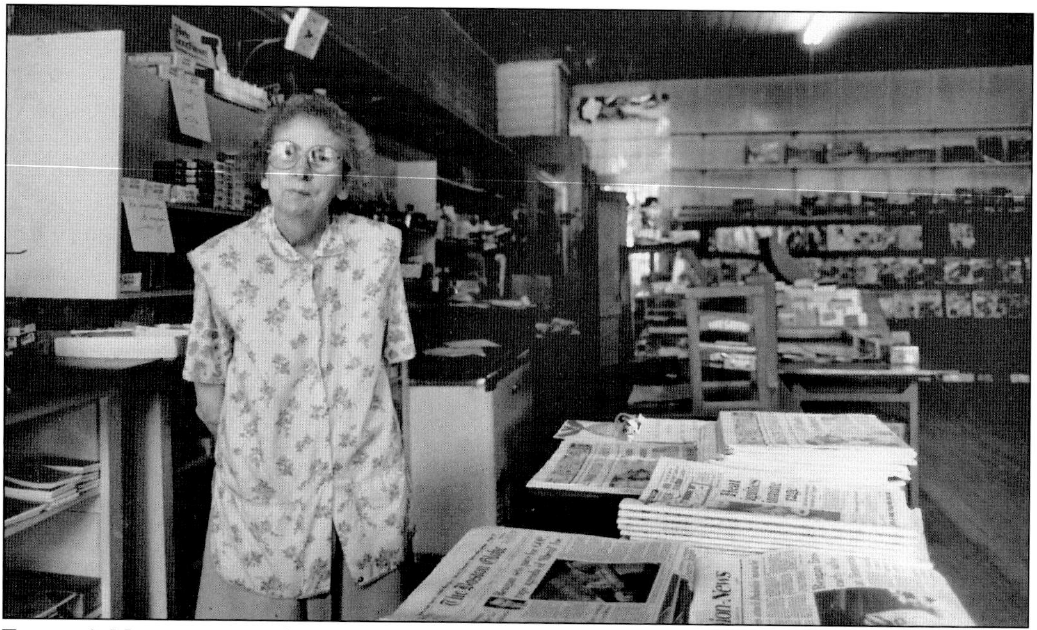

Frazier's News, 1988. Velma Frazier lived on Merrick Avenue and walked to her Central Street newsstand every day. The store was frequented by generations of townsfolk seeking newspapers, comics, candy, sundries, and greeting cards or looking to use the wooden telephone booth nestled against the back wall. Frazier's News was an institution for 64 years, started by Frazier's father, Hardy, in 1924. (Courtesy of Michael Seery and *Spencer New Leader*.)

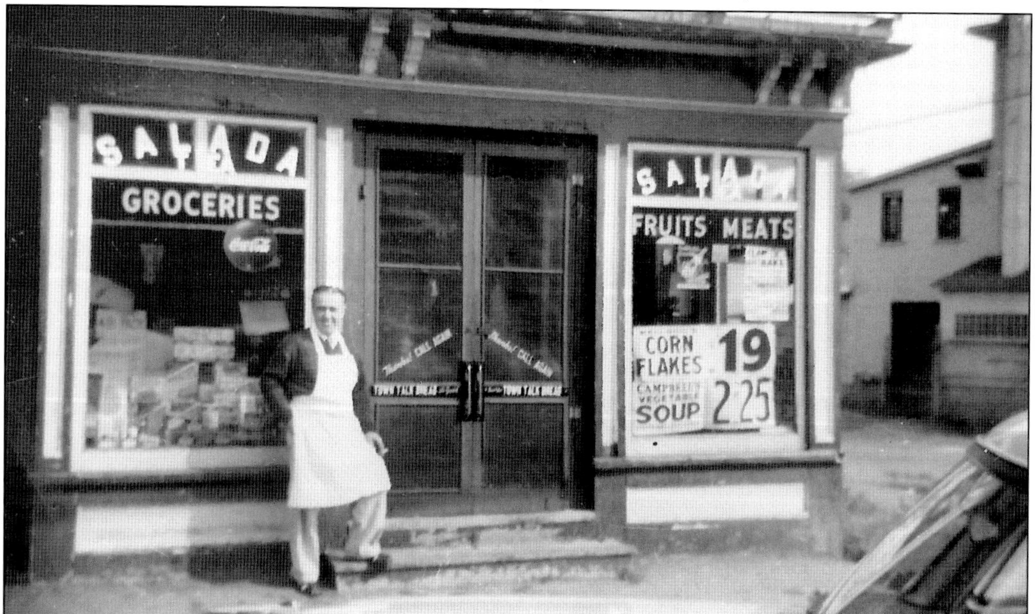

Clover Farm Store. Owned by Leon "Hoppy" Gaudette, this meat and grocery store at the corner of Central and Prouty Streets operated from 1934 to 1964. Gaudette delivered groceries to customers throughout town, and many paid on a tab system. Gaudette was involved in music and sports and served on the sheriff's department and as a warden for Kimball Street during World War II. (Courtesy of Donald Gaudette.)

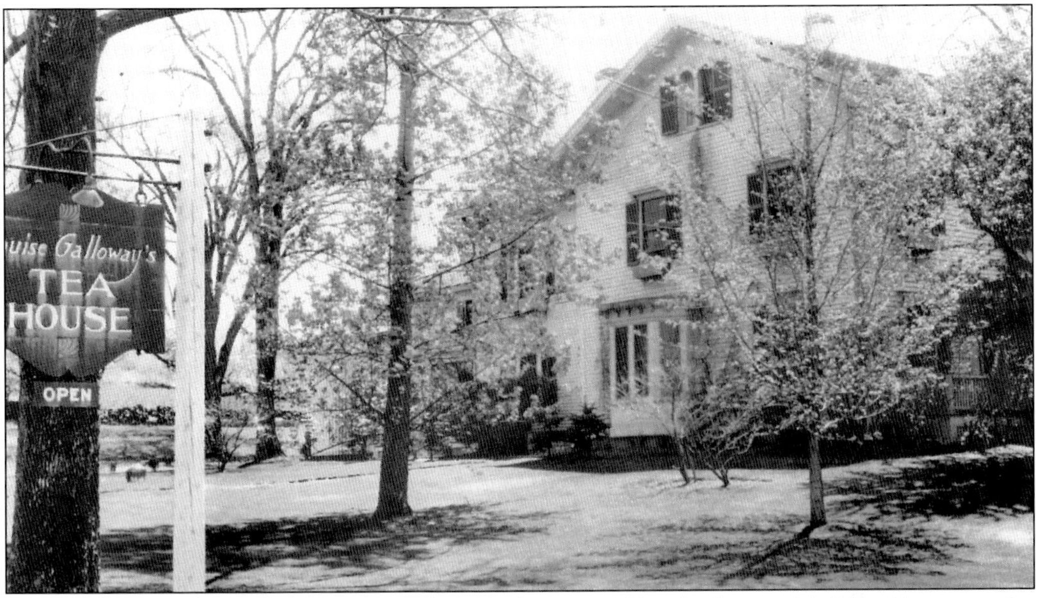

LOUISE GALLOWAY'S TEA HOUSE. Opened as a teahouse in 1924, the former Abel Reed house on the Boston Post Road became a destination for actors and sports celebrities. Louise Galloway, a Broadway actress who ran her own vaudeville company from 1911 to 1916, operated it. One of the dining rooms was painted with a lawn and flowers, so diners would feel they were outside. (Courtesy of MPL.)

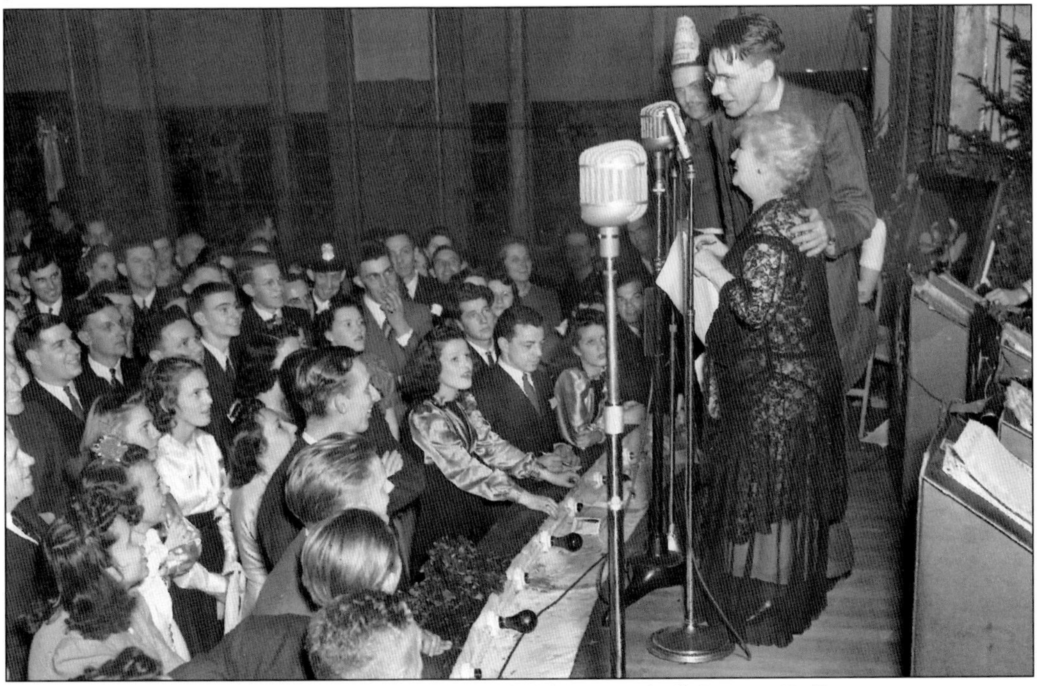

RECITATION, DECEMBER 1940. During a dance held at town hall, Louise Galloway recites a poem by William Carey Duncan celebrating Elsie the Cow's return to Brookfield. It was on this same stage in 1931 that Galloway began her summer playgroup, claimed to be the first in New England. Also onstage is Bob Pooley, the head of the orchestra that performed that evening. (Courtesy of May-Boyce Collection.)

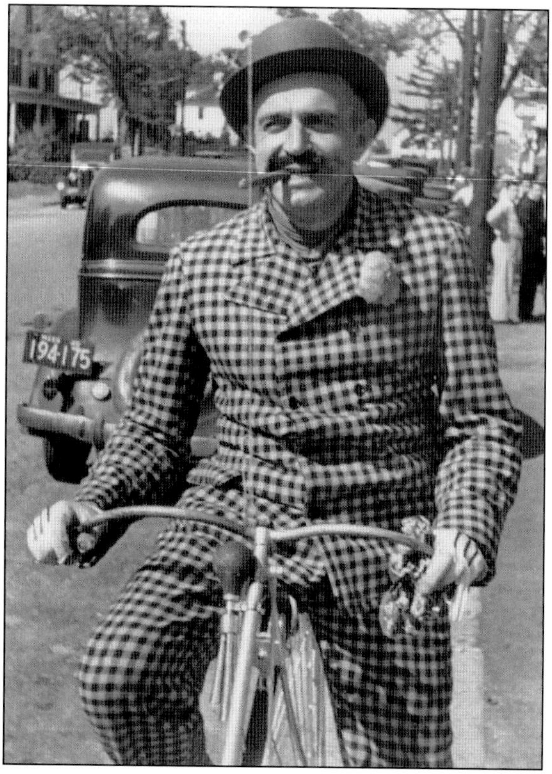

Founder, Gavitt Wire and Cable. The playful side of a most industrious man is revealed as Lester Gavitt tools down Central Street around 1948. He began his career in 1923 in West Brookfield, using textile braiding machines to produce shoestrings and buggy whips. By 1928, his Central Street plant in Brookfield was producing wiring for the new radio industry using the same techniques. (Courtesy of Harold R. Chesson Jr.)

Gavitt Wire and Cable Company. Women working in the cabling room are braiding multiwire cables for jukeboxes around 1960. Elsie Crawford faces the camera (rear center), while Mary Walulak (far left) operates a stripping machine. Consistently known for its made-to-order, quality operation, the innovative company has many applications for its products, including antennas, radios, microphones, and even wiring for NASA headsets. (Courtesy of Harold R. Chesson Jr.)

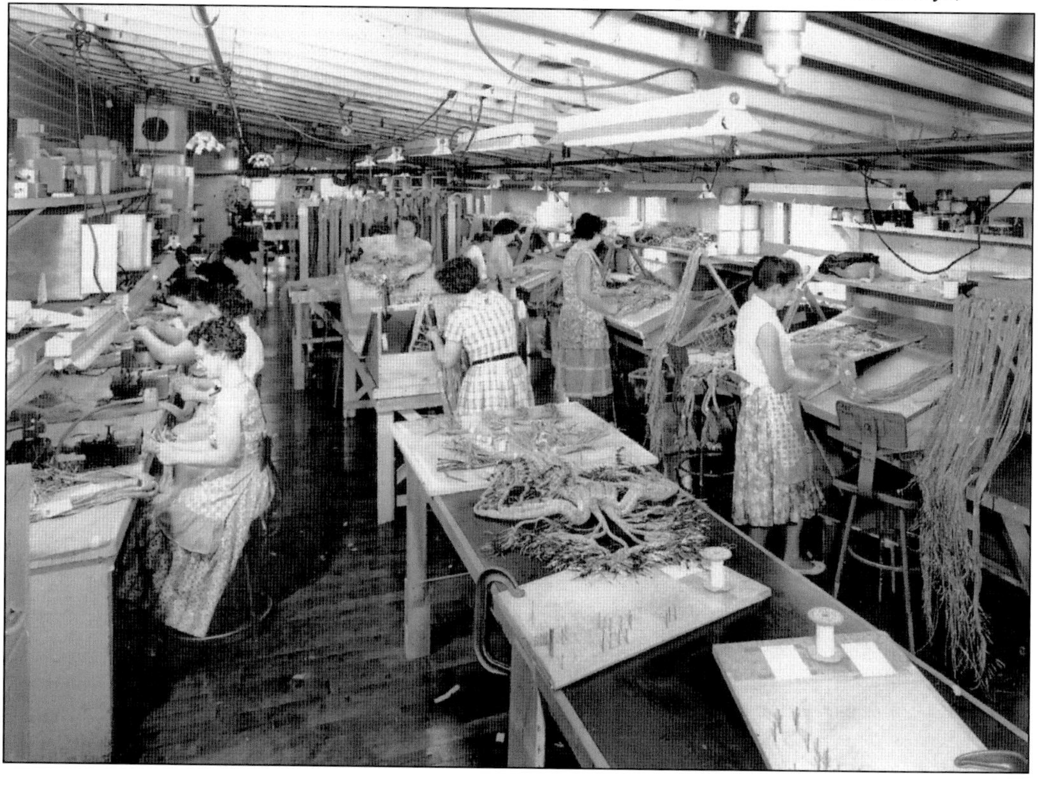

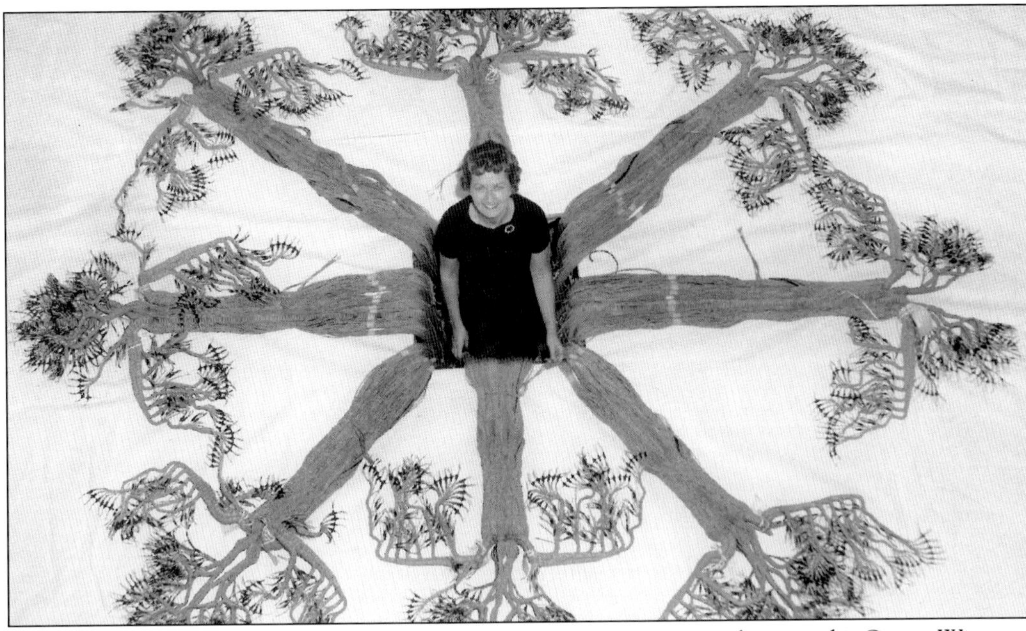

LINOTYPE MACHINE WIRING, C. 1960. Mabel Lyons Grimes was working in the Gavitt Wire and Cable Company office when she was asked to have her picture taken with this massive array of braided cabling. A special order for a linotype machine used in the printing industry required production to be extended through weekends and holidays in order to be completed on time. (Courtesy of Harold R. Chesson Jr.)

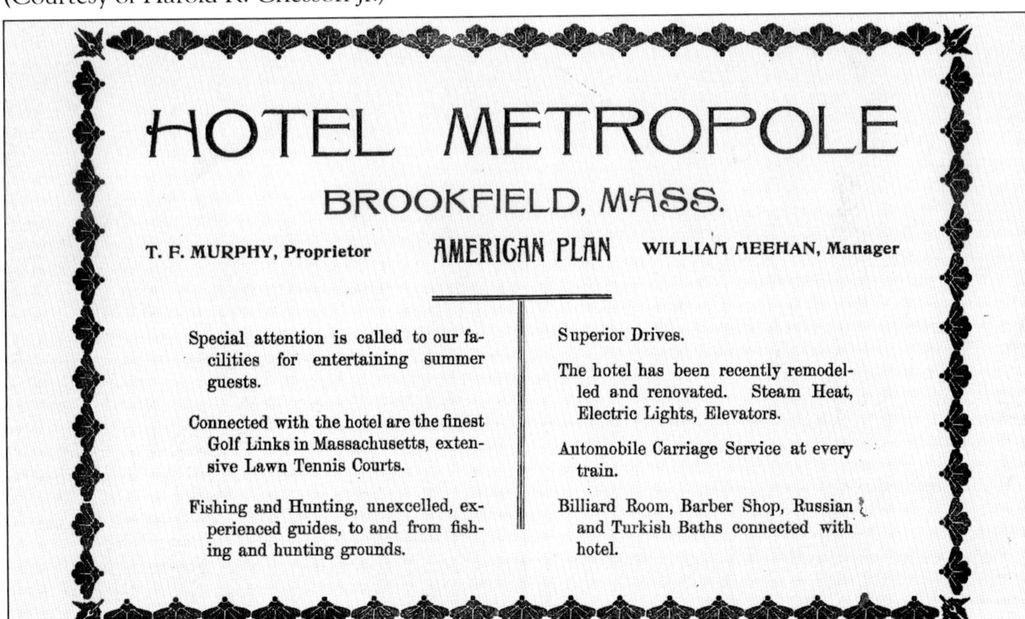

HOTEL METROPOLE. Brookfield native Thomas F. Murphy built his hotel on the corner of Pleasant and Hayden Streets around 1892, later moving it to Central Street near the Burt Shoe Factory. The railroad provided a stream of visitors, but fires eventually rendered the hotel unusable. Just a portion remains today, part of a private home next to Gavitt Wire's office building. (Courtesy of Loana Nichols Gadaire and Paula Gadaire Woodard.)

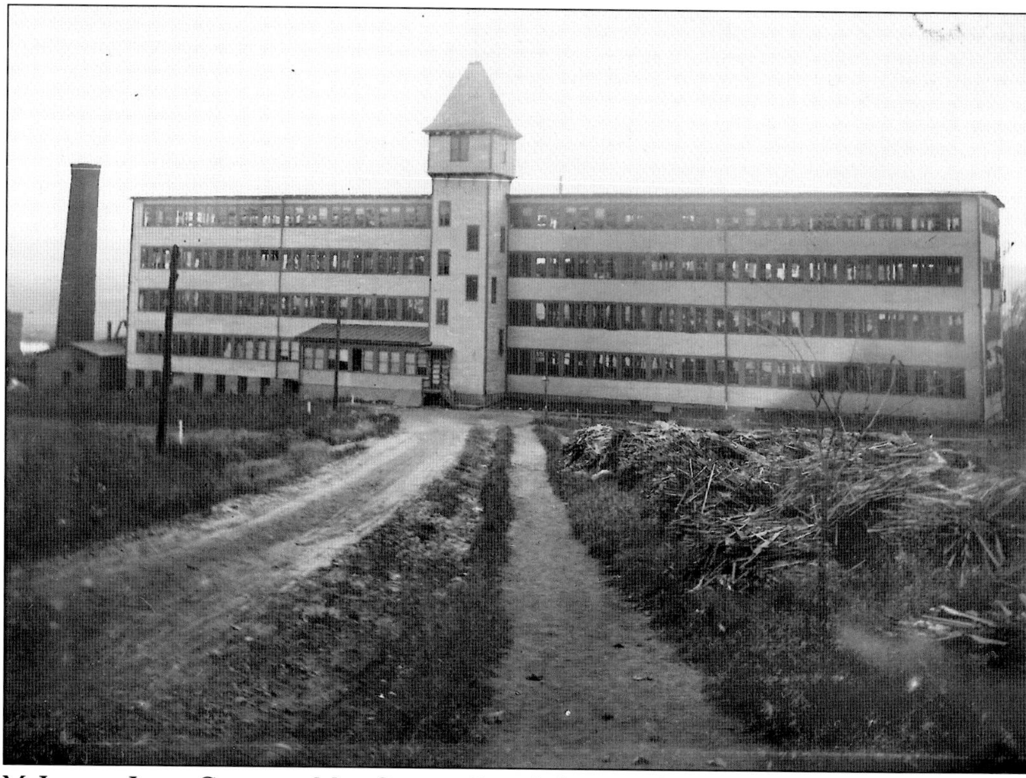

McLaurin-Jones Company, Mill Street. Founded in 1906 by William and John McLaurin to avoid tariffs imposed on products being sold from their father's mill in Scotland, the company was "the first to make surface coated papers, and among the first to apply adhesive coatings." McLaurin-Jones eventually expanded to a plant in Ware, leaving Brookfield's mill to produce gummed paper while the Ware plant manufactured specialty papers. (Courtesy of longtime resident.)

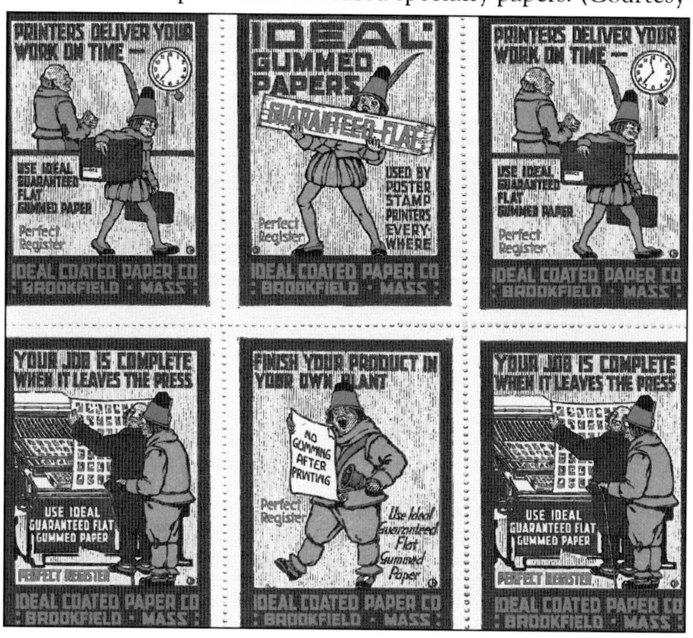

"Guaranteed Flat." A 1944 *Team-Mates* newsletter reported McLaurin-Jones Company's pivotal early innovation was being the first to "break'" the glue film on gummed paper, enabling gummed labels to remain flat regardless of humidity levels, whereas before they had a tendency to curl. The newsletter proudly noted, "All flattening processes in use in the gumming industry are an outgrowth of the original process developed by McLaurin-Jones Company." (Courtesy of William Jankins.)

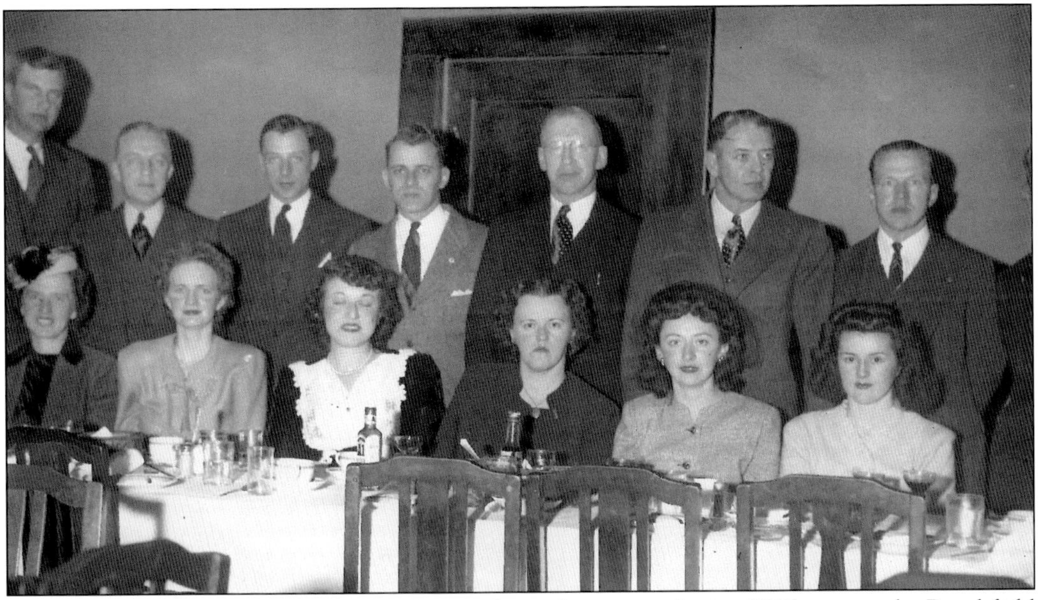

TEAM-MATES NEWSLETTER STAFF. In 1944, with employees numbering 350 between the Brookfield and Ware plants, McLaurin-Jones Company endeavored to facilitate communication among them. Meeting for dinner are, from left to right, (first row) Mary Weeks, Clare Broadbent, Philomena Petruzzi, Rita Murphy Cook, Mary Scott, and Neata Moore; (second row) unidentified, Philip R. Palamountain, Roger Levesque, George Adams, Frank Clark, Glenn Clark, Roy Clark, and Edward Ladue. (Courtesy of Neata Moore Campbell.)

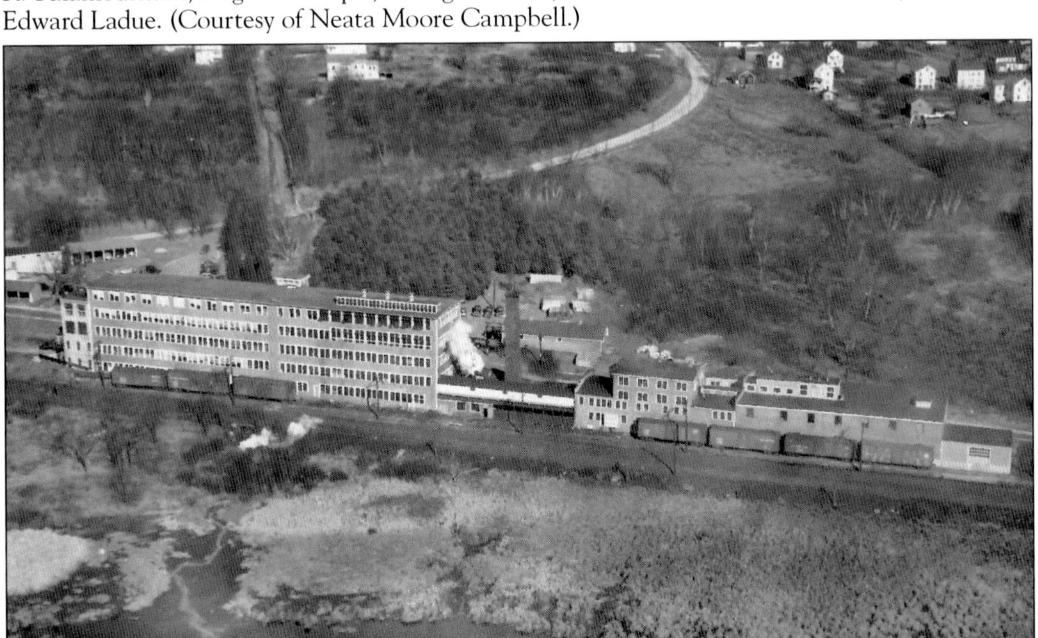

AERIAL VIEW, MILL STREET. Brookfield Shoe Factory was built in 1893, ceasing operations soon after 1900. In 1906, Ideal Coated Paper Company occupied the building, becoming one of the largest producers of gummed paper in the country before being consolidated into the McLaurin-Jones Company. After the 1950s, the building housed the Independent Box Company. In 2000, the main building on the left burned to the ground. (Courtesy of Barbara Clancy.)

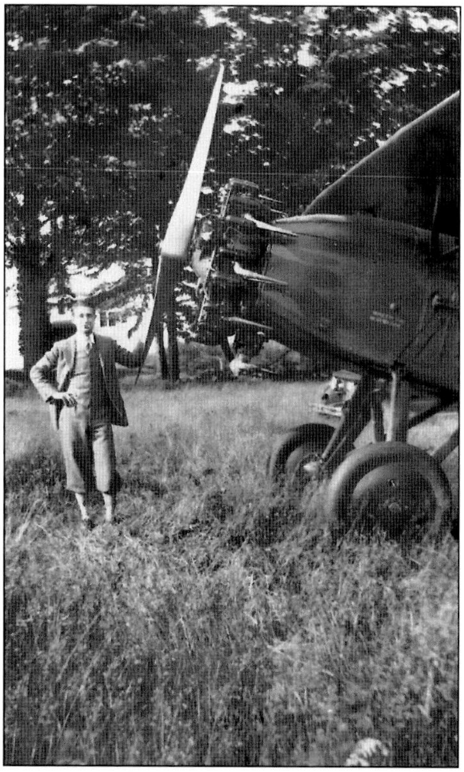

Pilot's License, c. 1935. Arthur Faugno of Lake Road had a long-standing interest in aviation as a young man. During the 1930s, he completed a course at the Aviation Institute of the USA in Washington, DC. After completing 50 hours of solo flying, he went to Boston and received his first-class pilot's license. (Courtesy of Gloria Achilles Faugno.)

Brookfield Airport. Located near the West Brookfield town line, the airport was part of the airmail system for the US Postal Service. Mail from the Brookfields was delivered to Westborough and relayed to Boston during the 1930s and 1940s. In existence since the early 1920s, the airport had a hangar on the property and offered flight instruction and passenger service using small planes. (Courtesy of Robert and Nancy Cronin Wilder.)

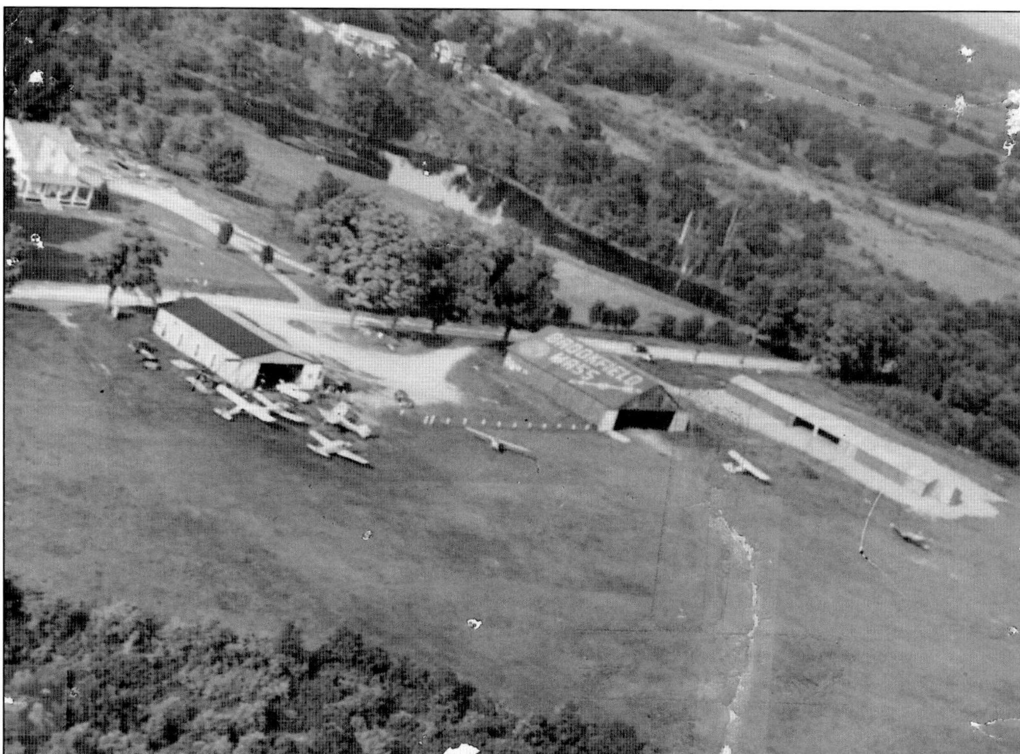

Seven

Lakes, Rivers, and Ponds

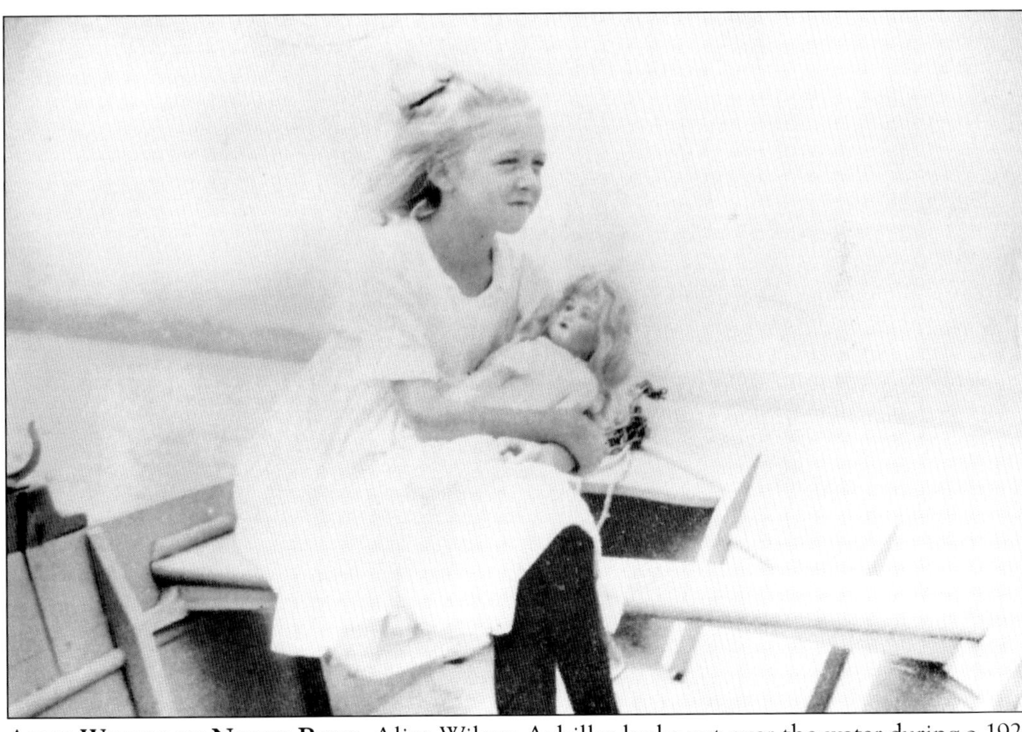

Alice Wilson on North Pond. Alice Wilson Achilles looks out over the water during a 1920 outing on Lake Quaboag, or North Pond, just off the shore of the Lake Road farm where her father, Arthur Wilson, worked. He was the manager of the Sibley farm, purchased in 1925 by George Jeppson and currently known as Oakholm. (Courtesy of Gloria Achilles Faugno.)

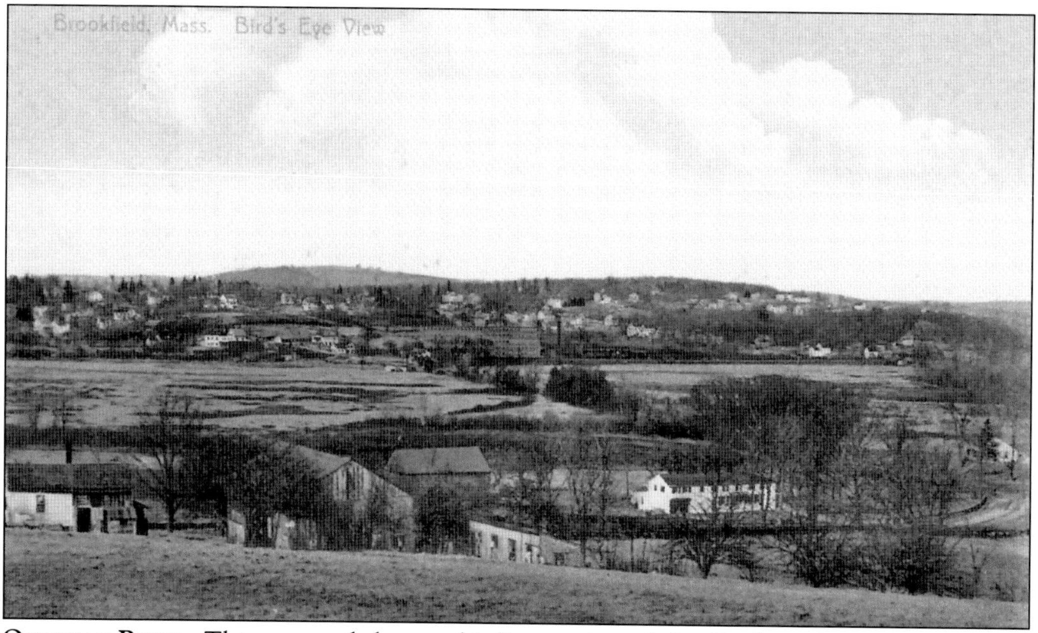

QUABOAG RIVER. This postcard shows a bird's-eye view of the Quaboag River and the land surrounding it. In the foreground are the houses at the foot of Long Hill Road, and in the distance are the houses and businesses leading up to the town center. This postcard was mailed in 1912 by Theresa Lane, who wrote, "The natural scenery is beautiful, as you can tell." (Courtesy of James Allen.)

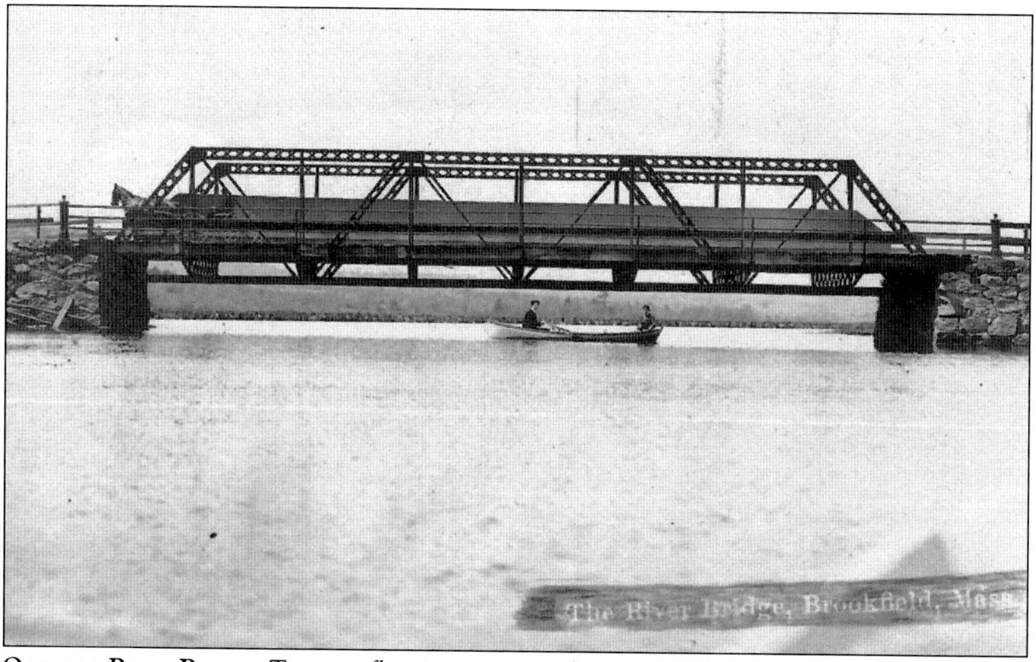

QUABOAG RIVER BRIDGE. Two men float in a canoe underneath the bridge over the Quaboag River, while a man drives over in a cart drawn by a horse. During both the flood of 1936 and the hurricane of 1938, this bridge completely flooded, leaving townspeople in one end of town cut off from the other end, with only boats to ferry them across the river. (Courtesy of Harris M. Gray.)

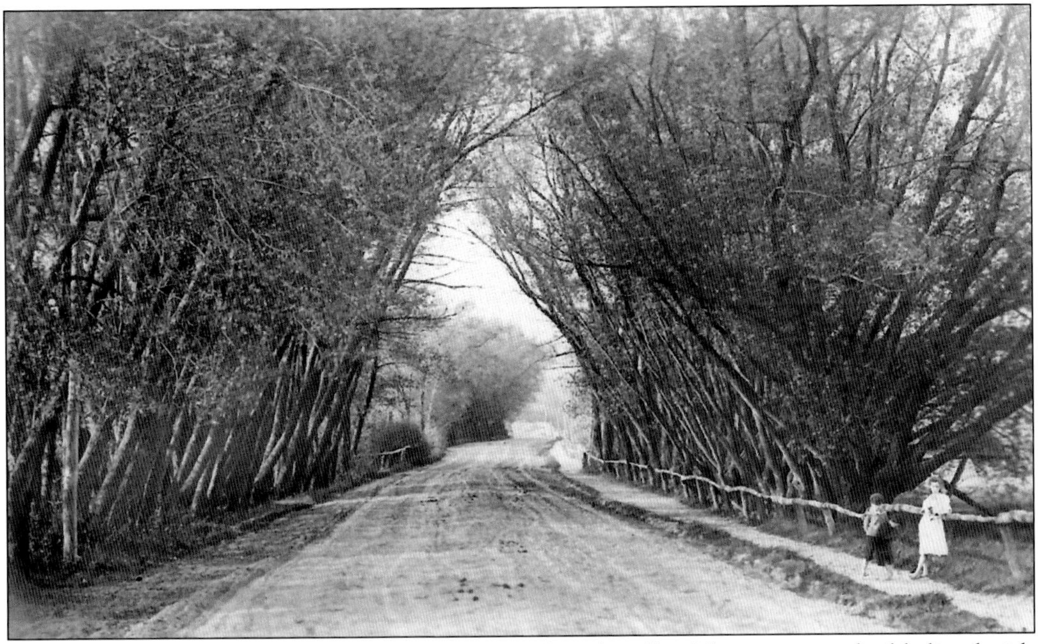

The Causeway. Three young children lounge on the sidewalk of the causeway thickly lined with willows in this view likely taken during the early decades of the 1900s. This path, on the road now known as Fiskdale Road on Route 148, connects the traditionally called Over-the-River section of Brookfield to the center of town. (Courtesy of James Allen.)

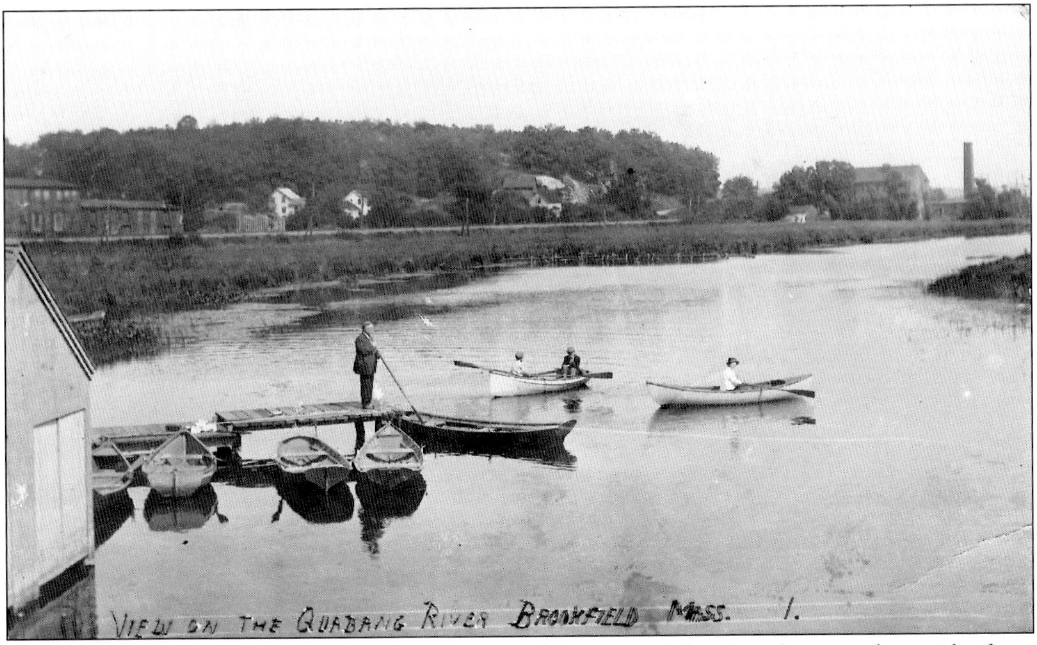

Donahue's Landing. Townspeople and visitors alike enjoyed Sunday afternoon boat rides from Donahue's Landing on the Quaboag River, just east of the river bridge, to North and South Ponds. This image was sent as a postcard around 1913 from a young girl named Mabel to her mother in Worcester; she wrote, "The man on the wharf is Mr. Donahue. We are having a dandy time." (Courtesy of James Allen.)

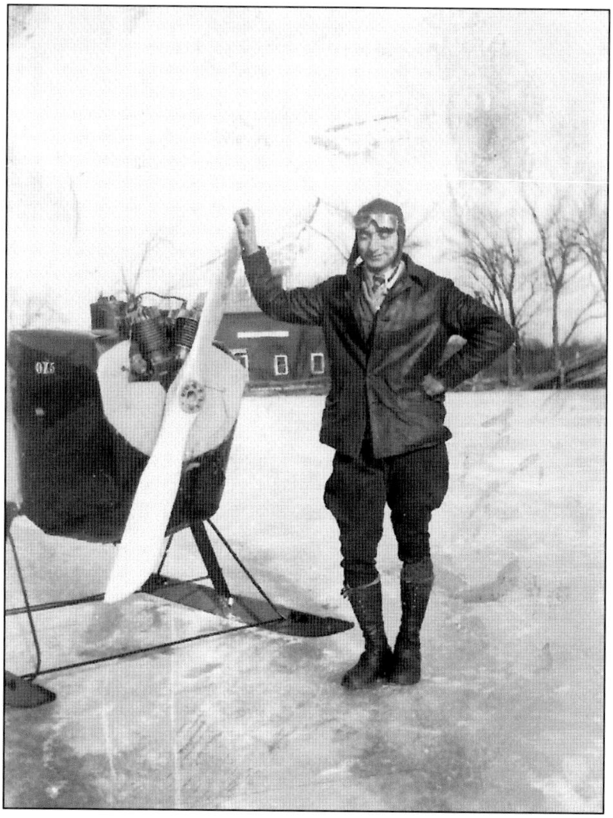

ICEBOAT. The lakes and ponds were used as diversions year-round. Arthur Faugno of Lake Road crafted this iceboat and used it to zip around during the winter on the ice at Mill Pond. He is shown here on the frozen pond in his pilot's gear in the late 1930s. (Courtesy of Gloria Achilles Faugno.)

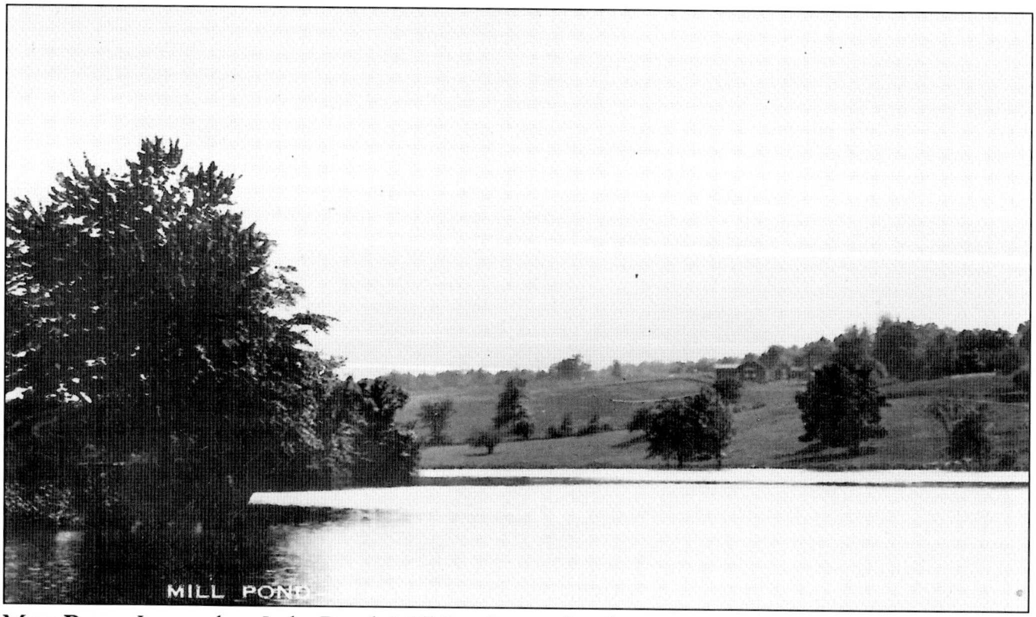

MILL POND. Located on Lake Road, Mill Pond in its heyday was surrounded by farmhouses with rolling pastures, a working sawmill, and Finney's icehouse, where ice cut from the pond during the winter was stored well into the summer months. This view, facing west, looks up the hill to Fiskdale Road and shows what is now Stepping Stone Stable. (Courtesy of Harris M. Gray.)

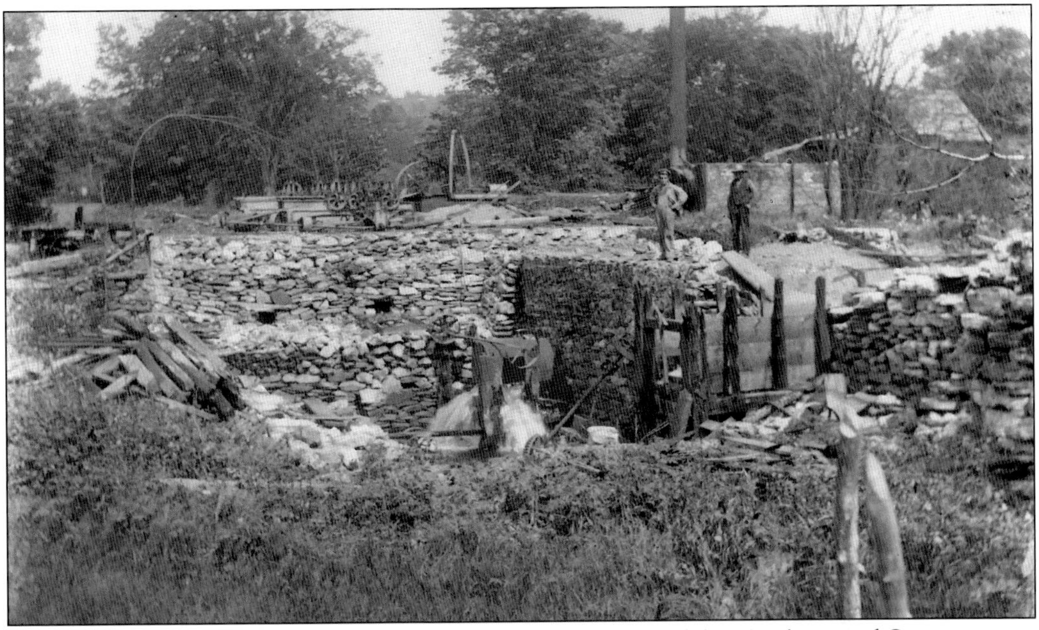

Brickworks. The brick-manufacturing complex on the banks of lakes Quaboag and Quacumquasit is shown here in the early 1900s. According to the *Brookfield Times* of August 23, 1889, a total of 1.5 million bricks were made the month before, which was only half the amount in demand. The brickworks met an accidental explosive end and now exist only in remnants scattered about the ponds. (Photograph by William Bullard; courtesy of Dennis LeBeau.)

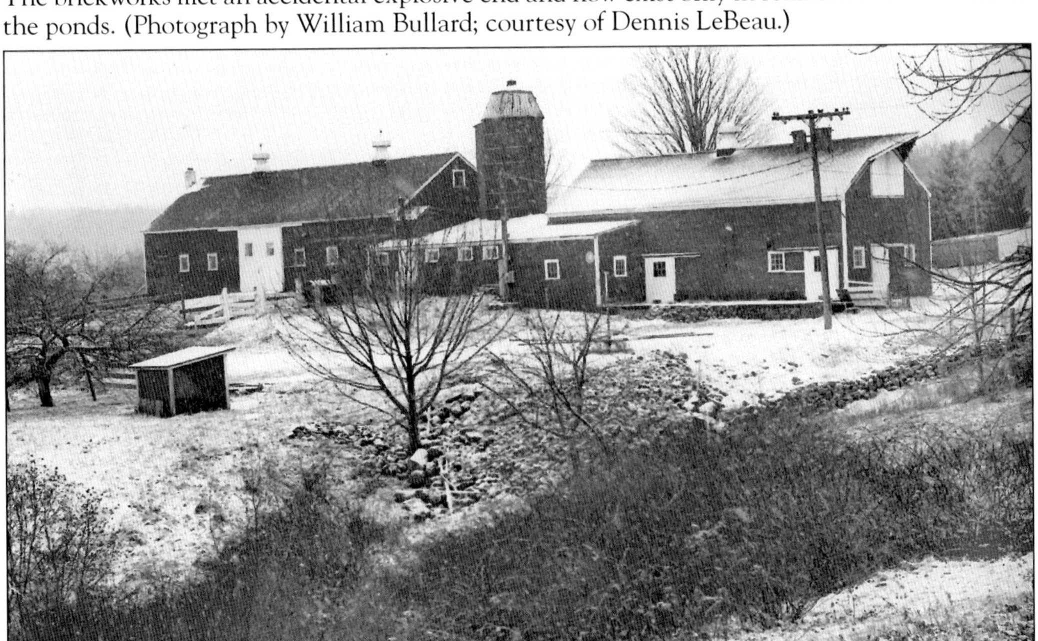

Poor Richard's. For almost two decades, beginning in 1950, Richard Sagendorph ran the Alta Crest dairy farm on Fiskdale Road, which was built as the Richardson farm in the early 1800s. In 1968, the stables were transformed into Poor Richard's, a collection of craft and gift shops. The site is now the home of Stepping Stone Stable. (Courtesy of Joan Derrick Sagendorph and *Worcester Telegram & Gazette*.)

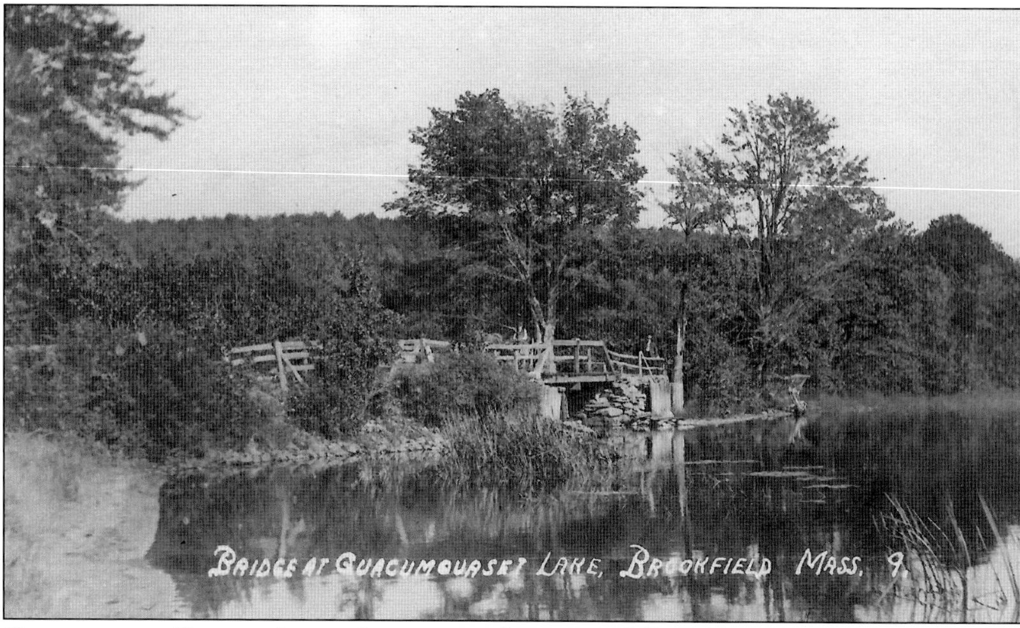

QUACUMQUASIT BRIDGE. A man driving a one-horse trap, followed by a man on foot, crosses the wood and stone bridge over Lake Quacumquasit in the early part of the 20th century. Also known as South Pond, this spring-fed body of water is deep and large, covering more than 200 acres. It was named for a Native American sachem. (Courtesy of William Jankins.)

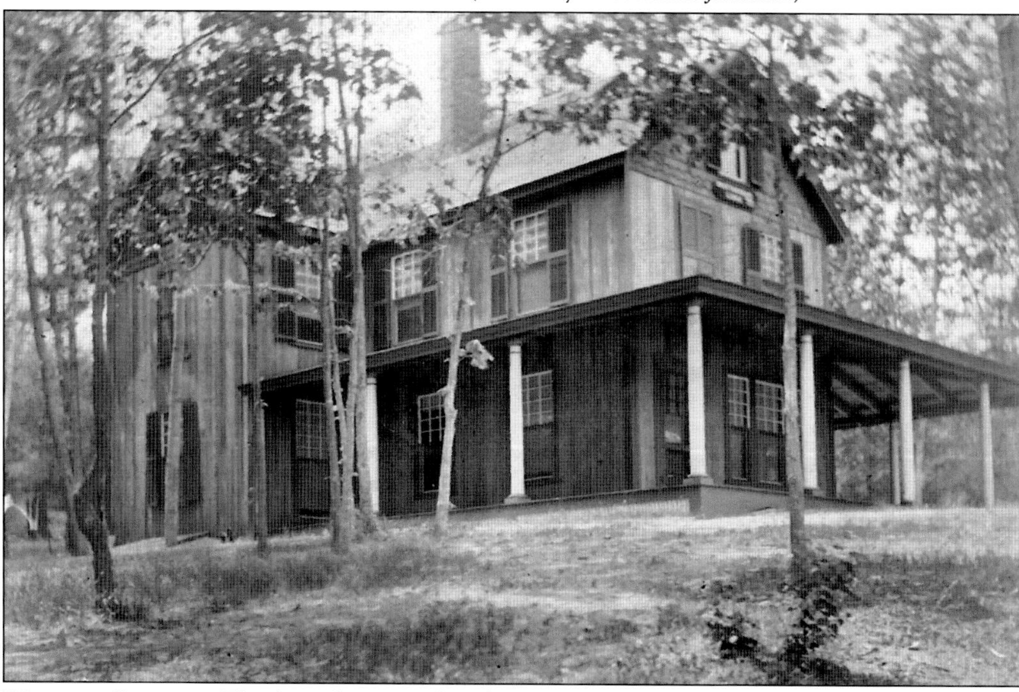

WEBSTER COTTAGE. This large house with a three-sided porch was built on Lake Quacumquasit, or South Pond, and while it looks modern, was actually one of the oldest houses on the Brookfield side of the water. Known as the Webster Cottage, it was in the Howard family for generations. (Courtesy of longtime resident.)

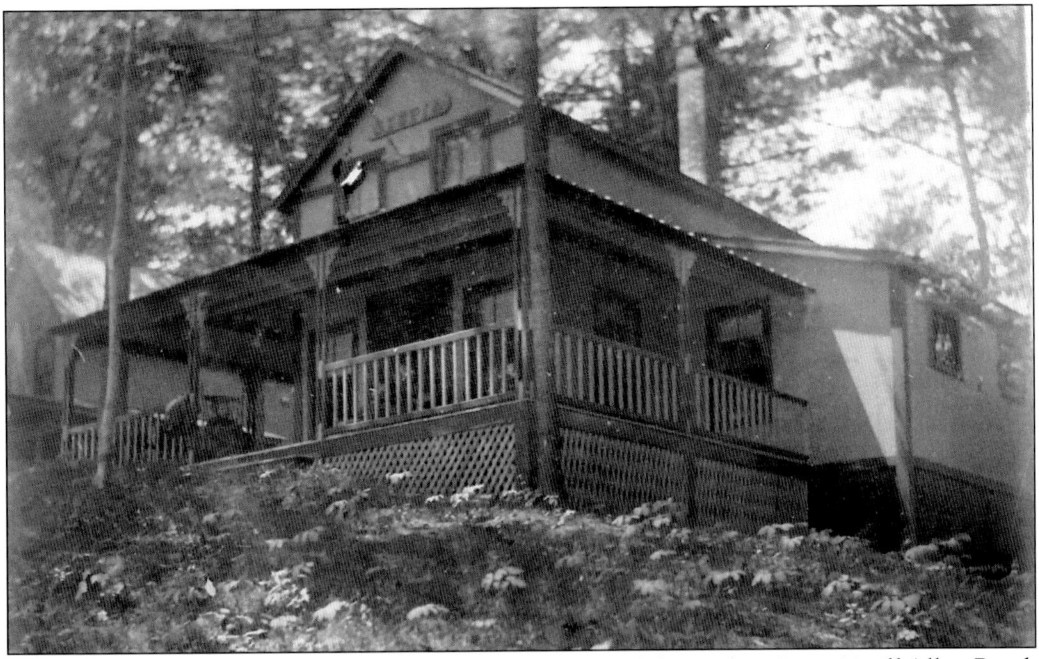

Utopia Cottage. This house on the shore of South Pond, located on Lane 21 off Allen Road, was originally recorded at the Worcester Registry of Deeds in 1871 as one of the "cottage lots at Quacumquasit Grove." Early owners included Albert Tattersall, the Hawes family, and Laurence and Edith Newell. The Jacques family currently owns it. (Courtesy of longtime resident.)

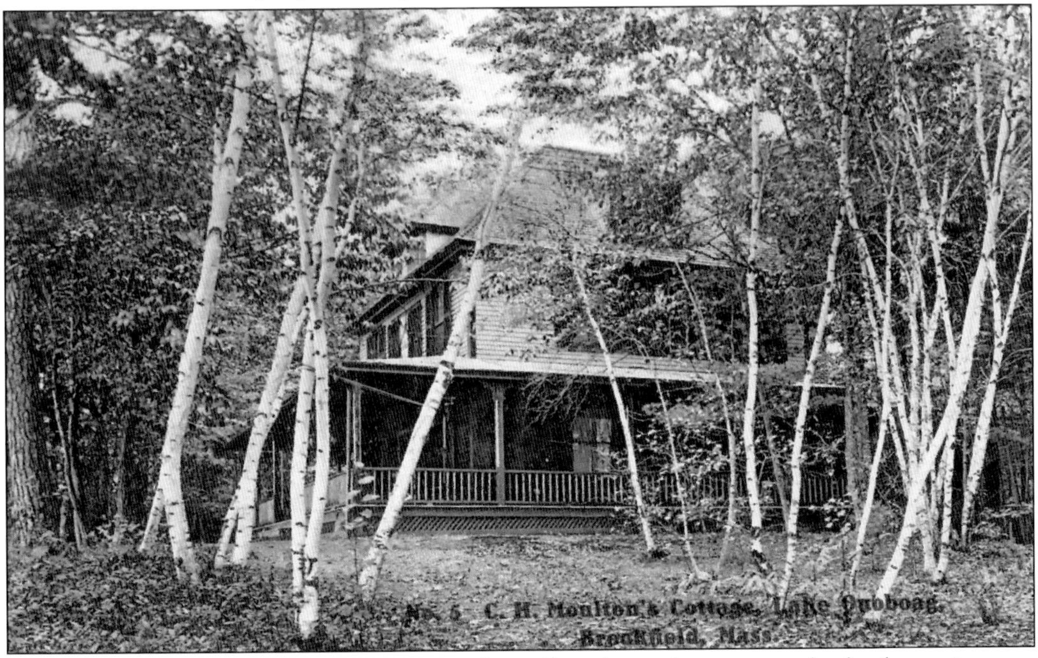

Moulton Cottage. It was not uncommon for well-to-do residents to own both a house in town and a cottage at one of the lakes. According to the town's 1900 record of valuation of taxes, C.H. Moulton owned both machinery and stock in trade for shoe and paper box companies as well as a "cottage at lake," which included a barn and a half-acre plot. (Courtesy of Sherril Cote.)

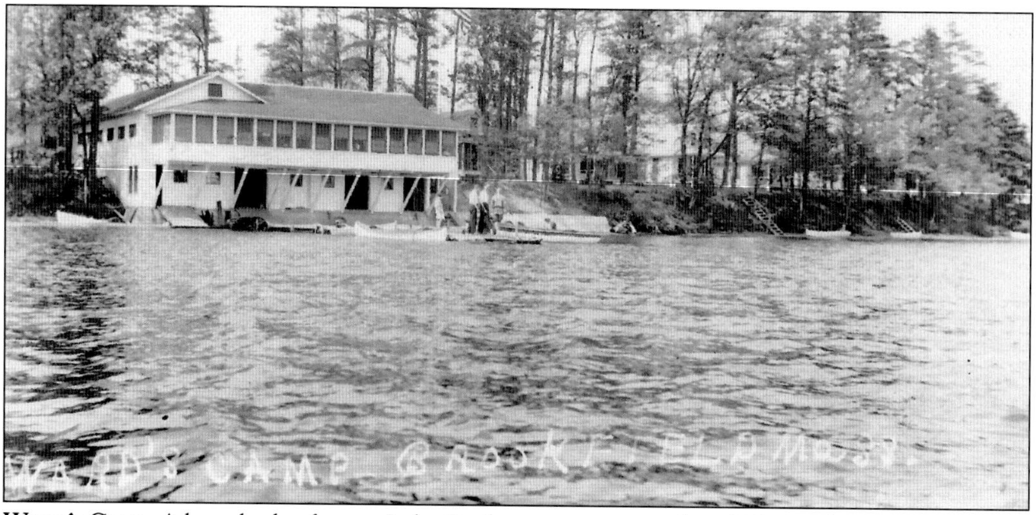

WARD'S CAMP. A large body of water, Lake Quaboag covers more than 500 acres but is quite shallow. The section of beach shown above, near Pine Lane, became a favored destination for swimmers and rowers, who often spent the whole day in and around the water. Cottages that lined the shores of the lake were rented to visitors, and townspeople and out-of-towners alike have fond memories of regular trips to the dance hall, which later became a roller-skating rink, where people could go skating, drink soda, and eat ice cream. As shown below, the place was known as the Quaboag Roller Rink at Ward's Beach but was often called just Ward's, after which it became Tobin's Roller-Skating Arena. (Above, courtesy of Harris M. Gray; below, courtesy of Sherril Cote.)

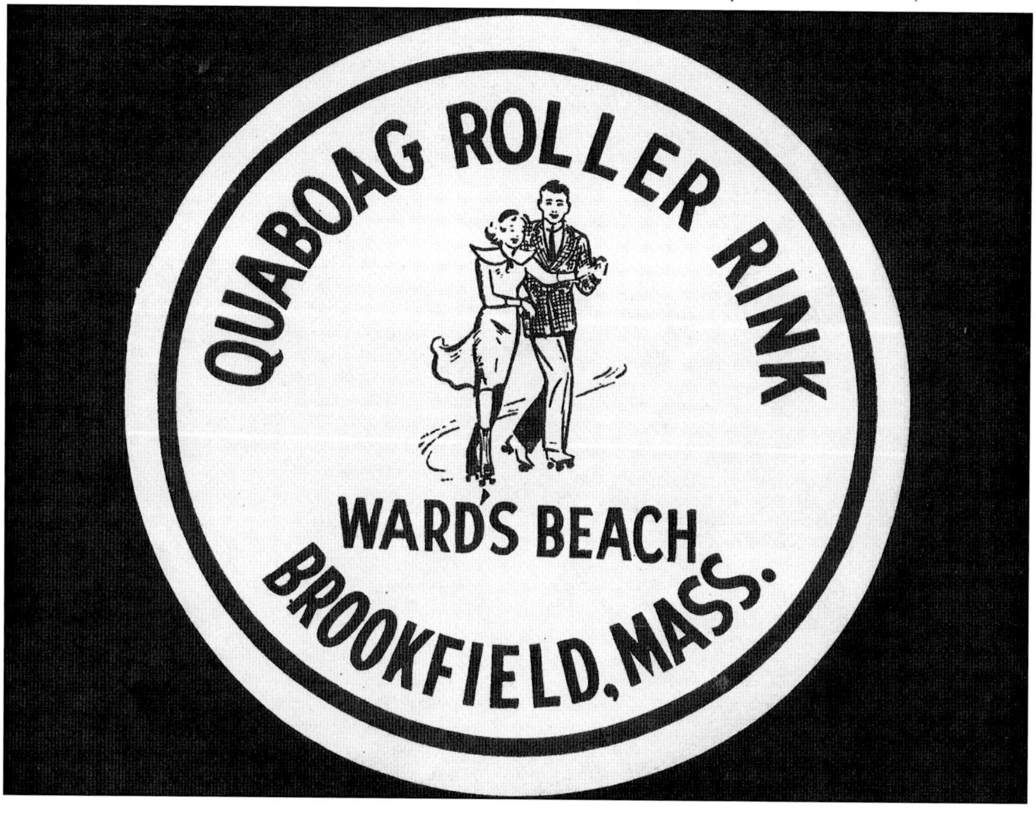

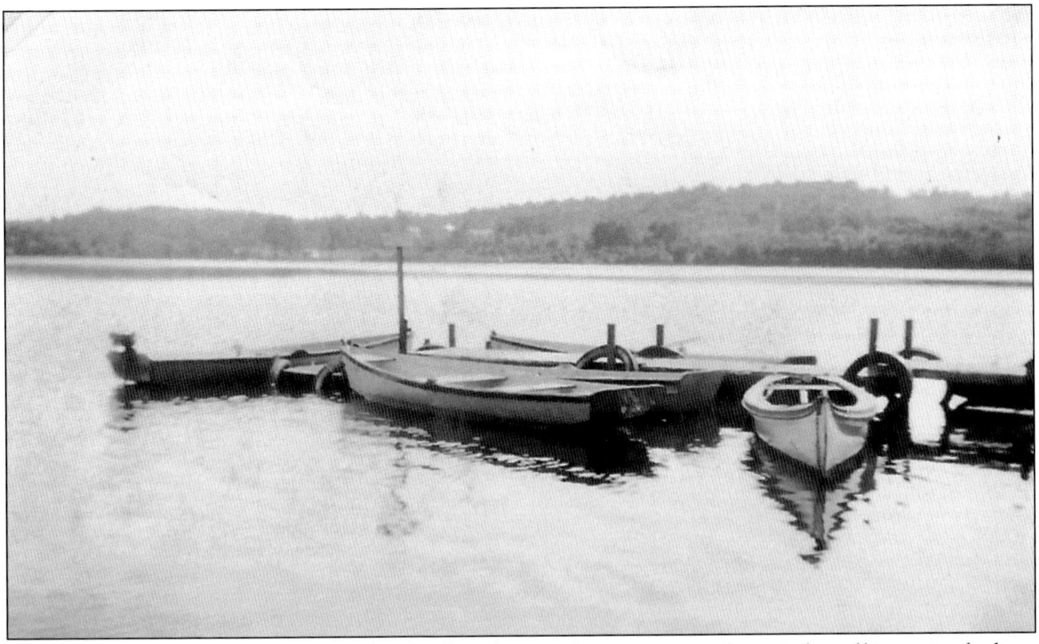

Lake Quaboag. The name of this body of water has many and varied spellings, including Quabuake, Quabauke, and Quabaug. Josiah Temple wrote in his history of North Brookfield that there was "little doubt the name of our place, as pronounced by Indians, was *Squapauke* or *Squabaug*. It is a compound word which signifies 'red water place' or 'red pond' so called from the reddish, iron stained gravel which forms the bottom and shores of the several ponds." Above, rowboats rest at the dock at Ward's Beach around 1930. Below is a view from the water of the cottages at Oakland Garden, a picnicking destination for groups such as the fire department, which held field days at the racetrack there. (Above, courtesy of May-Boyce Collection; below, courtesy of Harris M. Gray.)

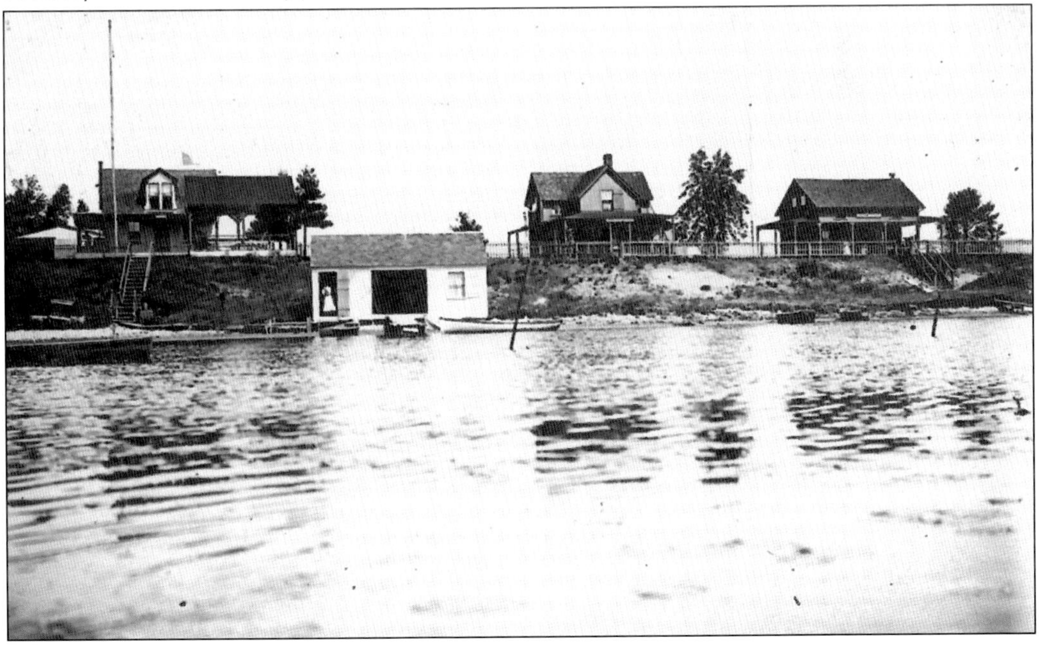

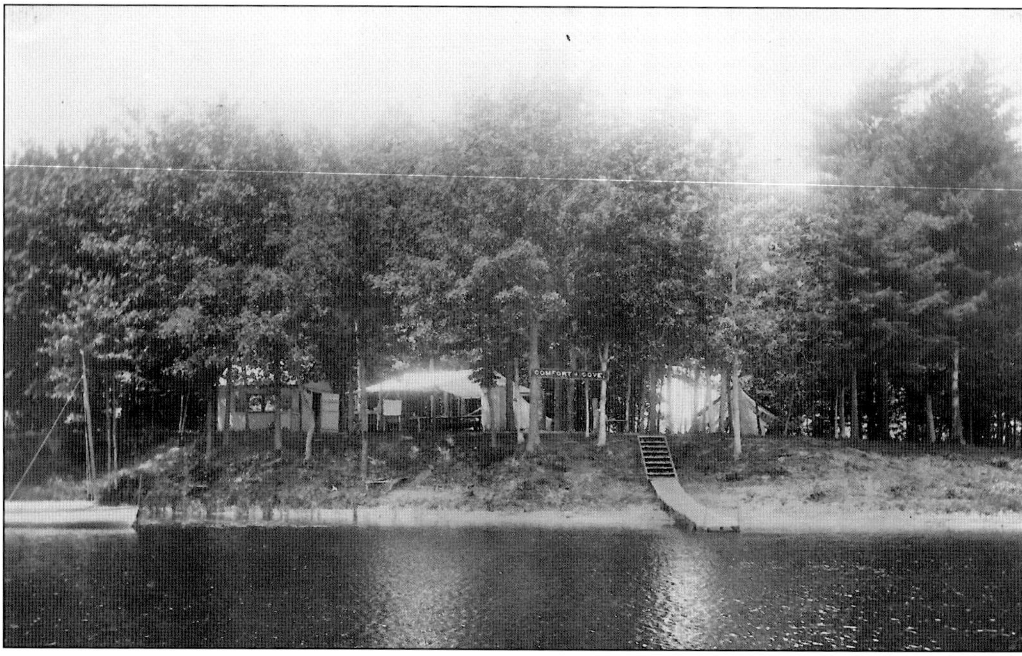

COMFORT COVE. Located on the western shore of Lake Quaboag, Comfort Cove was owned by George and Jane Meehan Chapin and seemingly offered a peaceful and relaxing place to eat, boat, and sleep. The Chapins lived in the Crosby mansion on West Main Street and, at the turn of the 20th century, operated the Brookfield Inn as well as a variety shop on Central Street. (Courtesy of longtime resident.)

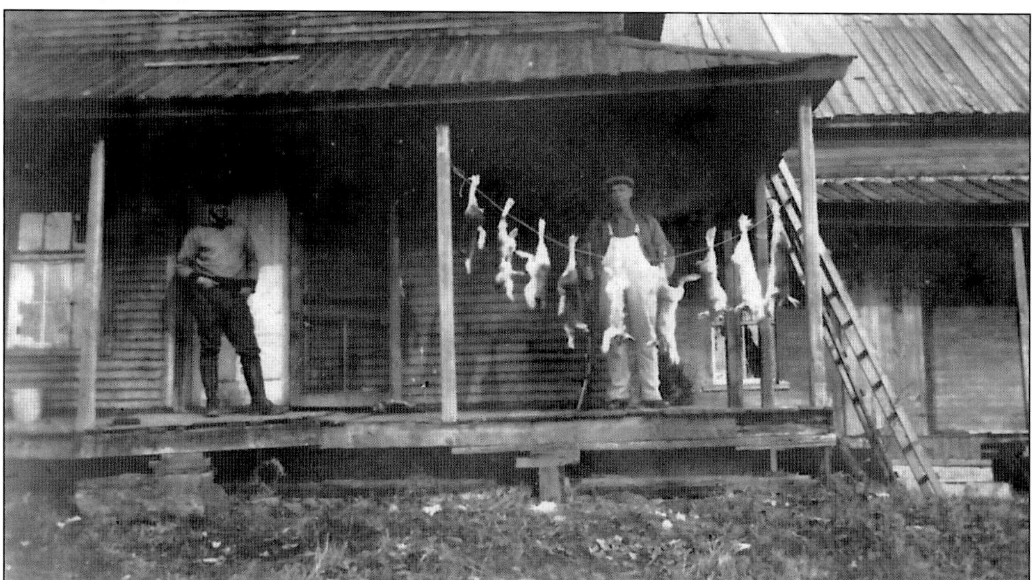

CAMP AT NORTH POND. Horace "Bus" May (left) and Paul Eugene Gadaire, shown about 1927, stand on the front porch of a North Pond camp, showing off their catch of rabbits. May was a longtime member of the fire department and was police chief during World War II; Gadaire was the co-owner, with his father-in-law, Charles Rice, of Rice and Gadaire Lumber Company on Central Street. (Courtesy of May-Boyce Collection.)

Eight

Celebrations

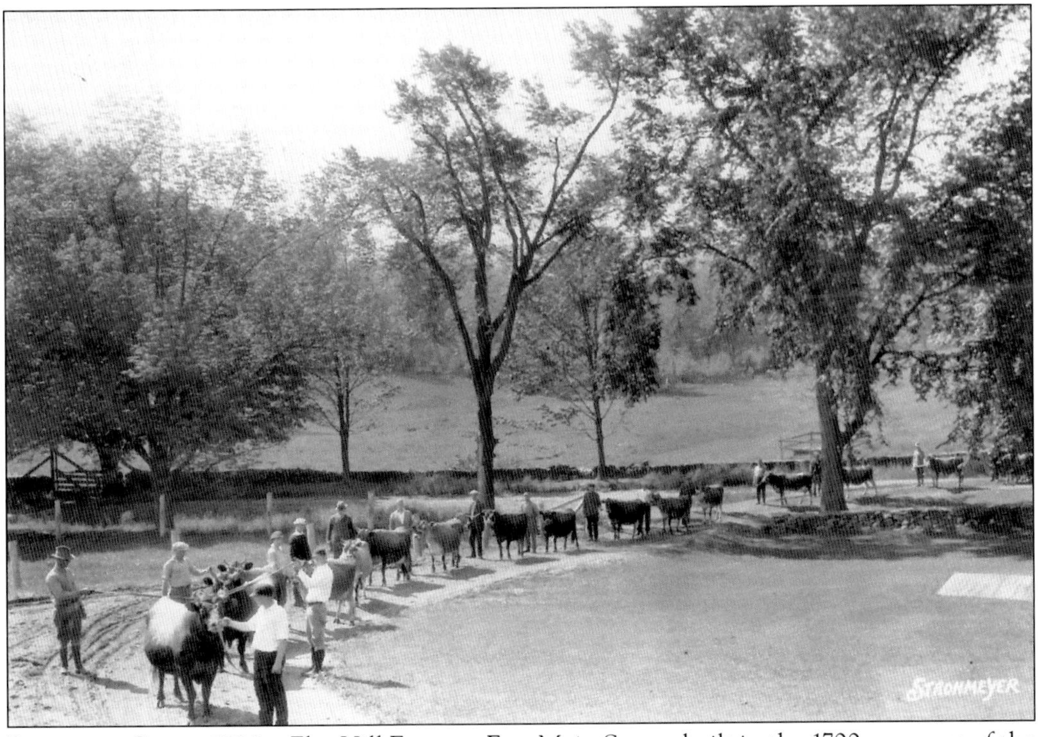

Parade of Cows, 1930s. Elm Hill Farm on East Main Street, built in the 1700s, was one of the largest working farms in the area, consisting at its peak of 1,300 acres of land, eight buildings, apple orchards, stables, and a purebred cattle operation. The farm's jersey cow "You'll Do Lobelia" was chosen to represent Borden Company as its mascot, Elsie the Cow. (Photograph by Strohmeyer; courtesy of Howard Whitcomb.)

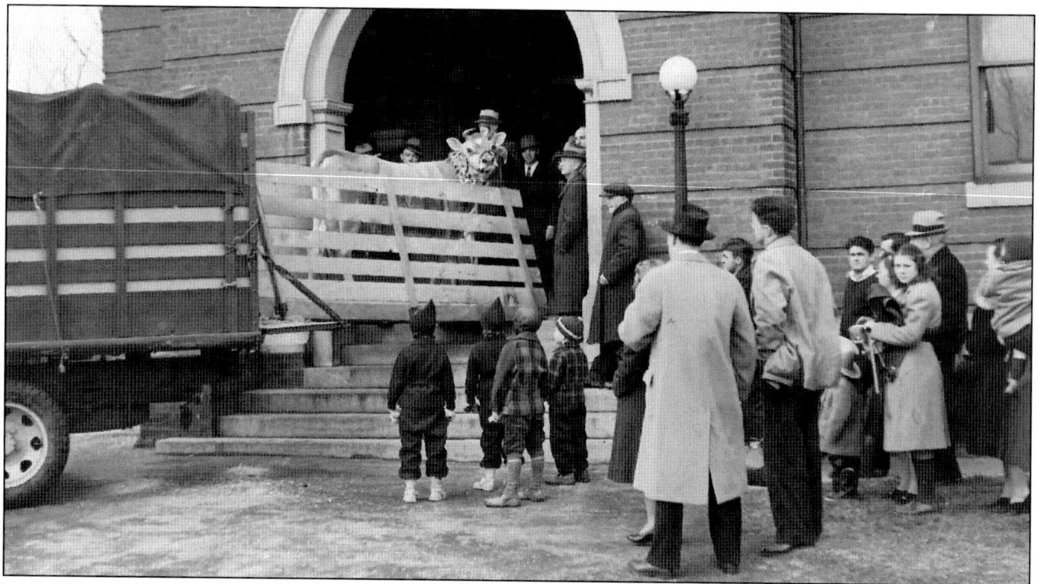

Elsie's Homecoming, December 1940. Elsie the Cow was feted with a grand party at town hall on her return home from Hollywood, where she appeared in *Little Men*, starring Kay Francis and Jack Oakie. Onlookers include Selectman Bellows (in doorway, at right), twins Nancy and Betty Cronin, high school principal Seavy Morse, Fred Corbett, and Estelle Chickering. (Courtesy of May-Boyce Collection.)

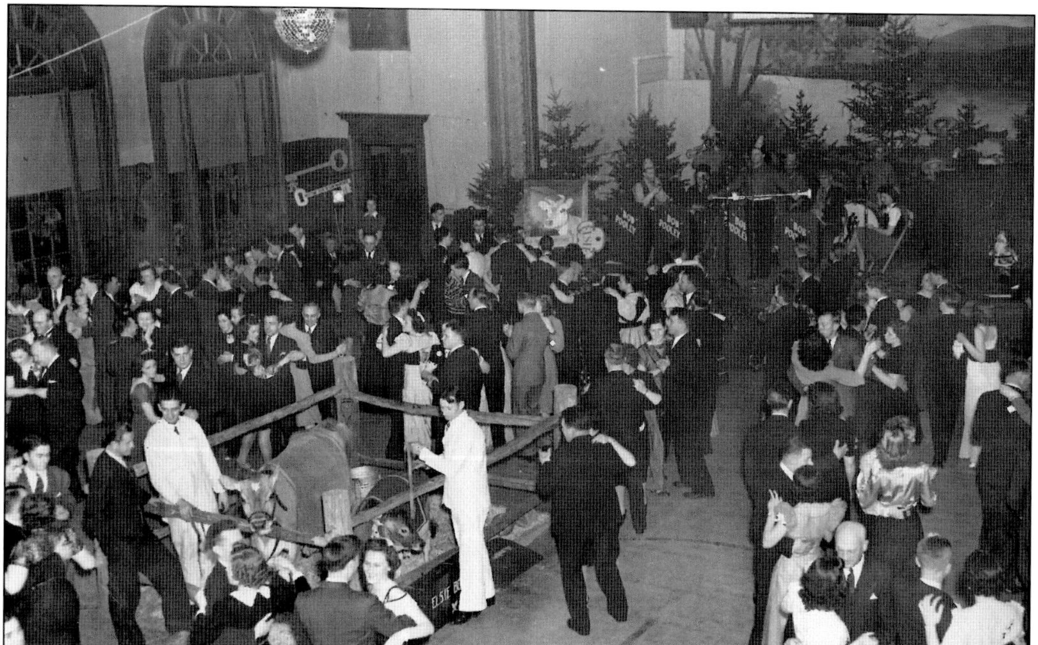

Great Hall, December 1940. More than 1,400 people from Brookfield and the surrounding towns poured into town hall to welcome home Elsie and her daughter Beulah. The dance was a fundraiser for the Firemen's Relief Fund. During her cross-country tour, Elsie collected hundreds of pounds of keys to different cities, including a five-foot-tall key to Brookfield. (Courtesy of May-Boyce Collection.)

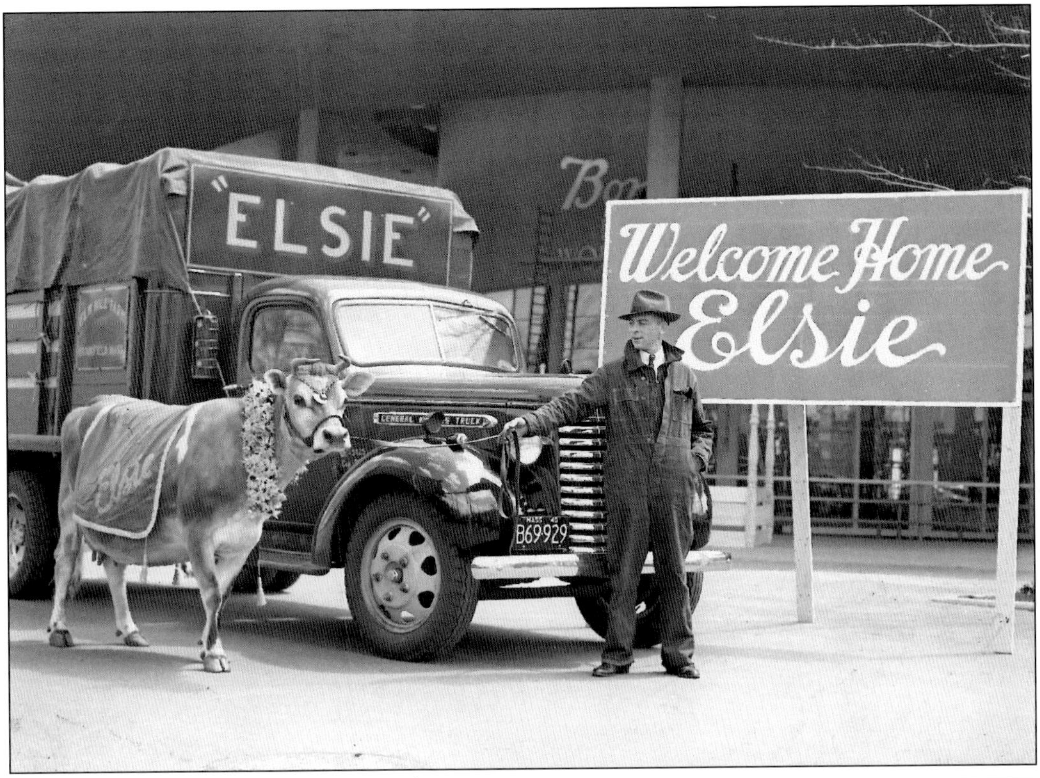

"WELCOME HOME, ELSIE," 1940. Earl Mayo, head herdsman at Elm Hill Farm, leads Elsie to a cocktail party at New York City's Roosevelt Hotel. She was chosen at the 1939 World's Fair after fairgoers wanted to know which cow was the real Elsie. She travelled cross-country in a specially equipped train car and was seen by an estimated 15 million people. (Courtesy of May-Boyce Collection.)

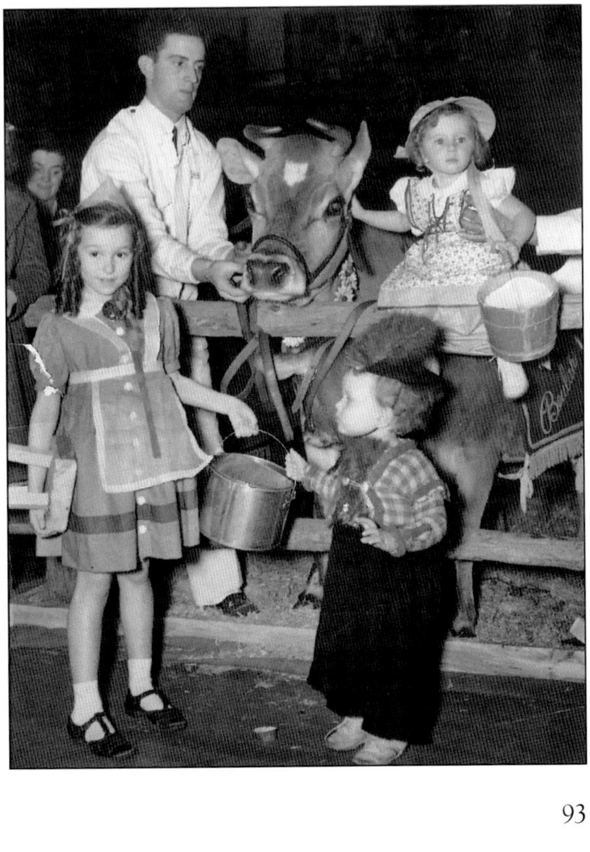

BEULAH IN TOWN HALL, 1940. Elsie's role in the film *Little Men* centered on the birth of her daughter Beulah. As part of the welcome home party for the famous bovines, 859 children dressed as farmers and milkmaids were served ice cream and cake. Barbara May Wilson (front left) is the granddaughter of Elm Hill Farm superintendent Lee Boyce, who travelled to Hollywood with Elsie. (Courtesy of May-Boyce Collection.)

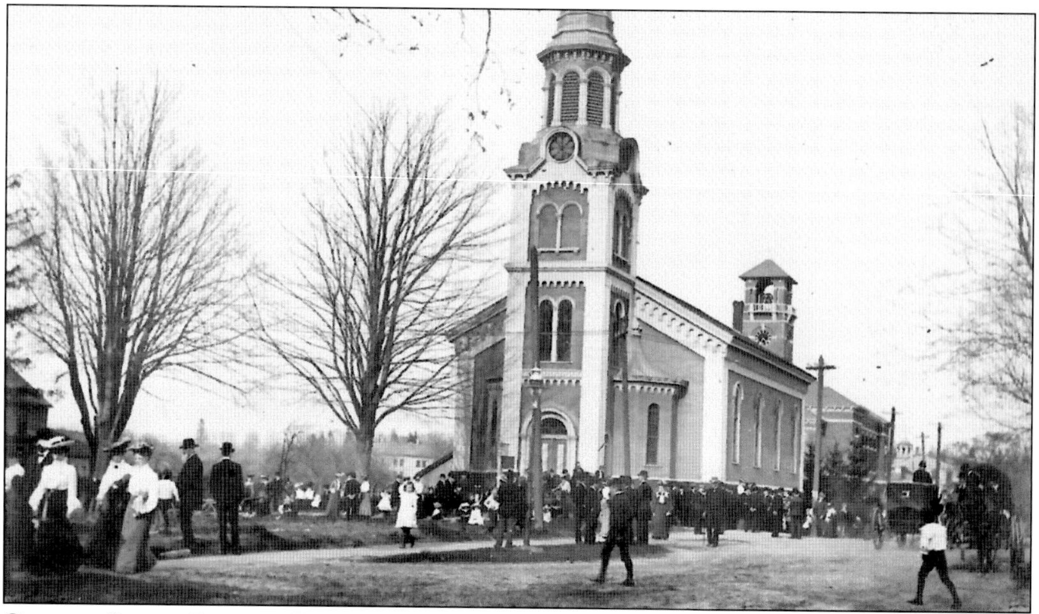

CENTRAL STREET, LOOKING EAST. Townspeople stream past the Congregational Church, perhaps to attend the open-air concert on the mall as part of the May 1904 dedicatory exercises for the new town hall. Designed by architect George H. Clemence, the $33,929.99 structure made from Brookfield bricks was deemed by building committee chairman George W. Johnson to be "thoroughly constructed of good material throughout in good architectural taste." (Courtesy of James Allen.)

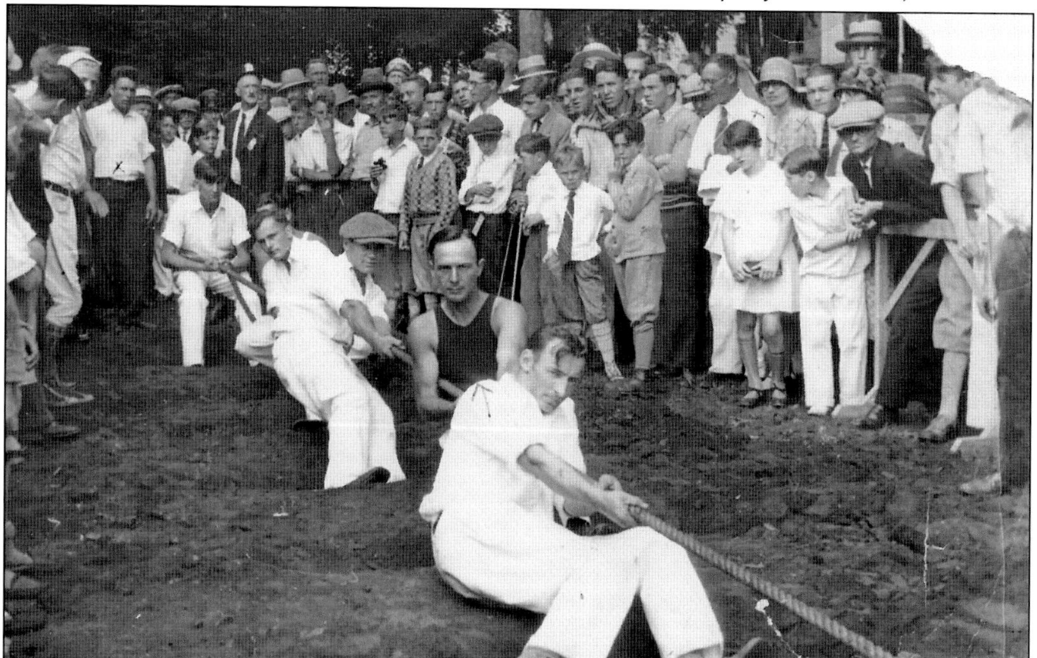

TUG-OF-WAR CONTEST, LATE 1930S. Albert D. Hooker Jr., in center wearing black tank top, and his white-clad teammates lean into their dug-out footholds during a tug-of-war contest on the common. Onlookers in the crowd include police chief Charles W. Brown, Peter Hazen, John Powell, and Oliver and Beatrice Steadman. (Courtesy of Olive Hooker Zadroga.)

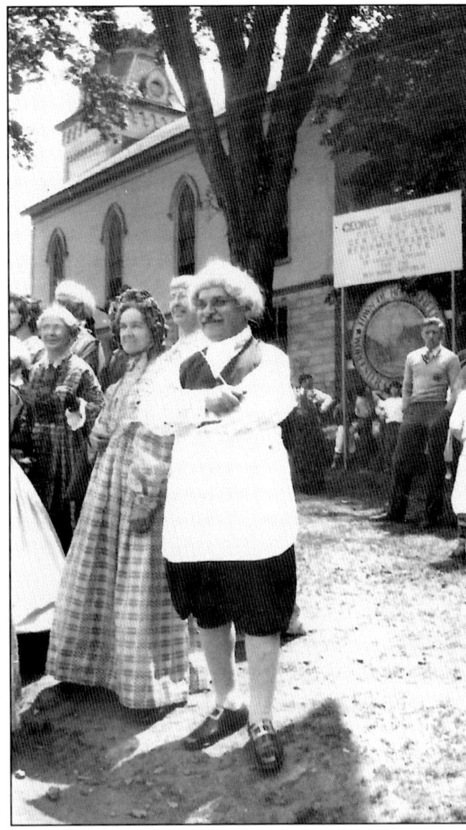

HENRY KNOX MEMORIAL INSTALLATION, 1927. In 1927, the Commonwealth of Massachusetts erected a memorial at the intersection of what is now Route 9 and Route 148 in honor of Gen. Henry Knox, which reads, "Through this place passed General Henry Knox in the winter of 1775–1776 to deliver to General George Washington at Cambridge the train of artillery from Fort Ticonderoga used to force the British Army to evacuate Boston." At right, costumed parade watchers stand by the Methodist Church, while below, celebrants pose in front of the Oliver Crosby house on West Main Street. (Right, courtesy of May-Boyce Collection; below, courtesy of Jeanne and Kermit Eaton.)

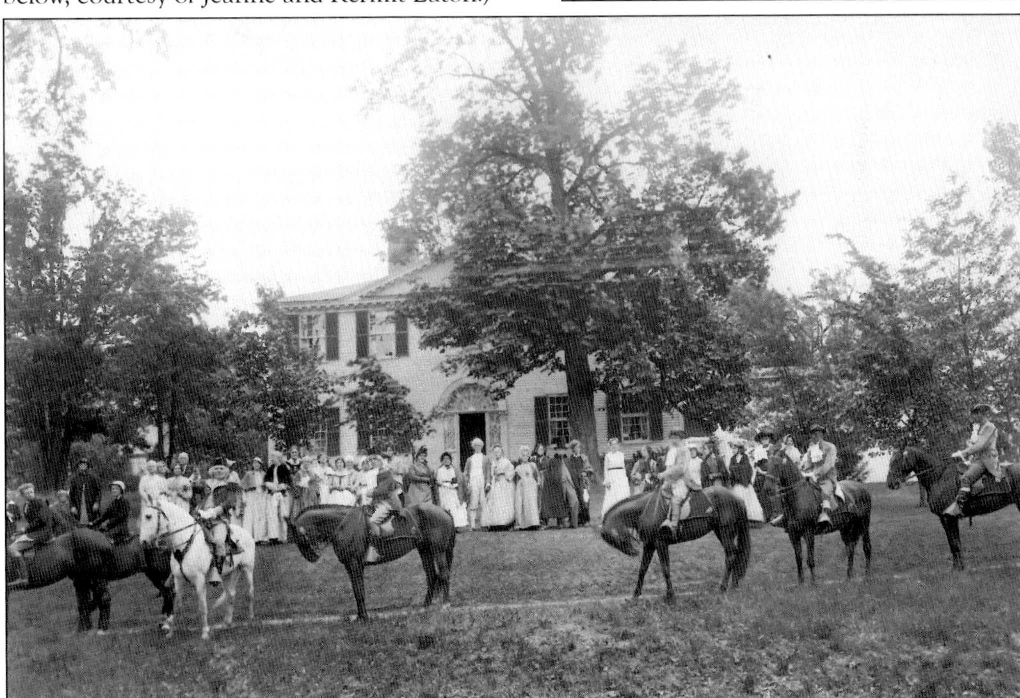

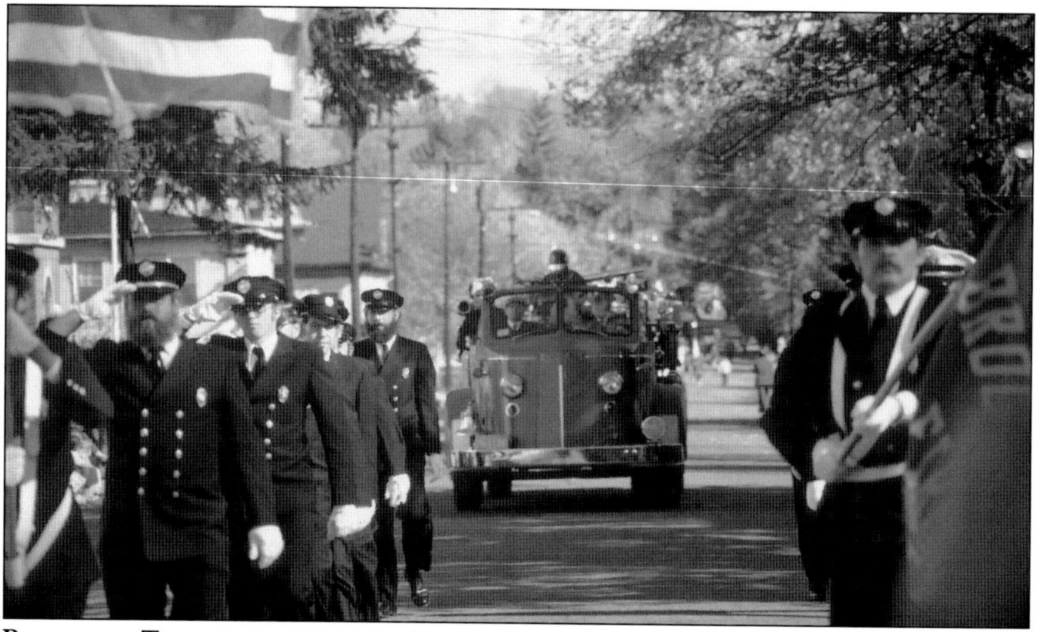

Brookfield Tercentenary, 1973. The 300th anniversary of the incorporation of Brookfield was celebrated in 1973 with a year-long schedule of events, including a weekend set aside as a Firemen's Day that included a chicken barbeque, musters, a firehouse tour, and band concert. Here, fire department members, including Alan Phipps, Alvin Brown, Harrison Achilles, and John Woodard, march down Central Street during the October 14 grand finale parade. (Courtesy of Dahler family.)

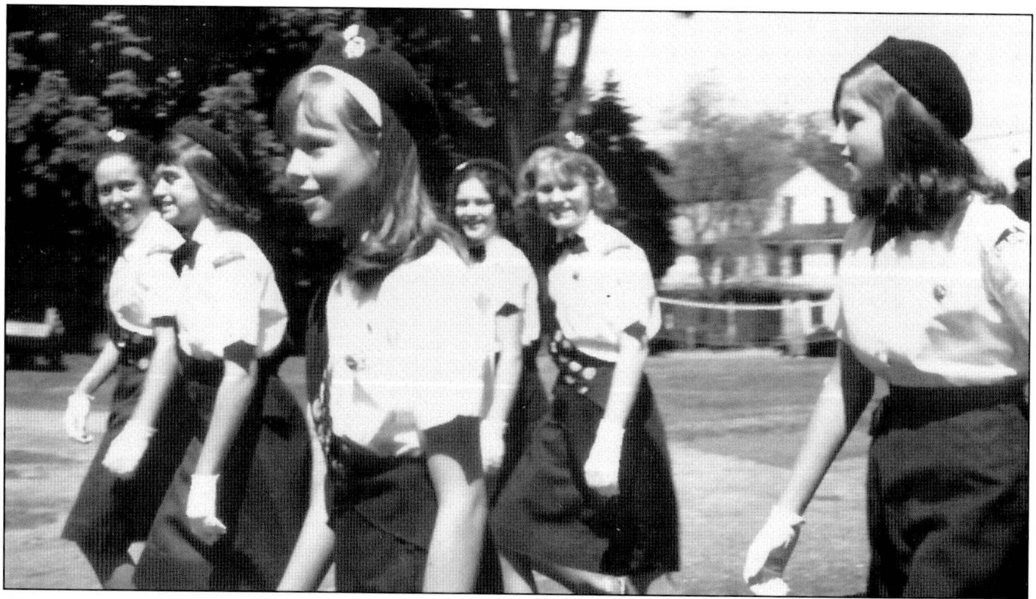

Girl Scouts Marching, c. 1961. From left to right, Girl Scouts Francis Ann Chaffee, Janice Terry, Laurel Glass, Barbara Turner, Sarah "Sally" Whitcomb, and Katherine Docwra march up River Street as part of the Memorial Day parade. The parade traditionally begins at Legion Square, where the American Legion once stood—now the site of the elementary school—and proceeds to the cemetery then the mall. (Courtesy of Docwra family.)

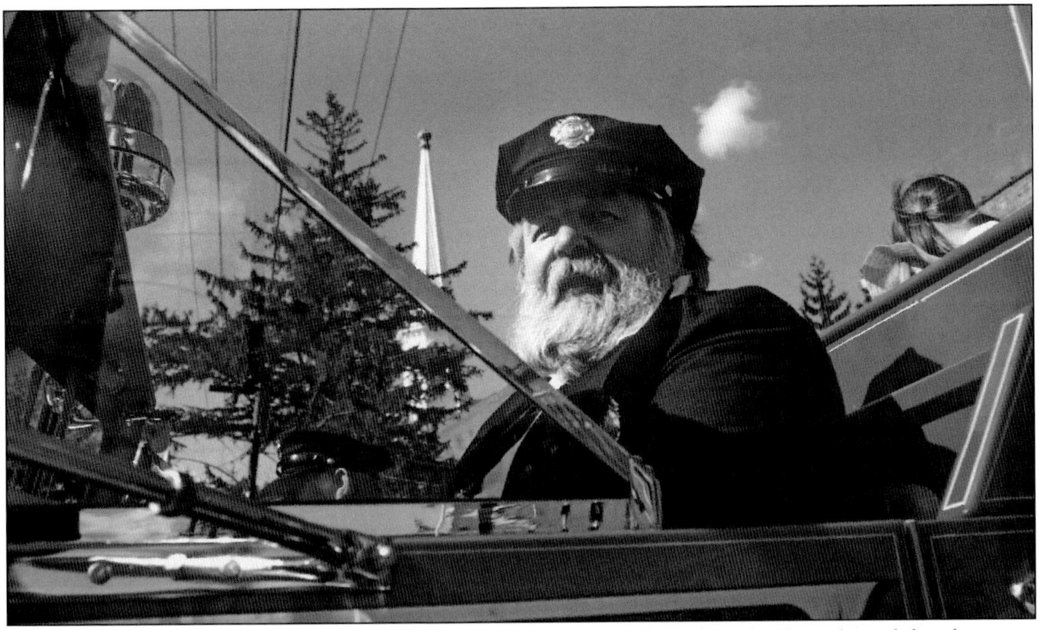

Anniversary Parade, 1973. Gordon Warman, winner of the best-looking beard for the year, rides in a fire truck past the Congregational Church as part of Brookfield's 300th anniversary parade. Warman was a member of the fire department for 36 years, serving as assistant chief. He was also much beloved by many youngsters in town who had him as a school bus driver. (Courtesy of Dahler family.)

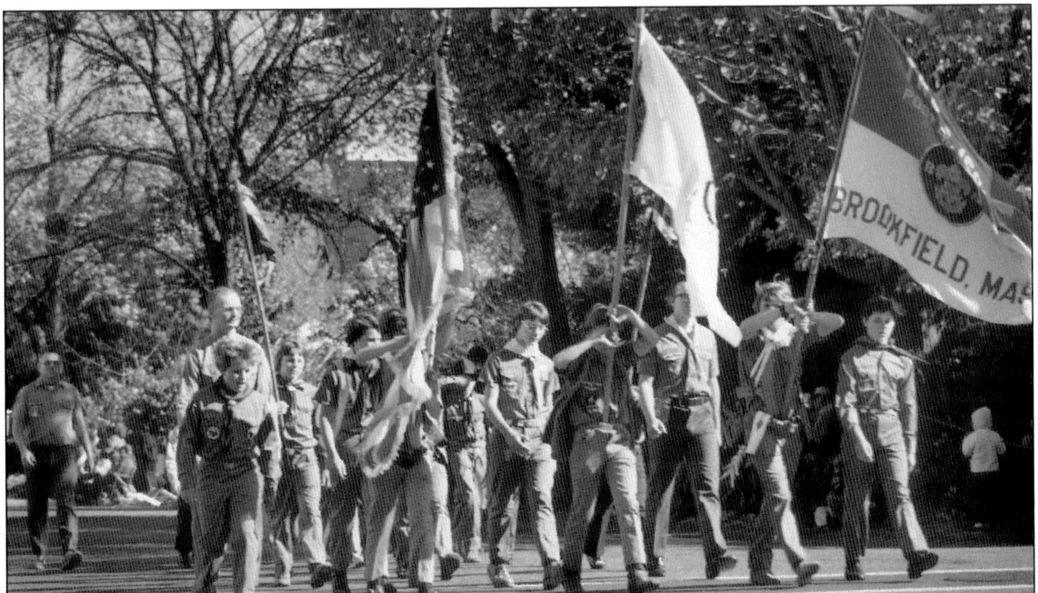

Boy Scouts Marching, 1973. Troop No. 159 marches in the 300th anniversary parade under the leadership of John "Pete" Marona. The parade concluded a year of dances, suppers, tours, and a beard-growing contest as well as Olde Home Day with doll carriage and bicycle parades, an ecumenical service on the common, and a Sportsmen's Day with canoe races, log rolling, a turkey shoot, and an archery contest. (Courtesy of Dahler family.)

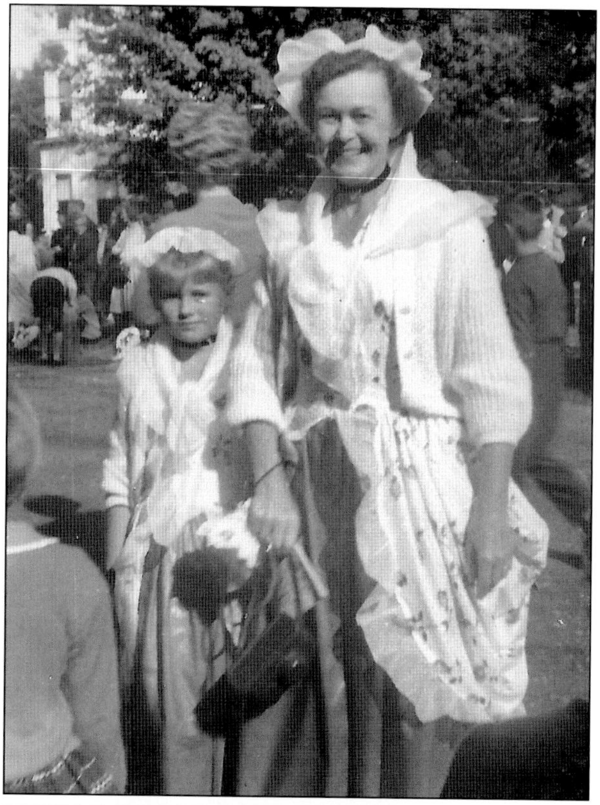

Quaboag Plantation Tercentenary, 1960. In 1960, the towns of Brookfield, East Brookfield, North Brookfield, Warren, and West Brookfield came together to celebrate the 300th anniversary of the founding of the Quaboag Plantation. The main program of events occurred September 16–18, 1960, with a homecoming weekend comprised of a massive parade viewed by an estimated 30,000 people, musters and drills, a concert, marathon, square dance, fireworks, a historical pageant, water show, and historical open houses. At left, Sarah "Sally" Whitcomb (left) and her mother, Barbara Whitcomb, who helped plan the festivities, enjoy the celebration. Below, from left to right, Madelyn Docwra, Ann Terry, and Winifred Broughton, all Brookfield Post Office employees, take time out for a photograph in their colonial costumes. (Left, courtesy of Andrea Campbell Faugno; below, courtesy of Docwra family.)

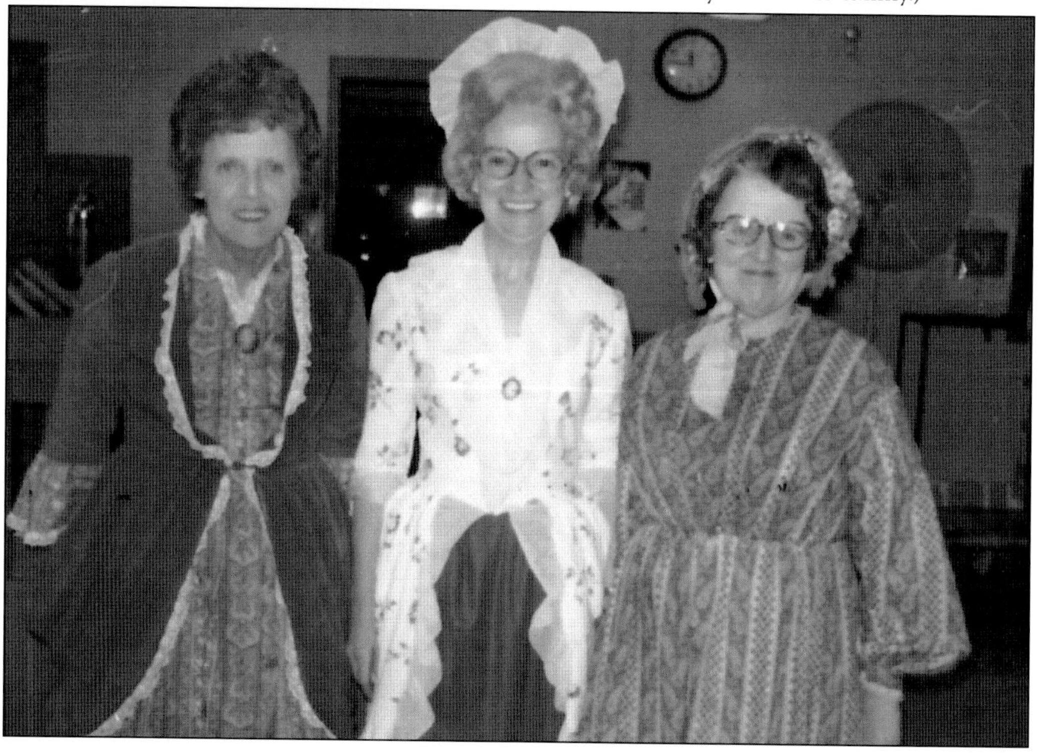

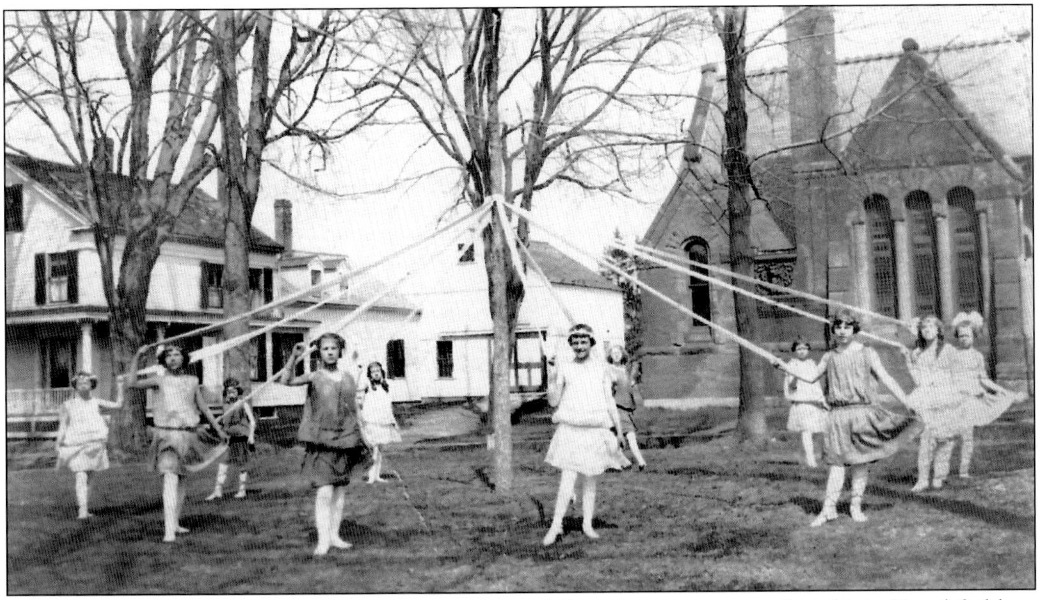

Maypole Celebrations on Common. May Day celebrations span many decades in Brookfield, as shown by these two photographs taken 50 years apart. Above, a group of young girls, including Barbara Vivian Boyce May (fifth from the left), poses on the common in front of the Merrick Public Library during the 1920s. Below, members of the local Brownie Troop, with a crowd of onlookers, tie maypole ribbons on the mall on May 19, 1973, as part of Brookfield's 300th anniversary celebration. May baskets were also auctioned off that day, and dancing continued until midnight. (Above, courtesy of May-Boyce Collection; below, courtesy of MPL and *Worcester Telegram & Gazette*.)

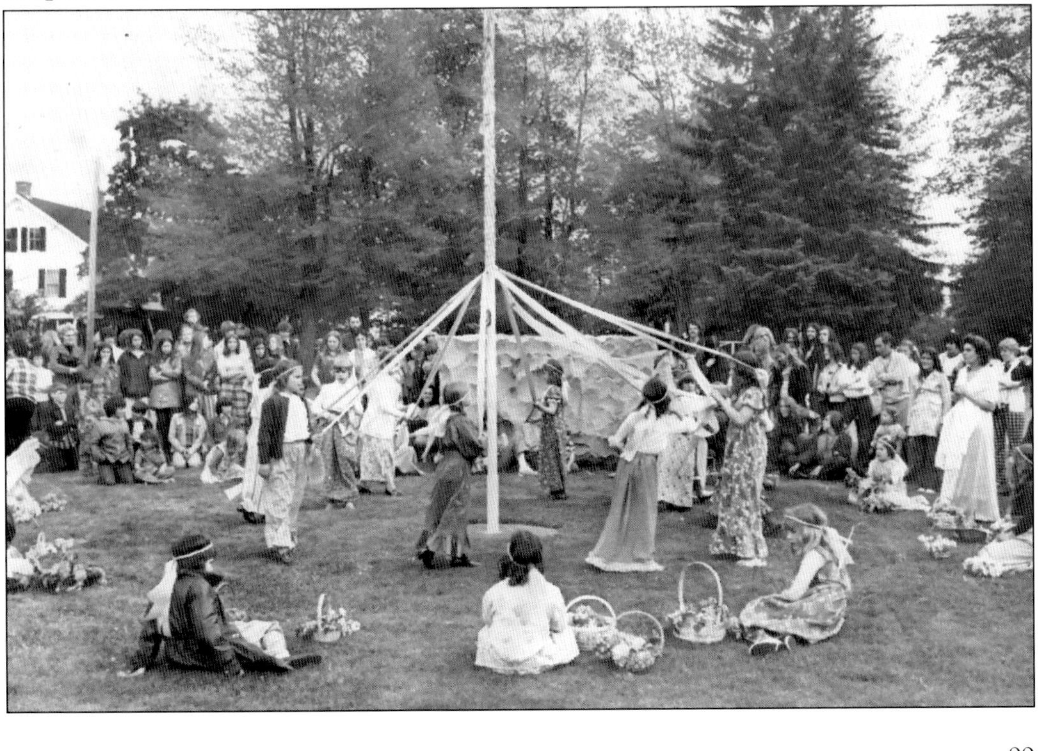

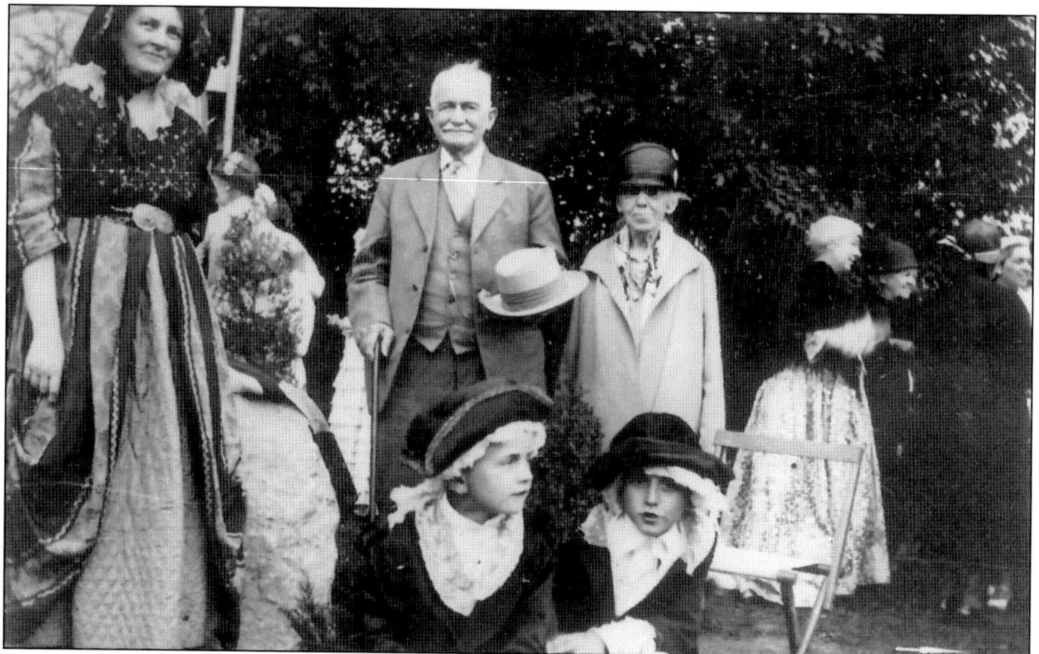

George Washington's Bicentennial Birthday, 1932. Brookfield residents gather to celebrate the 200th anniversary of the birth of George Washington. From left to right are (kneeling) Larry Durkin (left) and James Seery; (standing) Mary Frazier and Mr. and Mrs. Sumner Reed. (Courtesy of Michael Seery.)

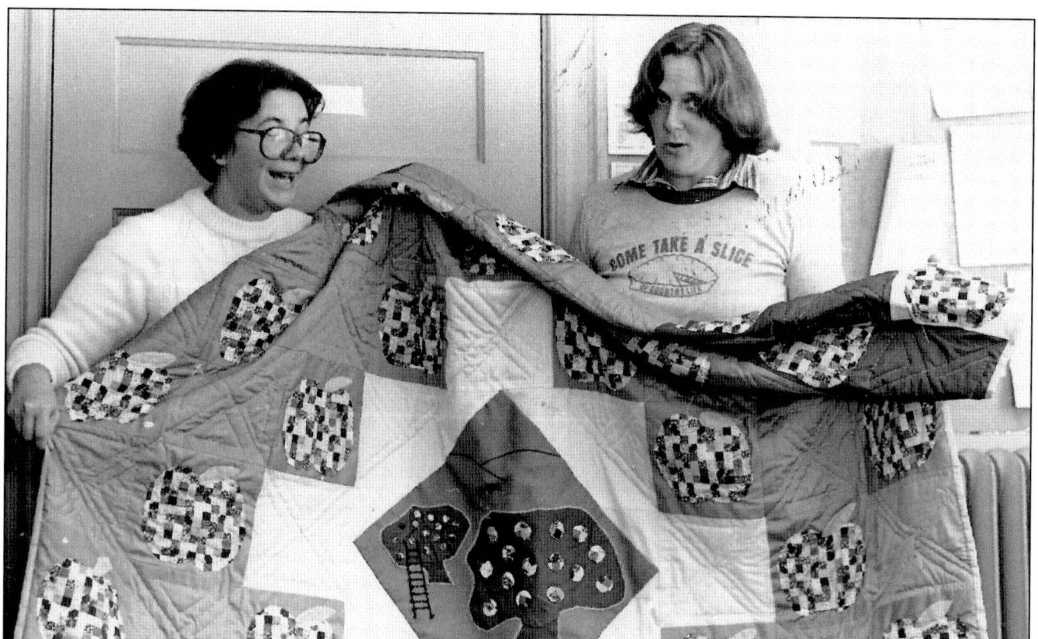

Apple Country Fair Quilt. Since 1979, the Brookfield Community Club has been organizing the Apple Country Fair, with a quilt handmade by the community as first prize in the fundraising "rapple." Diane Martell (left) and Carol Plumb display the quilt designed by Gwen Campbell and quilted by many Brookfield hands. (Courtesy of Carol Plumb and *Spencer New Leader*.)

Nine

DISASTERS

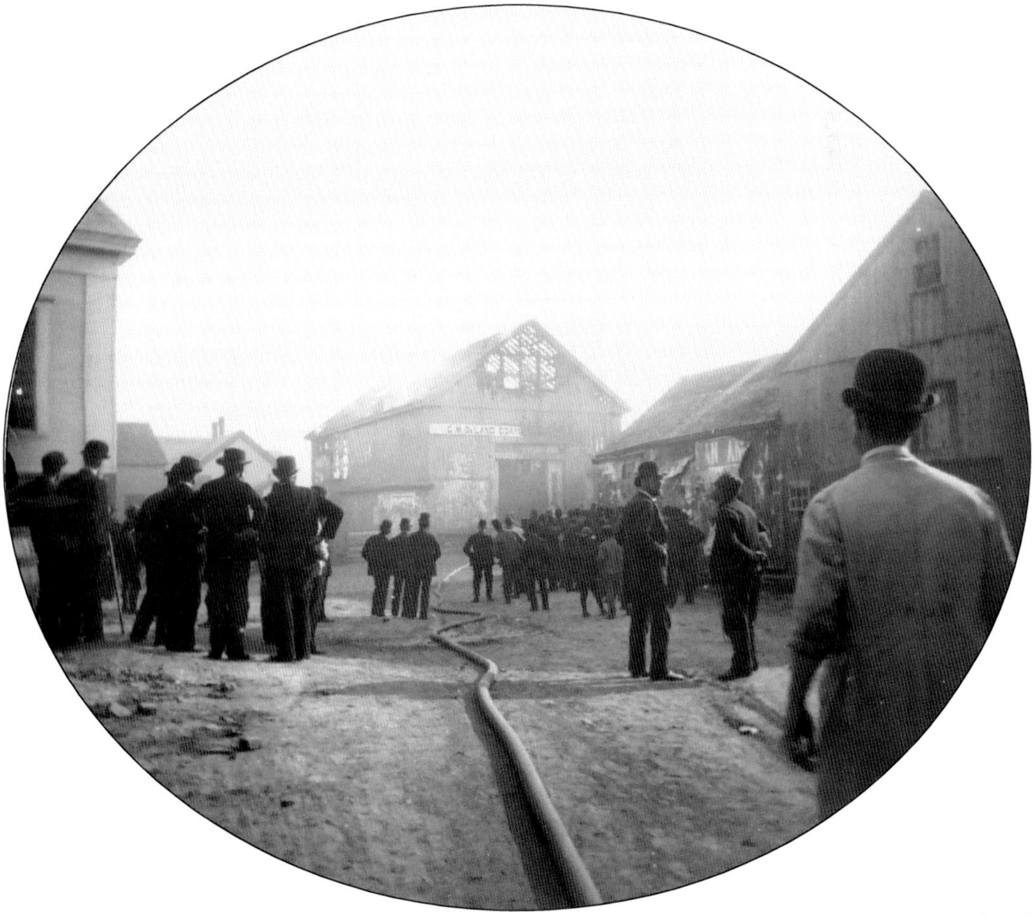

BOARDING STABLE BURNS. This c. 1890 image displays what amounts to standing around and watching a building burn when water and materials were not available to the fire department. Fire engineer's reports for 1902 through 1906 state both Steamer Nos. 1 and 2 companies had 40-foot extension ladders, "but no means are at hand for forwarding them to a fire." (Photograph by Charles P. Blanchard; courtesy of Blanchard Means Foundation.)

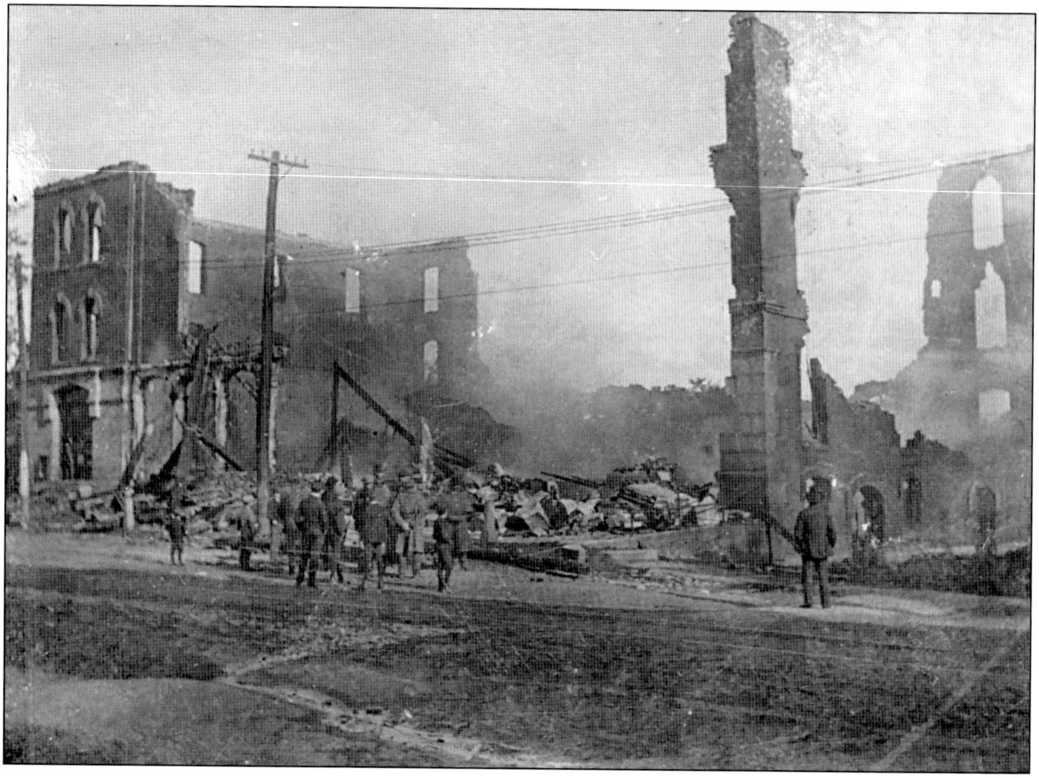

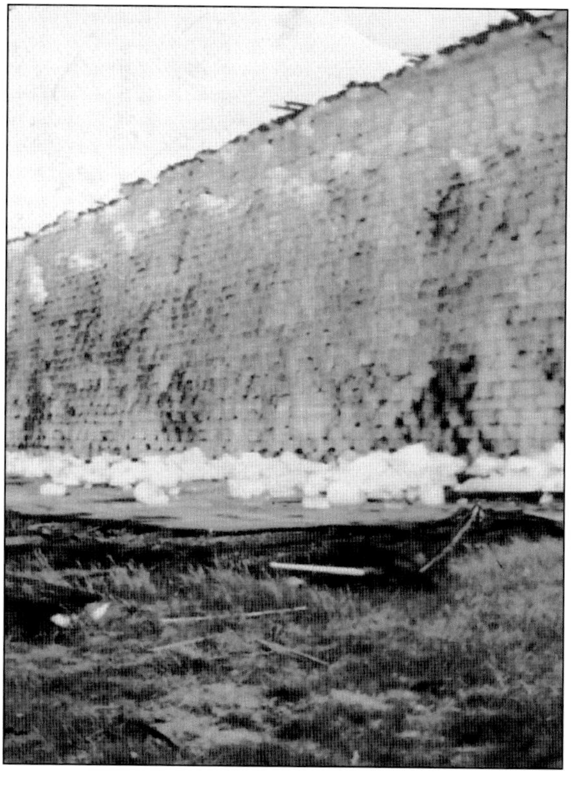

Town Hall Remnants, 1902. A 1903 report published by the state public records commissioner says, "The town hall was destroyed by fire September 1902. Most of the town records were in the vault and were uninjured. A safe used by the board of selectmen was left in the ruins for about two months, the contents of which were wet but not destroyed." (Courtesy of James Allen.)

Finney's Icehouse Fire. Large chunks of ice were harvested from Mill Pond during the winter and stored in the icehouse, packed in sawdust, for use throughout the year; some of the ice blocks were loaded onto trains and sent to Boston. Here, on August 16, 1944, a charred wall of the icehouse still stands and chunks of melting ice lay scattered about. (Courtesy of May-Boyce Collection.)

Colburn's Boathouse, Quaboag River. The great flood of 1936 occurred during the month of March. A winter of heavy snowfall, sustained rains, and ice dams combined to form a destructive force, which resulted in 10 deaths, 50,000 people homeless, and over $200 million in damages across the state of Massachusetts. (Photograph by Louise Menard Bemis; courtesy of Sheila Pronto McCarthy.)

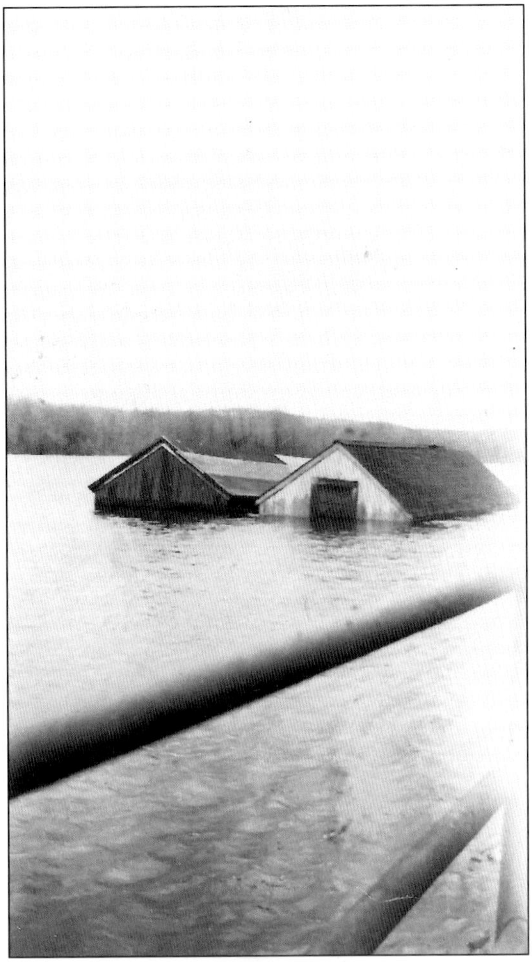

Route 148, Flood of 1936. The flooded causeway at Quaboag River isolated the Over-the-River district from the rest of town. Dairymen brought their milk to town center by rowboat and horse-drawn wagon, driving a mile in water as deep as four feet. (Photograph by Louise Menard Bemis; courtesy of Sheila Pronto McCarthy.)

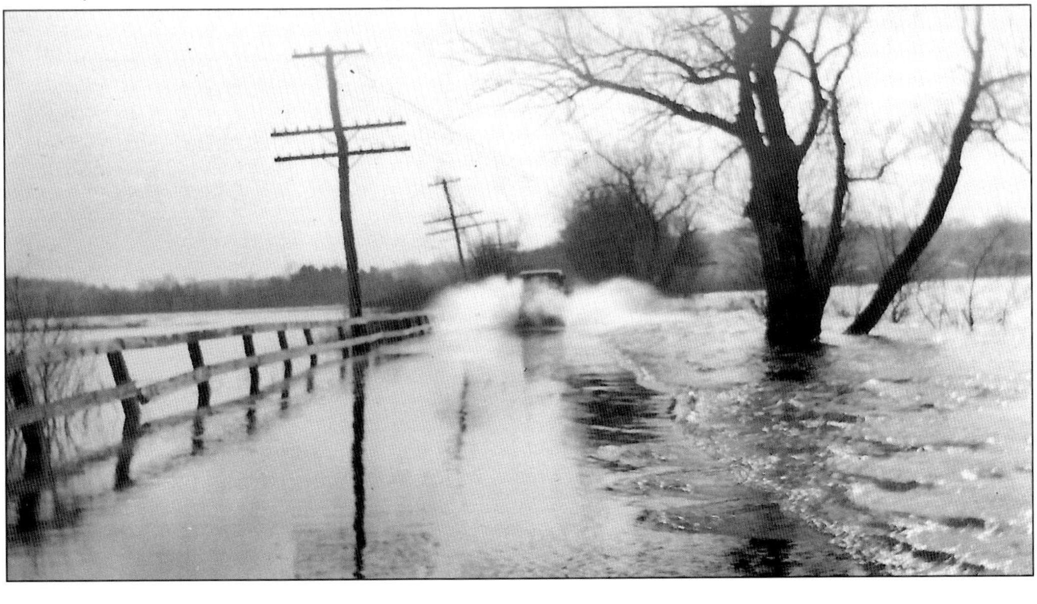

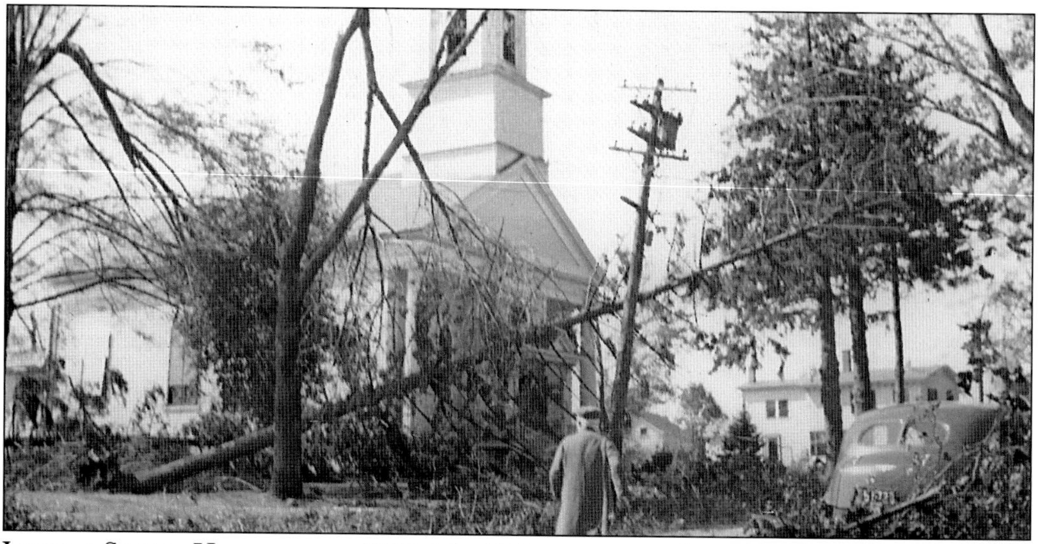

Lincoln Street, Hurricane of 1938. John K. Leamy surveys hurricane damage in front of St. Mary's Church, which lost its steeple and its stained-glass windows over the altar. According to the *Spencer Leader* of September 30, 1938, parishioners were a little blue, as "they had seen their little church redecorated and were justly proud of its appearance." (Photograph by Louise Menard Bemis; courtesy of Sheila Pronto McCarthy.)

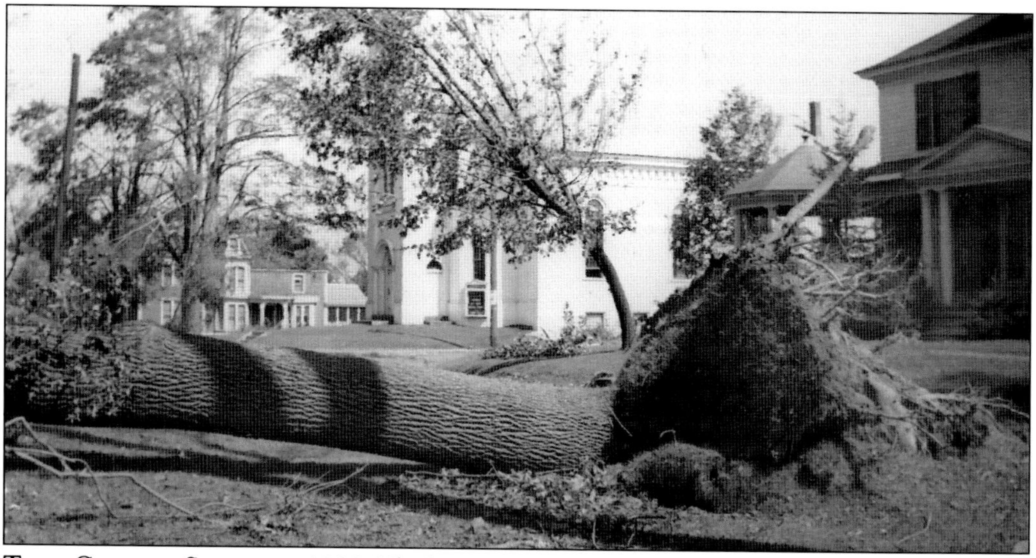

Town Common, September 1938. The hurricane of 1938 was also known as the great hurricane and "the Long Island Express." A profusely wet summer had kept streams, rivers, and ponds bursting at their banks, and when the cyclonic winds and precipitation of the hurricane hit, the flooding commenced and, with it, extensive damage to life and property. (Photograph by Louise Menard Bemis; courtesy of Sheila Pronto McCarthy.)

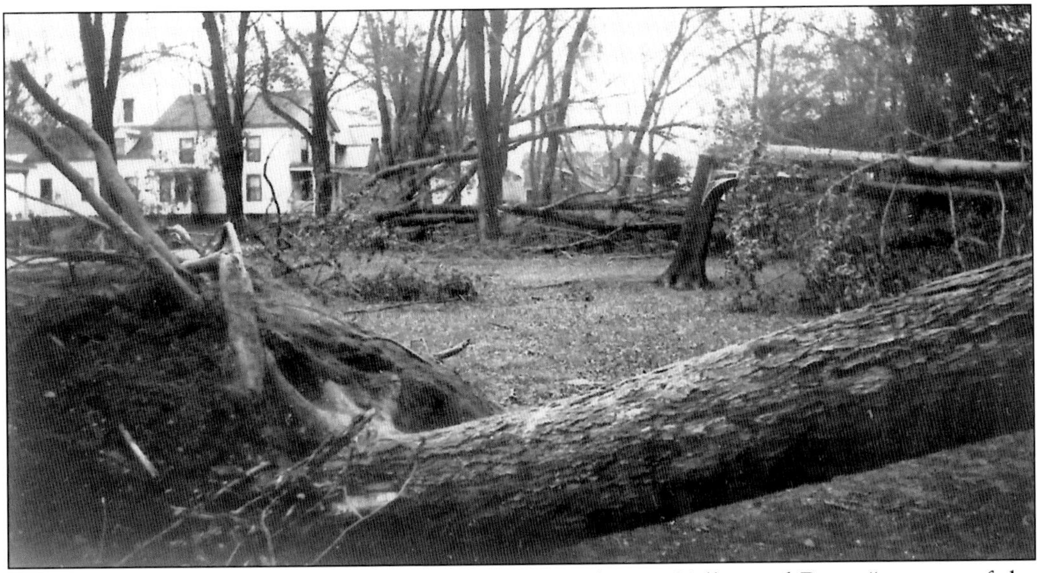

Town Common, 1938. The hurricane of 1938, according to Vallee and Dion, "was one of the most destructive and powerful storms ever to strike Southern New England . . . unlike most storms, this hurricane did not weaken on its way." Sustained winds of 121 miles per hour were recorded. In this view of the common looking south, the library is barely visible behind the mass of upturned trees. (Courtesy of May-Boyce Collection.)

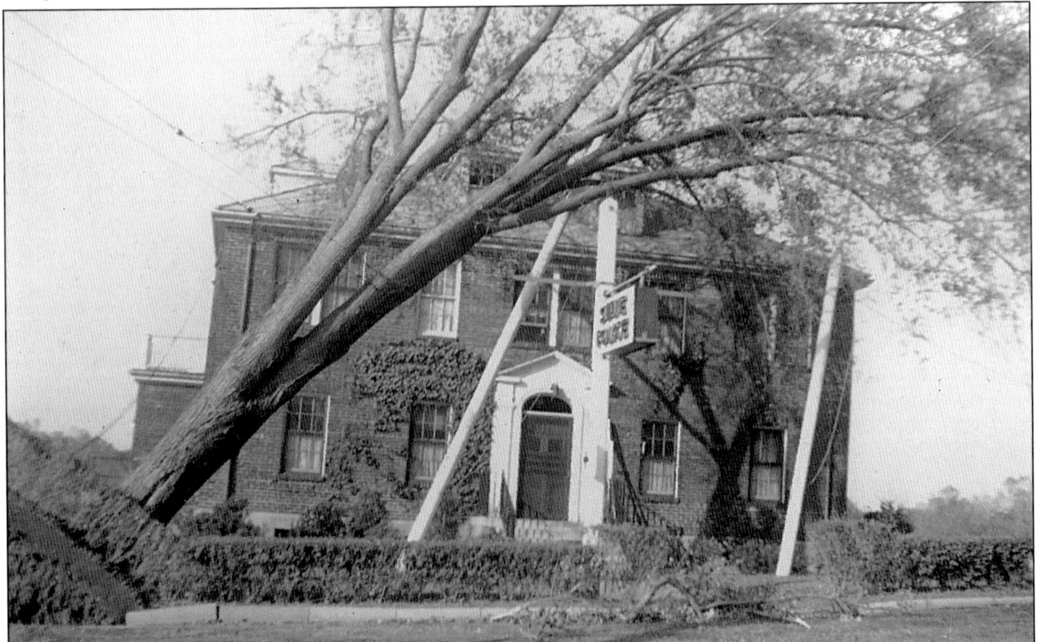

State Police Barracks, South Maple Street. With Routes 9 and 148 both flooded, the state police, although on dry land, were marooned. The *Spencer Leader* of September 28, 1938, shows a photograph of Trooper Nelson of the Brookfield barracks battling currents while trying to make a landing on the northern end of Lake Lashaway in East Brookfield. (Photograph by Louise Menard Bemis; courtesy of Sheila Pronto McCarthy.)

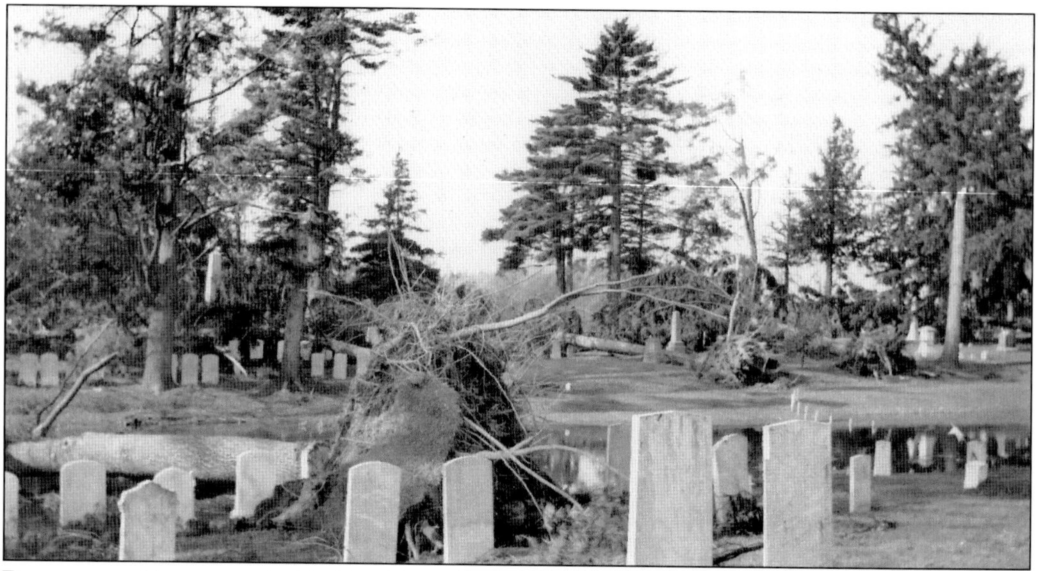

Brookfield Cemetery, 1938. The Brookfield tree warden noted in his 1939 report that many hanging limbs broken by the hurricane of 1938 were trimmed and carted away, including 43 in the cemetery, 50 on Fiskdale Road, 30 on Rice Corner Road, 12 on River Street, 12 on the causeway, and 10 on the common. (Photograph by Louise Menard Bemis; courtesy of Sheila Pronto McCarthy.)

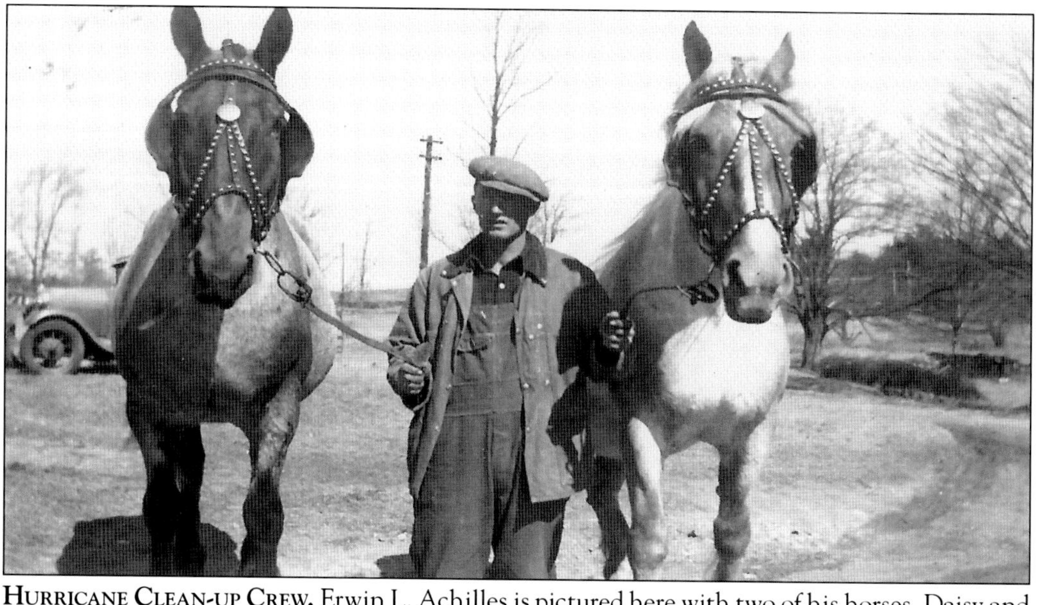

Hurricane Clean-up Crew. Erwin L. Achilles is pictured here with two of his horses, Daisy and Lady. Achilles and his team of workhorses assisted the highway department with clearing trees from the town roads after the hurricane of 1938. (Courtesy of Gloria Achilles Faugno.)

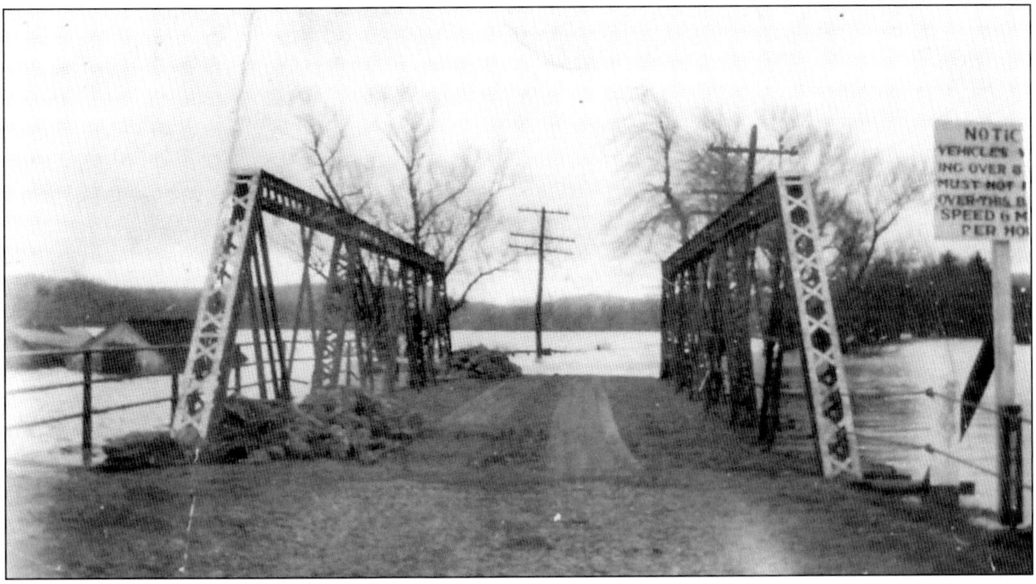

Railroad Bridge, 1938. The *Spencer Leader* of September 23, 1938, reported, "A million tons of water from Lake Lashaway went raging down to Lake Quaboag to raise the level of the lake at least twelve feet above normal high water. [At 11:00 a.m.] the great bridge on the main line of the B&A Railroad was completely washed out and all transportation by rail was halted." (Courtesy of May-Boyce Collection.)

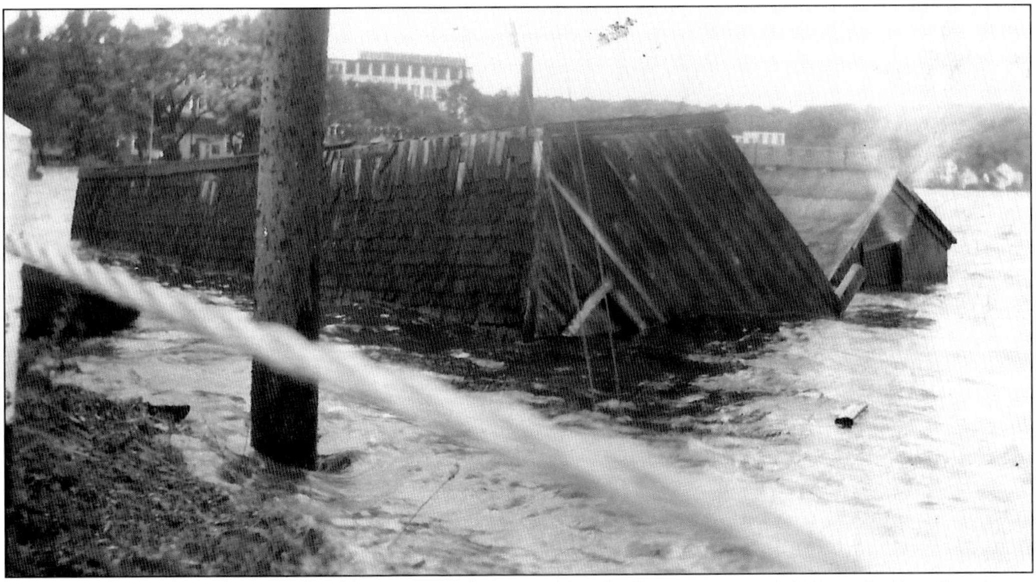

Boathouse Topples. Many buildings were destroyed by the hurricane of 1938, including Quaboag River boathouses. The Worcester County Extension Service surveyed 33 towns in Worcester County after the hurricane and provided the following brief facts in the *Spencer Leader* on September 30, 1938: 298 farm buildings damaged with many barns blown over, 21 silos demolished, 310 hen houses collapsed, and 123 cows killed. (Courtesy of Michael Seery.)

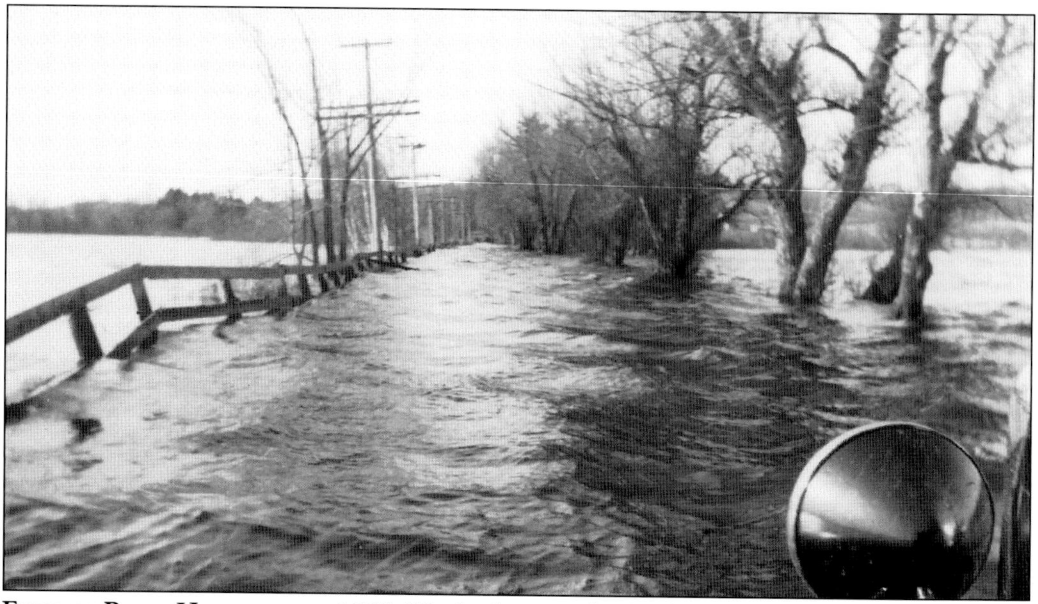

Fiskdale Road, Hurricane of 1938. The bridge over the Quaboag River was completely washed out, and the *Spencer Leader* of September 30, 1938, reported the following: "Snakes take to trees! Up until Sunday afternoon trees left standing along Quaboag River were filled with thousands of snakes twined in the branches." Hundreds more were floating on the river. (Photograph by Louise Menard Bemis; courtesy of Sheila Pronto McCarthy.)

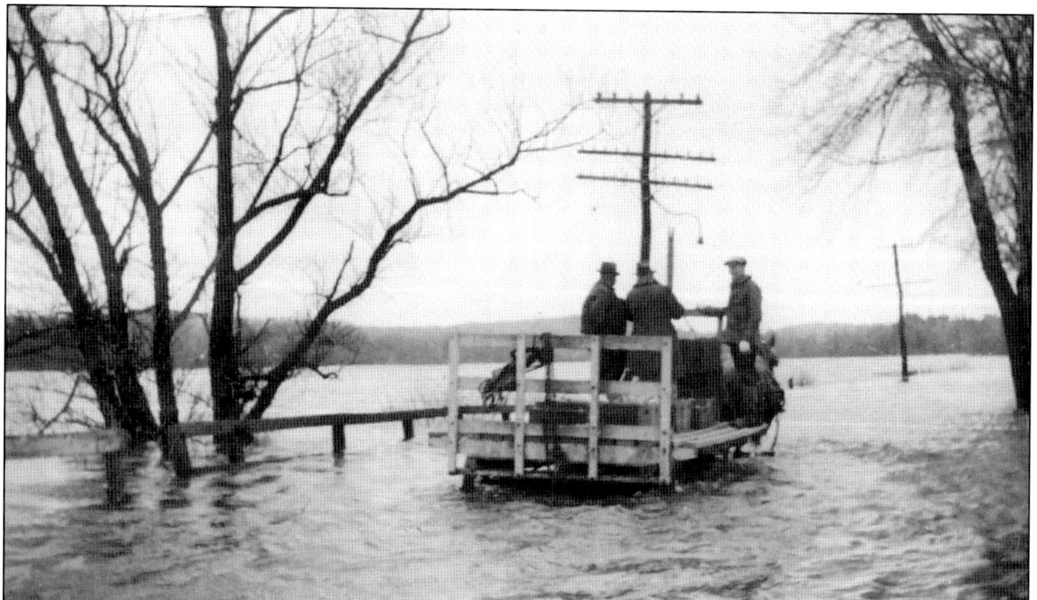

Causeway, September 1938. Fiskdale Road was one of many streets that flooded. The *Spencer Leader* of September 30, 1938, noted that "on Wednesday morning residents of Mill, lower Kimball, and lower sections of Pleasant and River Street and Donahue Avenue found their yards a seething river. Water poured through Kimball Street woods. . . . The home of Joseph J. Maxfield stood between two raging torrents of water." (Courtesy of May-Boyce Collection.)

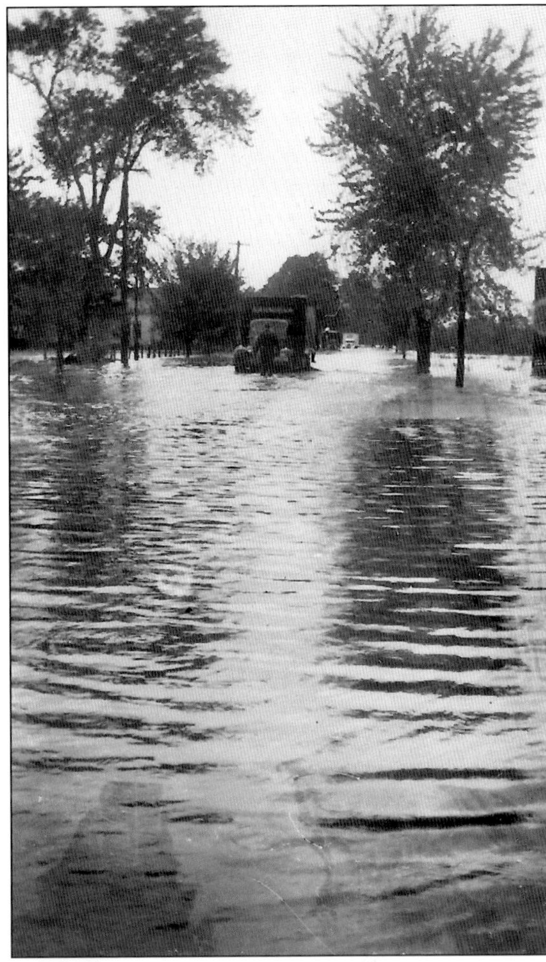

State Road at Brown's. The *Spencer Leader* of September 1938 reported that a "special permit was received by phone to leave food at local store. Boats carried cargo from a point on Post Road east of Brown's to a point near Post Road Inn. A bread truck was on this side of the flood as was a milk truck and were used for days to bring food into town from boats." The fire department was called "to aid in moving the poultry of Police Chief Charles W. Brown, Boston Post Road, to higher ground. No boxes or crates were available, every second counted, on a chance 2,500 hens were placed in relays in a boat; all but about 400 were saved." (Right, courtesy of May-Boyce Collection; below, photograph by Louise Menard Bemis; courtesy of Sheila Pronto McCarthy.)

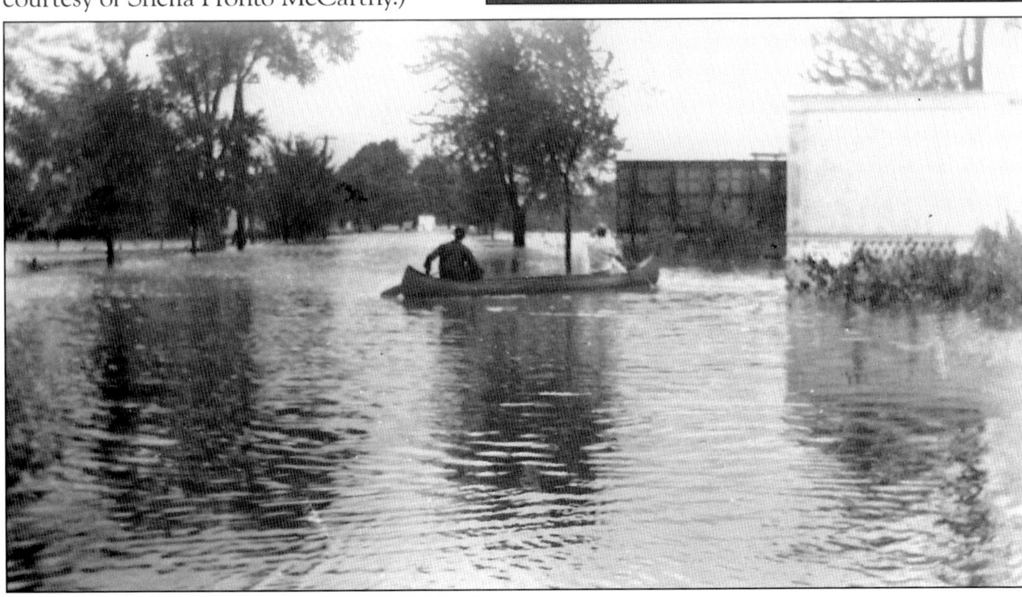

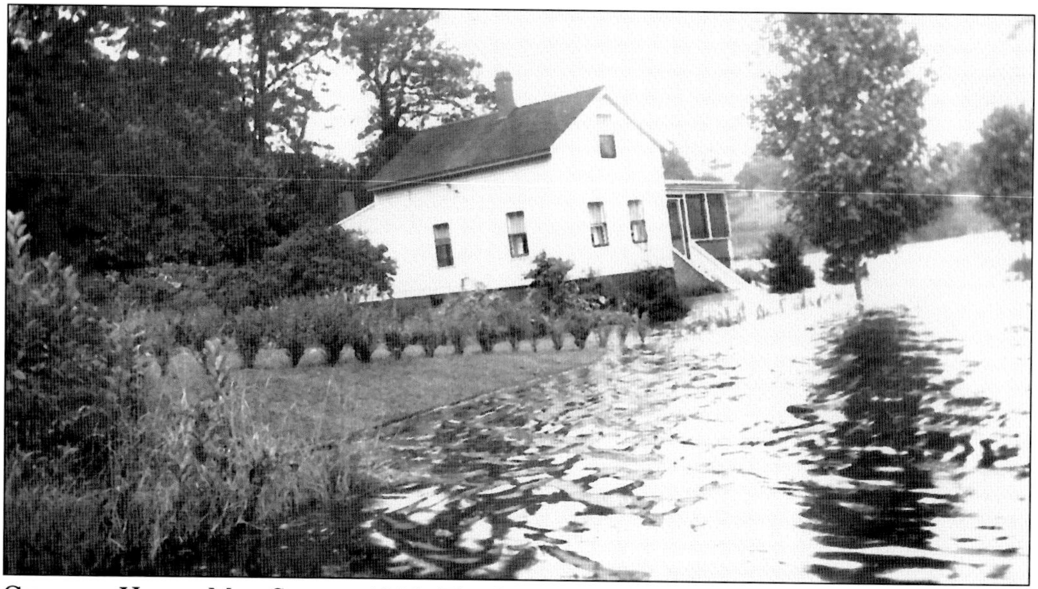

Charron House, Mill Street, 1938. The *Spencer Leader* reported the following conditions on September 21, 1938: "At 3 o'clock all phone connections out of town ended. Lights went out about 4 p.m. . . . The Sharon [*sic*] family on Mill Street, Mundell family on River Road, Green family, Stone family on Donahue Street had to evacuate. Then the tornado started with its night of terror." (Photograph by Louise Menard Bemis; courtesy of Sheila Pronto McCarthy.)

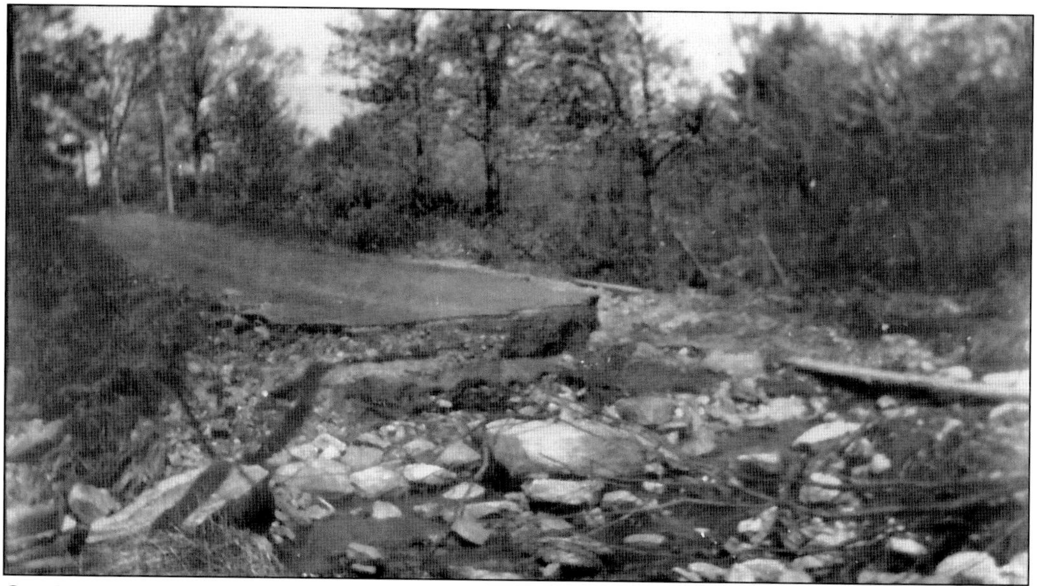

Old North Brookfield Road, 1938. Under the "Hurricane Hits" section of the *Spencer Leader* of September 28, 1938, it was noted that the town was "completely isolated except for pedestrians over back roads and fields from North Brookfield. Brookfield flats under four feet of water. Lake Quaboag at least ten feet above normal level." (Photograph by Louise Menard Bemis; courtesy of Sheila Pronto McCarthy.)

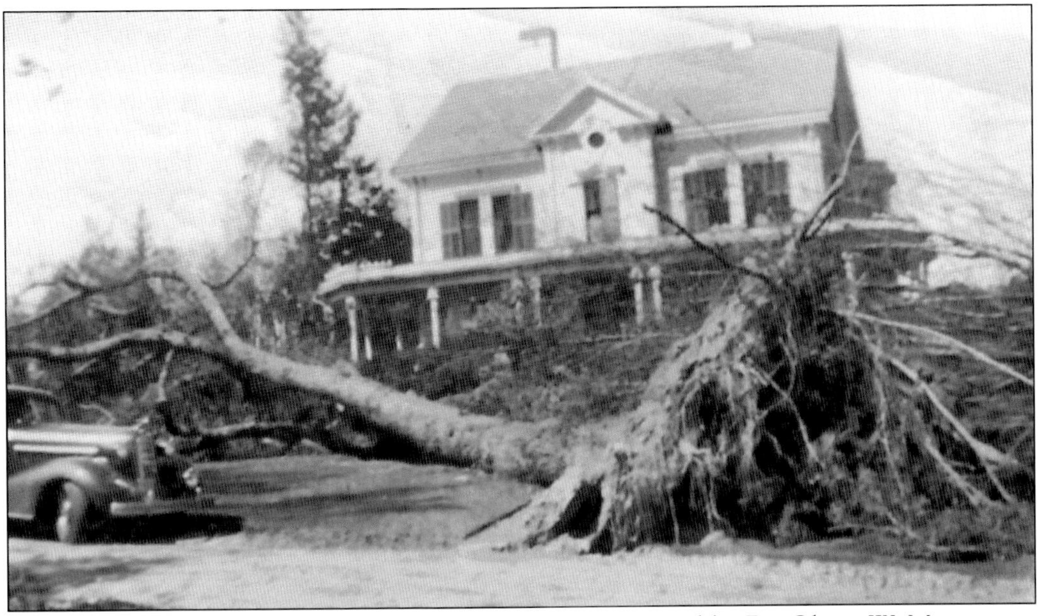

Elm Hill Farm. Hurricane damage at Elm Hill Farm, owned by Dr. Oliver W. Means, was extensive. The *Spencer Leader* of September 30, 1938, recorded that barns were damaged and the apple orchard lost more than 1,000 trees and "two elms dating before the Revolutionary War . . . torn by the roots. The blacksmith shop was found a distance away against a wall." (Courtesy of May-Boyce Collection.)

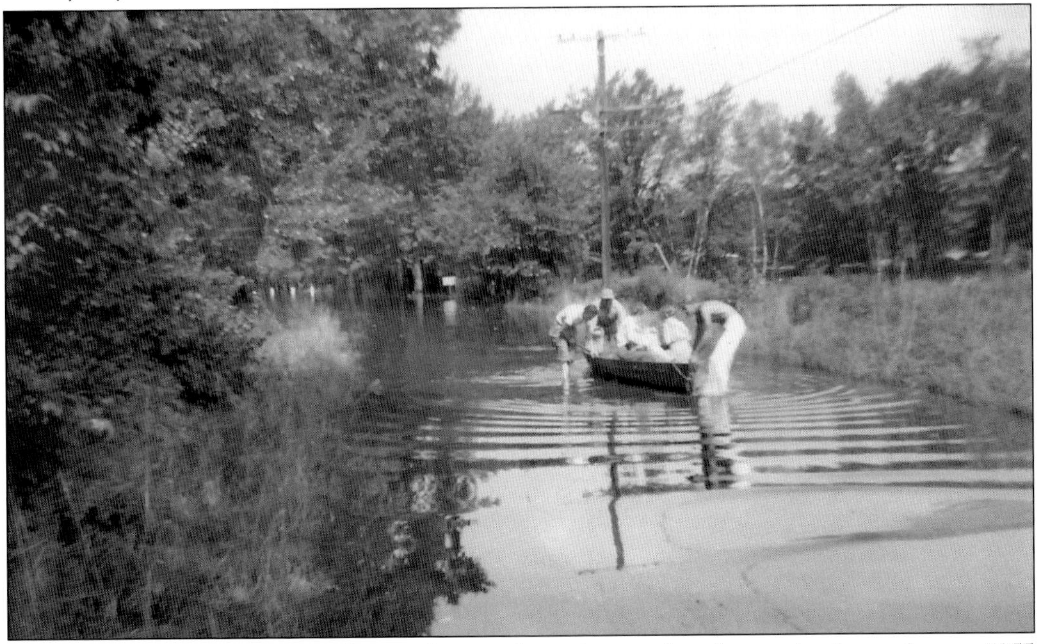

Quaboag Street, 1955. Residents take to a boat during the aftermath of two August 1955 hurricanes. Hurricane Connie produced four to six inches of rain in southern New England. The ground was saturated, and river and lake levels were above normal when a week later Hurricane Diane added 20 inches of rain over two days. (Courtesy of Grace Boynton Prizio and Linda Prizio Lincoln.)

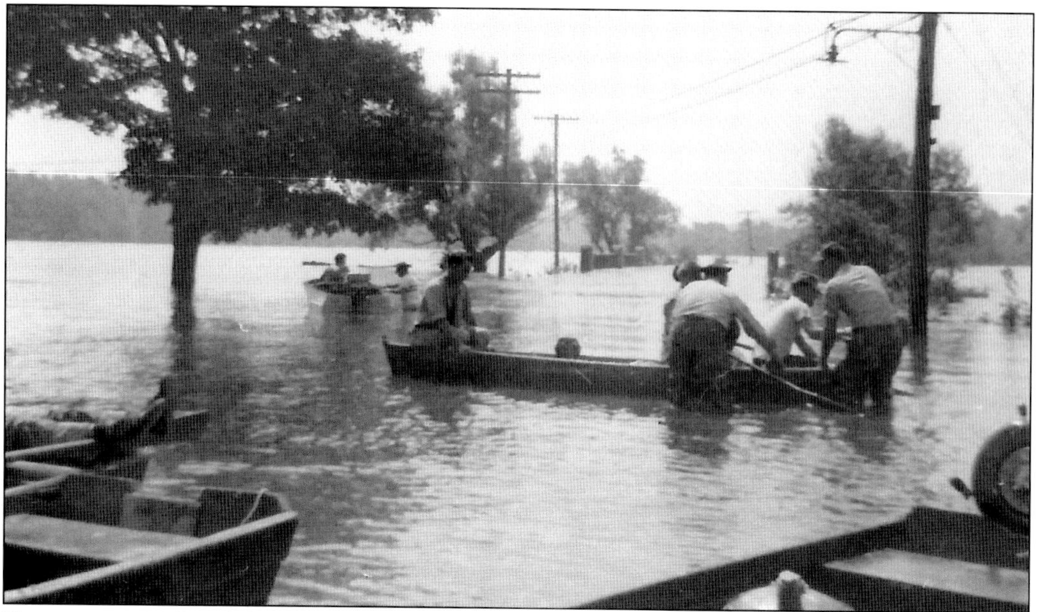

Flood of 1955. Brookfield was flooded again in 1955, as shown above at the causeway and below at the train depot. The *County Courier* of August 1955 reported, "Residents were completely isolated over the weekend by floods rising to heights of seven to ten feet along the Causeway leading into Brookfield, by the washout at Mill Pond and Long Hill Road and Brookfield Road to Route 20." In anticipation of such isolation, the fire department moved several fire trucks to the Over-the-River district, and boat transportation was provided across the causeway by residents, including Warren Campbell (above left). The police department was equally vigilant and took care to protect victims of flooding on North and South Ponds, patrolling to keep looting to a minimum, restricting boating, and keeping sightseers away to prevent wake damage. (Both, courtesy of Carolyn Potter Murray.)

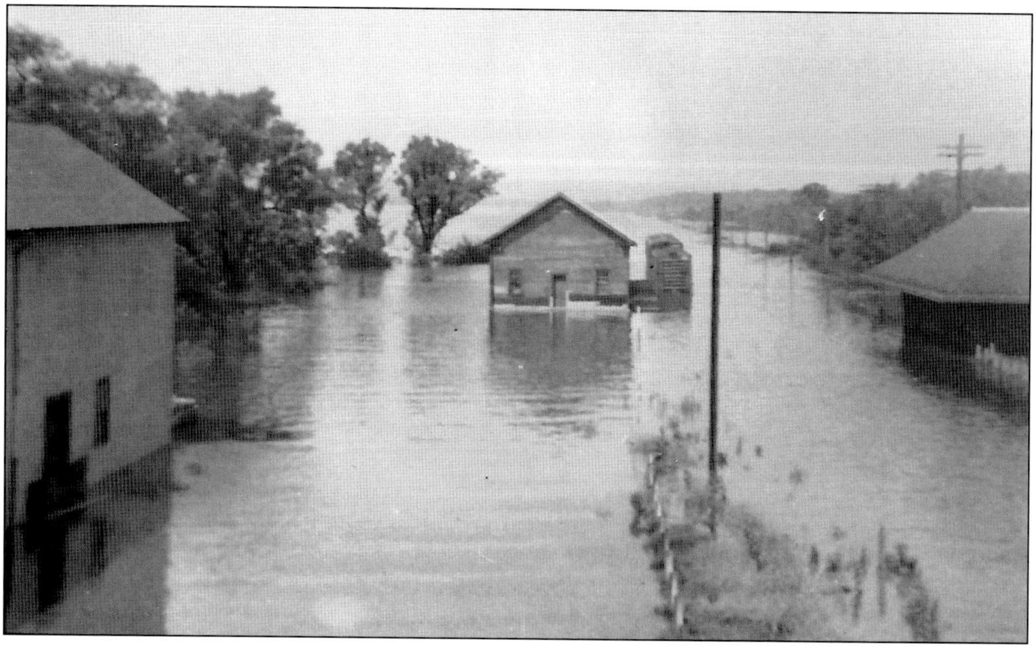

Ten

Service to Community and Country

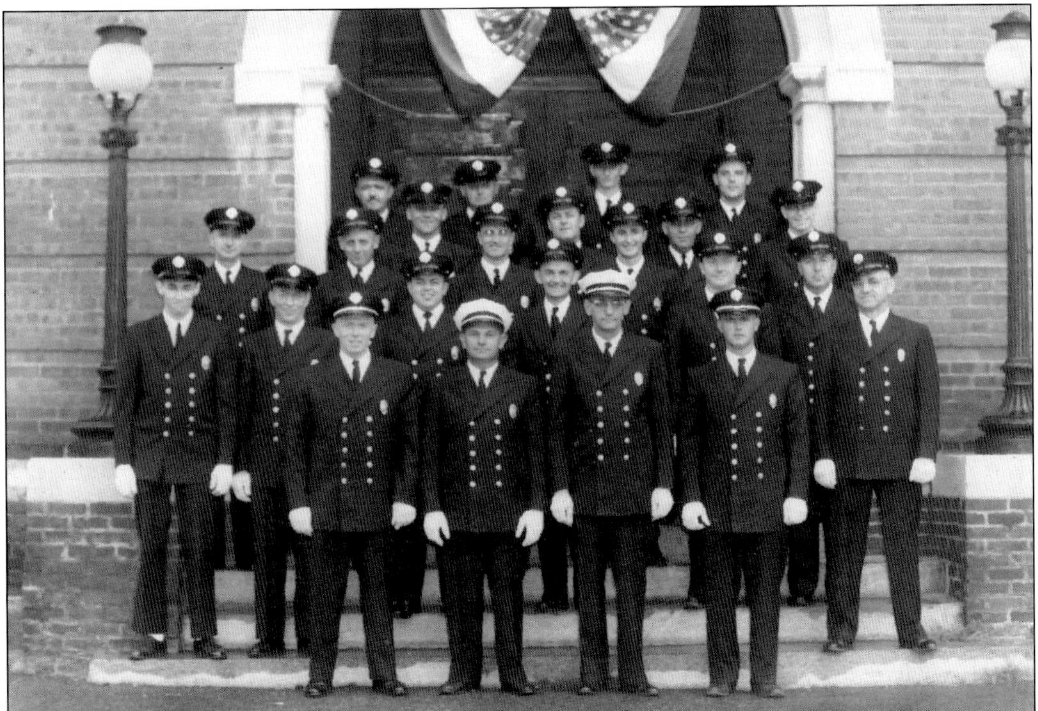

Fire Department, 1960. In their new uniforms are, from left to right, (first row) Capt. George Clancy, Assistant Chief Lewis Terry, Chief William Gero, and Lt. Alvin Brown; (second row) Curtis Bullard, Howard Woodard, Robert Turner, Robert Terry, Joseph Murray, Gordon Warman, and Horace May Sr.; (third row) Arthur Faugno, George Herbert, Horace May Jr., Richard Robinson, George Boynton, Richard Howe, Edgar Gregory, and William Tourtellotte; (fourth row) Gilson Merriam, Charles Herbert, Richard Finney, and Bruce Gadaire. (Courtesy of Gloria Achilles Faugno.)

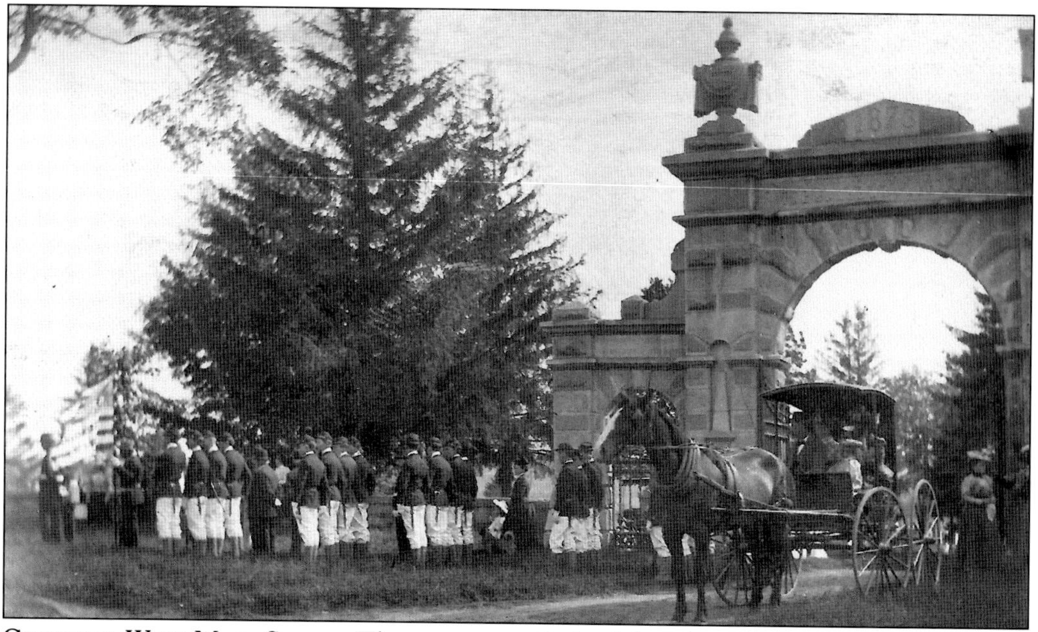

Cemetery, West Main Street. The town set aside land for a burial ground in 1718 as part of the original Quaboag Plantation, and in 1756, it was enlarged to five acres. In 1873, Otis Hayden and William A. Banister presented the town with this majestic gate, shown above, inscribed, "Until the day break and the shadows flee away." These photographs depict the large celebration held to commemorate the service and sacrifice of Brookfield soldiers. The monument in the photograph below stands at 16 feet tall in the Grand Army section of the Brookfield Cemetery and is dedicated to the "loyal sons in the war for preservation of the Union, from 1861–1865." (Both, courtesy of longtime resident.)

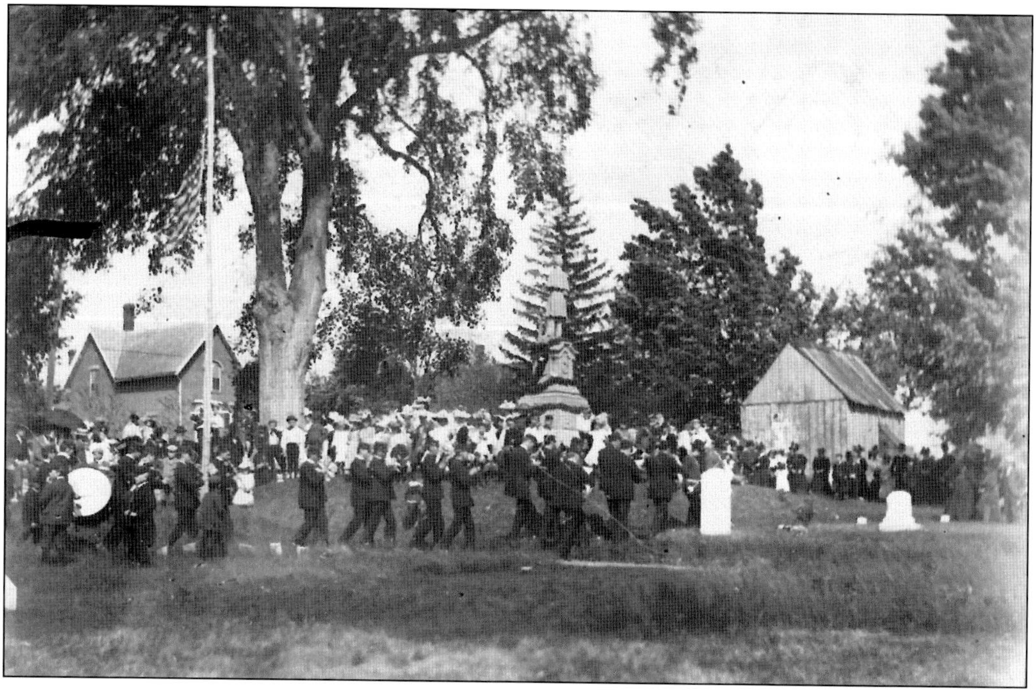

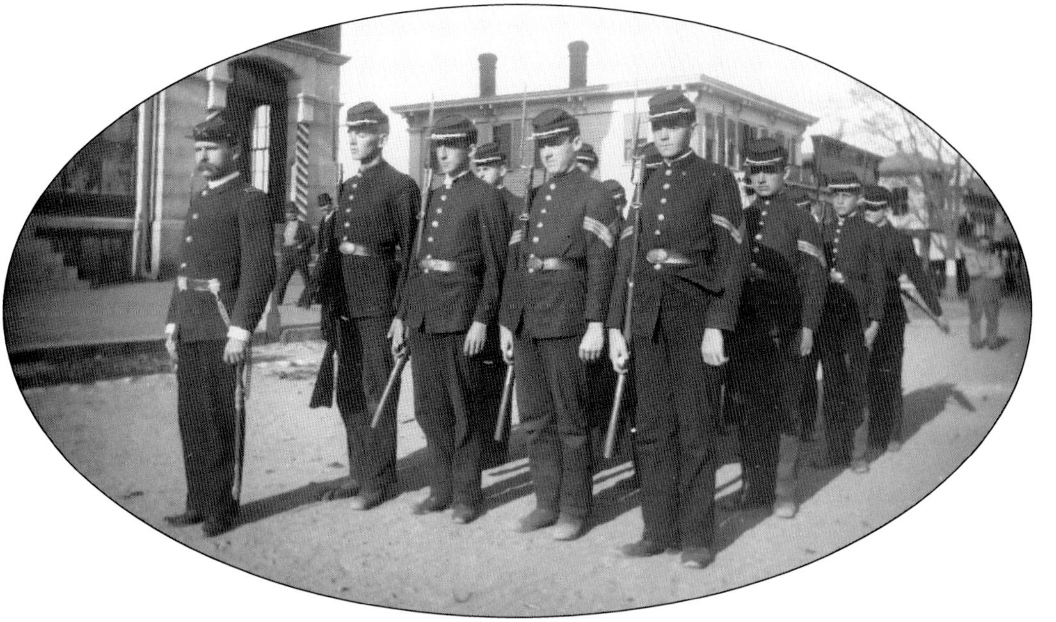

CIVIL WAR MARCHERS. The *Brookfield Times* of July 11, 1890, reported that on July 4, 1890, the dedication of the Civil War monument took place to much fanfare with a program, parade, and donation to the town of the Grand Army of the Republic Record Book, where the "names and service history of each man enlisted from Brookfield' 61–'65 should be reported." The book was to be kept by Dexter Post No. 38 as long as it existed and then be available to future generations at the Merrick Public Library, where it resides today. The Brookfield High School Cadets, shown below in the late 1800s, had 18 members march in the Quaboag Plantation 250th anniversary parade in 1910. (Above, photograph by Charles P. Blanchard; courtesy of Blanchard Means Foundation; below, courtesy of longtime resident.)

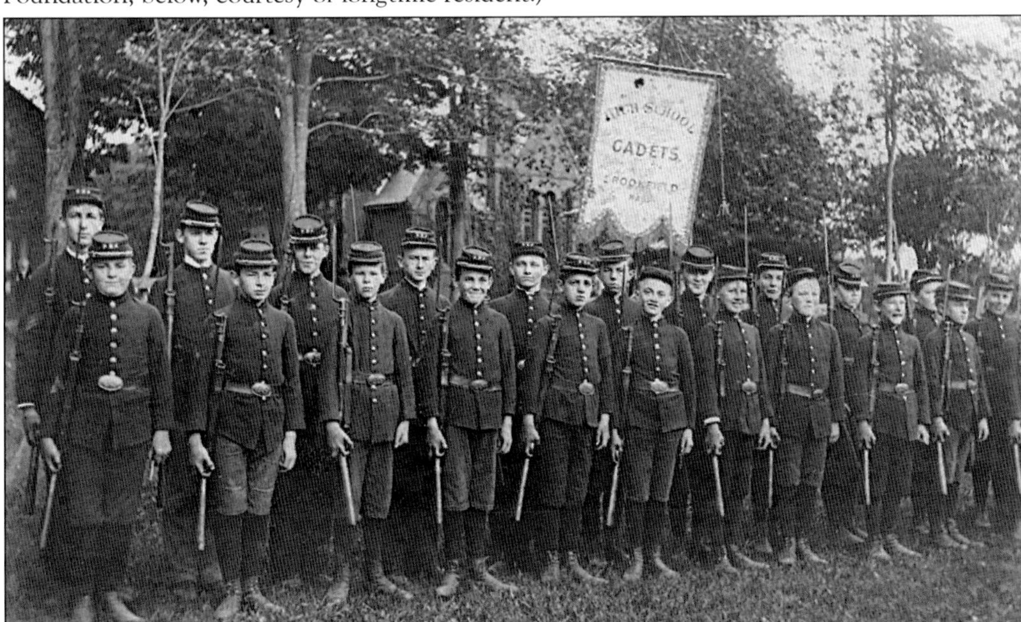

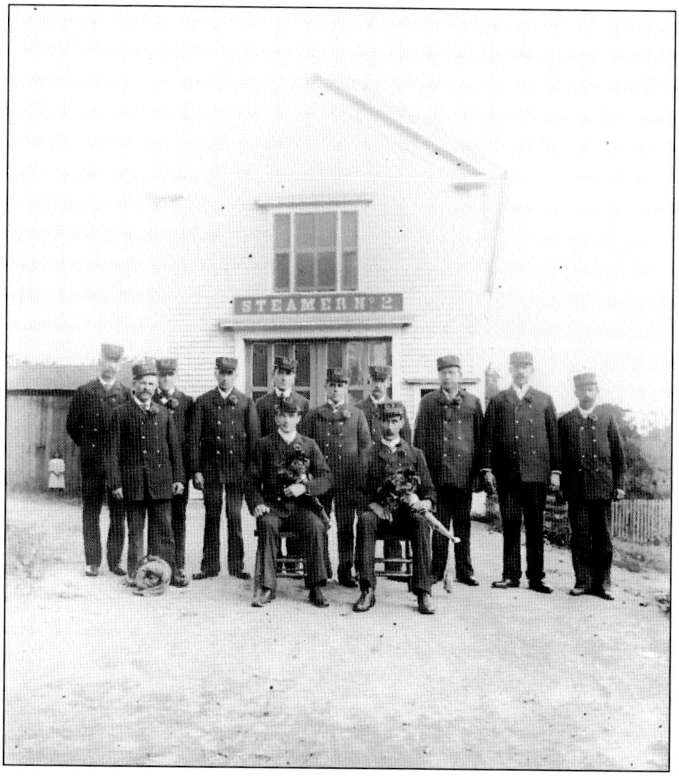

STEAMER NO. 2. This building, situated in the center village, housed the new Amoskeag steamer, purchased in 1899. In 1902, two serious fires nearby on Prouty Street and at the town hall caused much damage and some personal injury to firemen. The engine house itself was also burned. (Courtesy of May-Boyce Collection.)

CATARACT NO. 2. This piece of equipment, purchased by the fire department in 1855, was pulled by a group of men who would then insert a hose into a body of water or a well. Pumping would be done by hand, with much effort, in order to produce a stream of water. (Courtesy of Reta Priest Warman.)

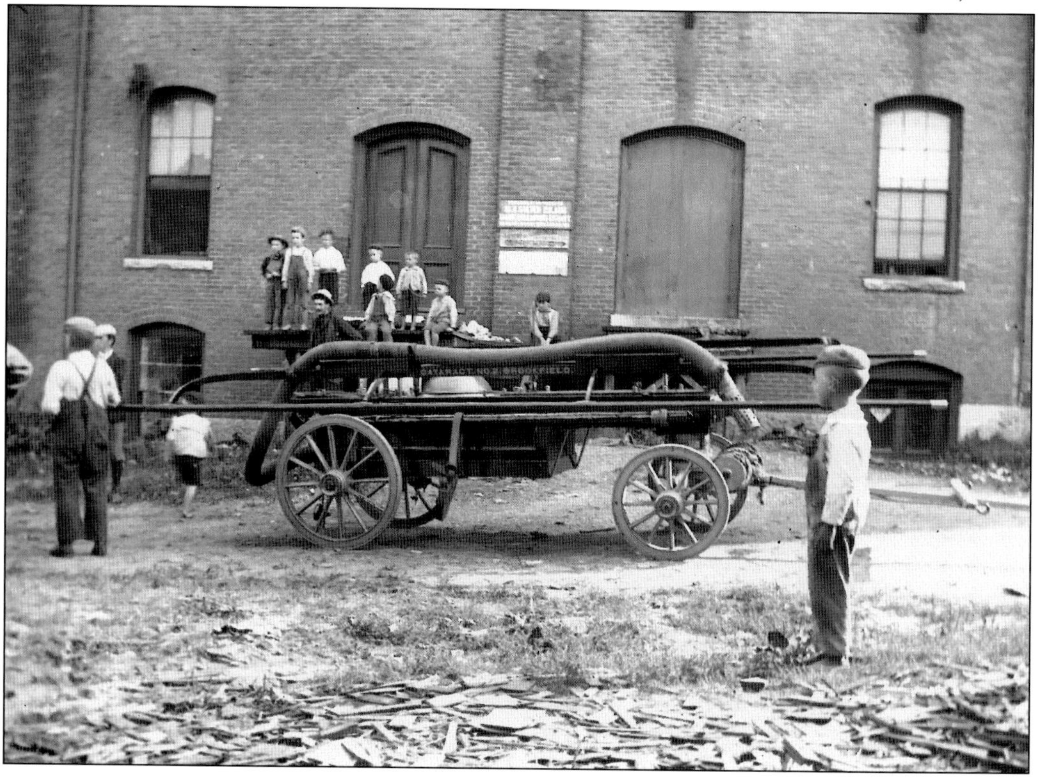

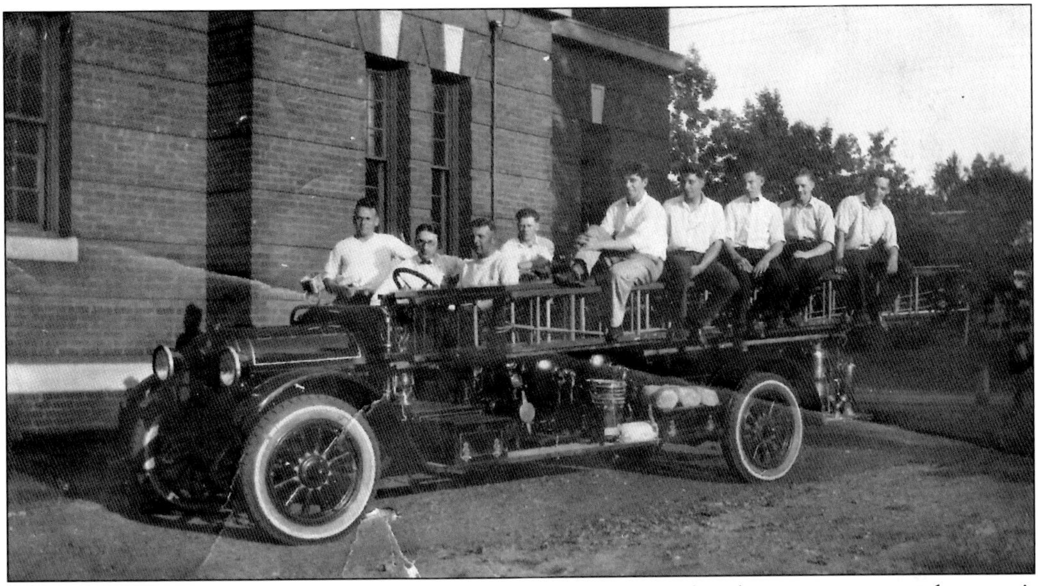

A 1924 Reo Combination Truck. Members of the volunteer fire department sit on the town's first motorized piece of firefighting equipment, parked next to the town hall. From left to right are Harold May, Benjamin Faugno, Walter May, Red Sullivan, Leon "Hop" Gaudette, Winfield Howe, John "Jack" Ryan, unidentified, and Horace "Bus" May. (Courtesy of May-Boyce Collection.)

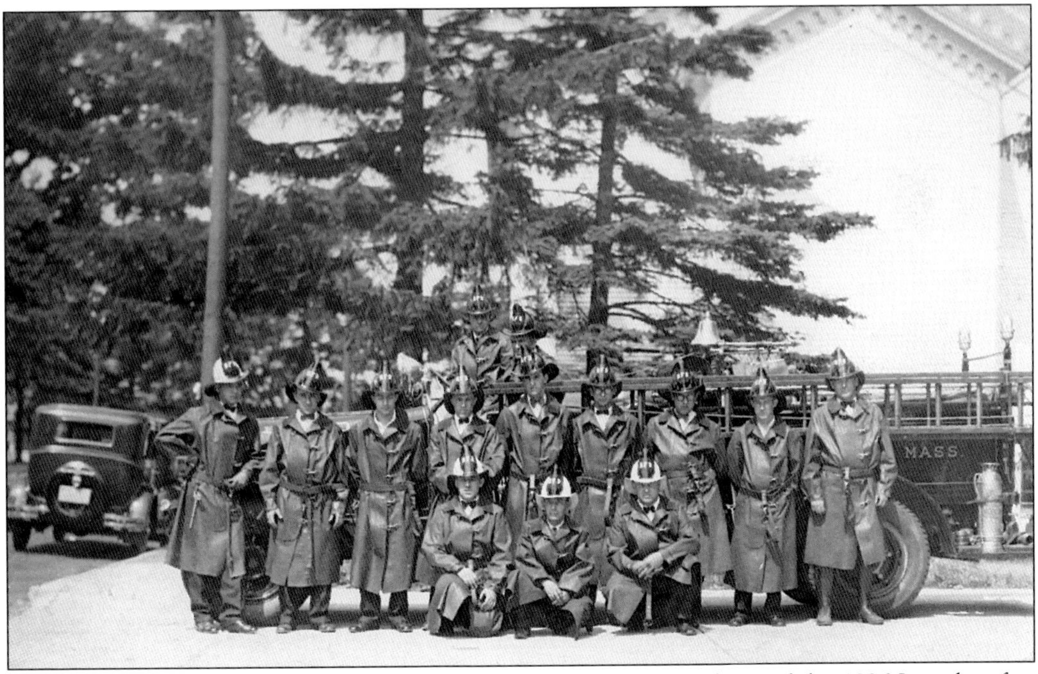

Fire Department, c. 1930. Arrayed in their waterproof gear in front of the 1926 Larrabee fire truck are, from left to right, (first row) Wilfred Gaudette, William Byron, and Lester Priest; (second row) Horace May, Leon "Hop" Gaudette, Romeo Faugno, Ernest Robidoux, Arthur Howe, Sidney May, Clifford Gadaire, Harold Wright, and Harold May; (third row) unidentified and Philip Boynton. (Courtesy of May-Boyce Collection.)

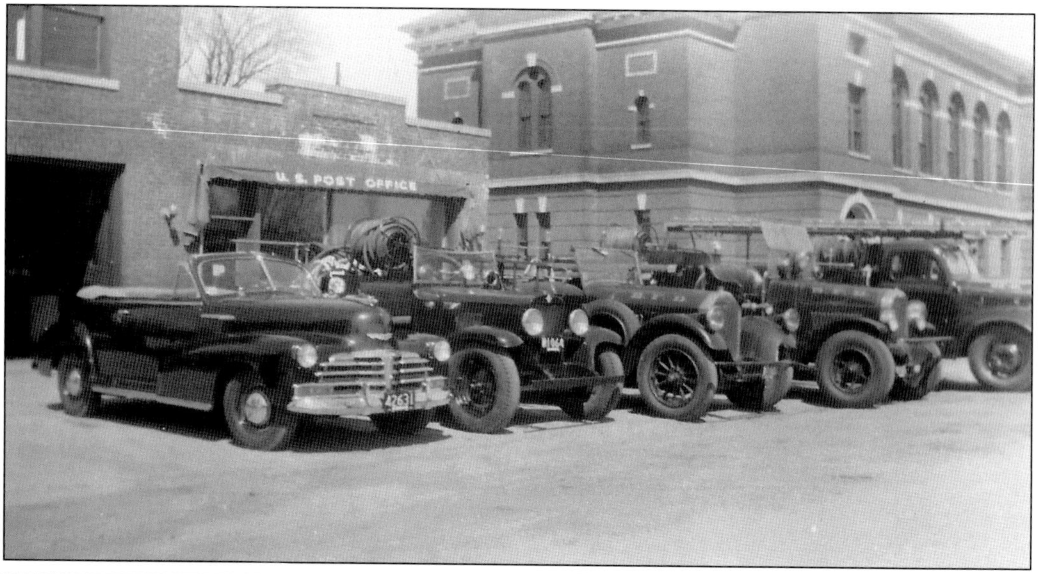

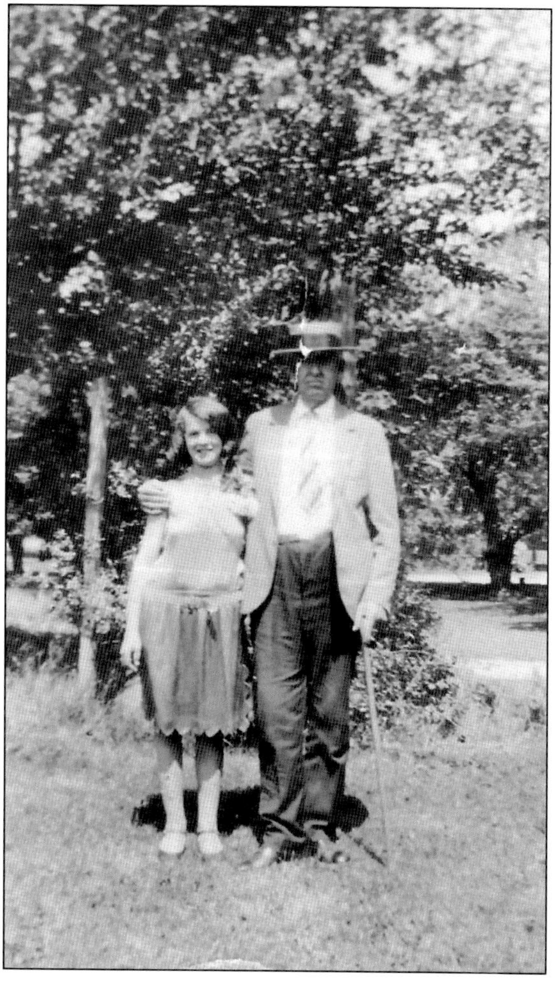

FIRE DEPARTMENT VEHICLES. A display of firefighting vehicles is lined up on Central Street, probably in the early 1950s. A far cry from hose carriages, hand tubs, and horse-drawn steamers, the department's motorized vehicles included a 1926 Larrabee that could pump 750 gallons of water per minute and a 1947 "Big" Dodge pumper that could pump 500 gallons of water per minute. (Courtesy of Barbara Clancy.)

JOHN F. CROTTY, 1926. Chief of police John Crotty and his wife took on the guardianship of Grace Boynton Prizio, shown in this photograph at age 16. Julia Stone Boynton, Grace's mother, passed away at the age of 27, leaving seven children. All of the children were taken in by friends of the family. (Courtesy of Grace Boynton Prizio and Linda Prizio Lincoln.)

MASSACHUSETTS STATE POLICE. At right, Sgt. James E. Cronin sits astride his new Indian motorcycle in front of his home at 23 Kimball Street around 1933. Motorcycles came into great favor as policing vehicles, as they were versatile and economical in the growing agency. Below, newly built in 1931, the Brookfield State Police barracks houses an arm of Troop C, previously operating from a building on High Street. The state police have the distinction of being the first statewide law enforcement agency in the nation, founded in 1865, to address issues arising in the post–Civil War years, such as lawlessness surrounding Prohibition, concealed weapons, union unrest, and violence in increasingly industrialized city areas. Burgeoning motor vehicle ownership required roadway monitoring for safety and order on the highways. (Both, courtesy of Robert and Nancy Cronin Wilder.)

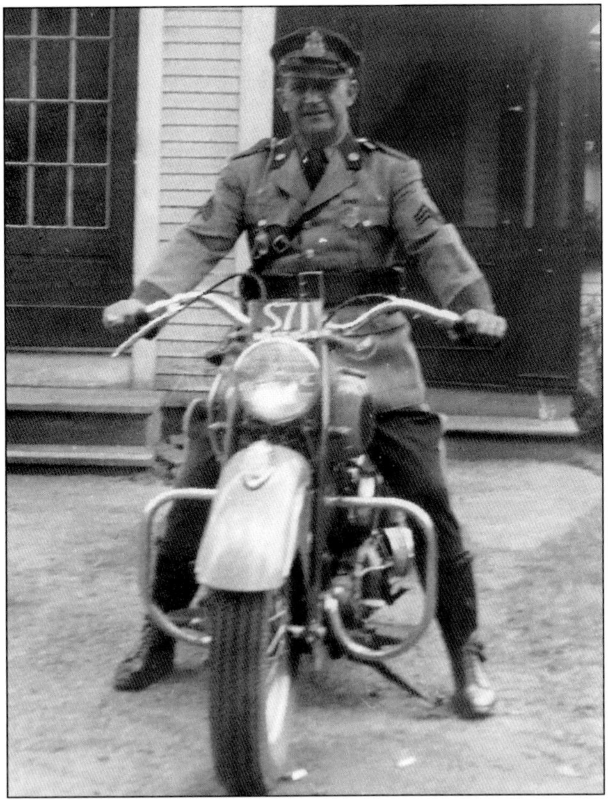

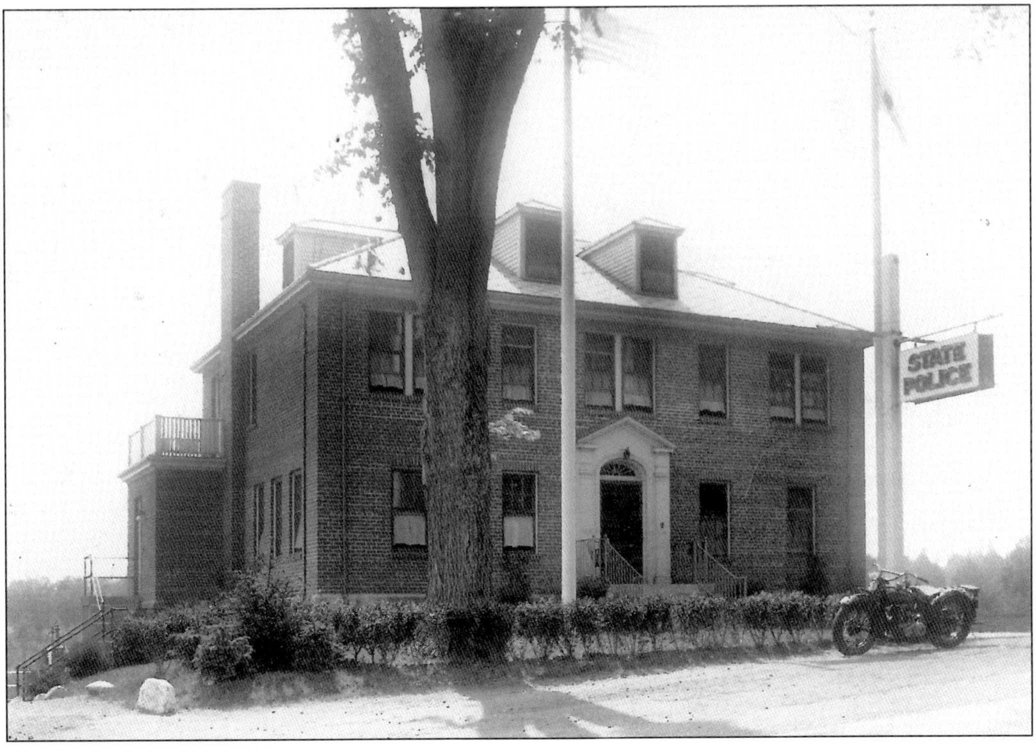

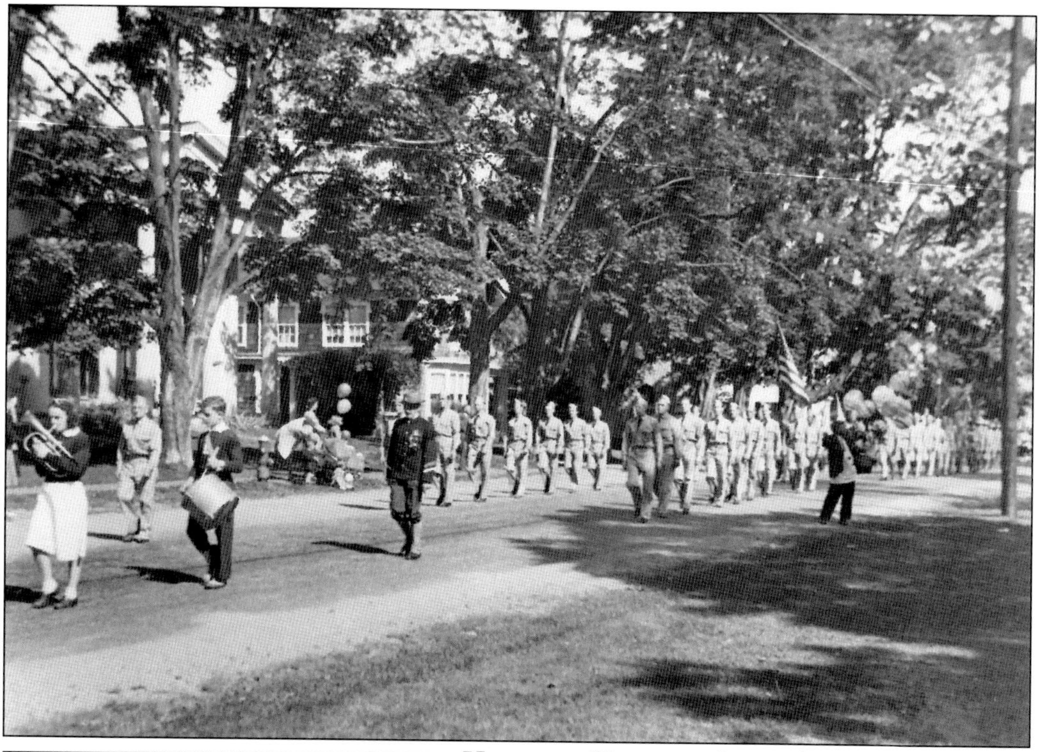

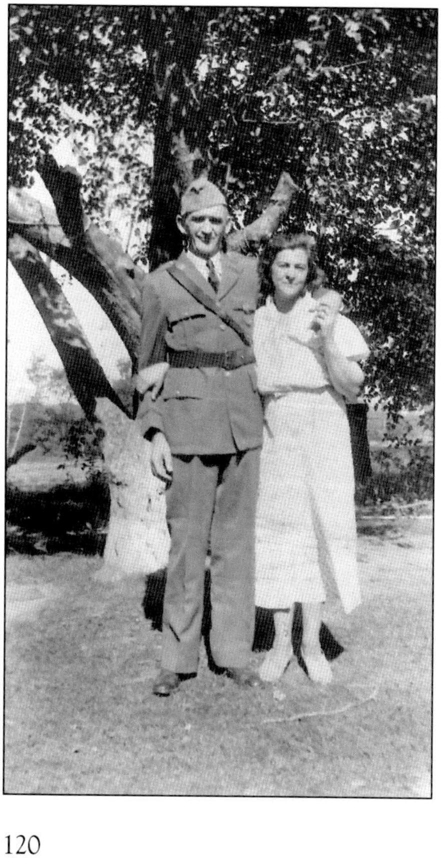

Honoring Veterans. Lines of veterans parade by Memorial Square along the common on River Street. The town lost two men during World War I, and nine men died while in service during World War II. The service and sacrifice of all men and women in the armed forces are kept alive in this small town with ceremonies, such as this one. (Courtesy of May-Boyce Collection.)

Seerys, 1938. Edward J. Seery, a veteran of World War I, established the Veterans of Foreign Wars Post No. 530 in 1944. His wife, Winifred Gaffney Seery, emigrated from Galway, Ireland, in 1915 at the age of 17. They were married soon after and had eight children, including war hero John J. Seery Sr. (Courtesy of Michael Seery.)

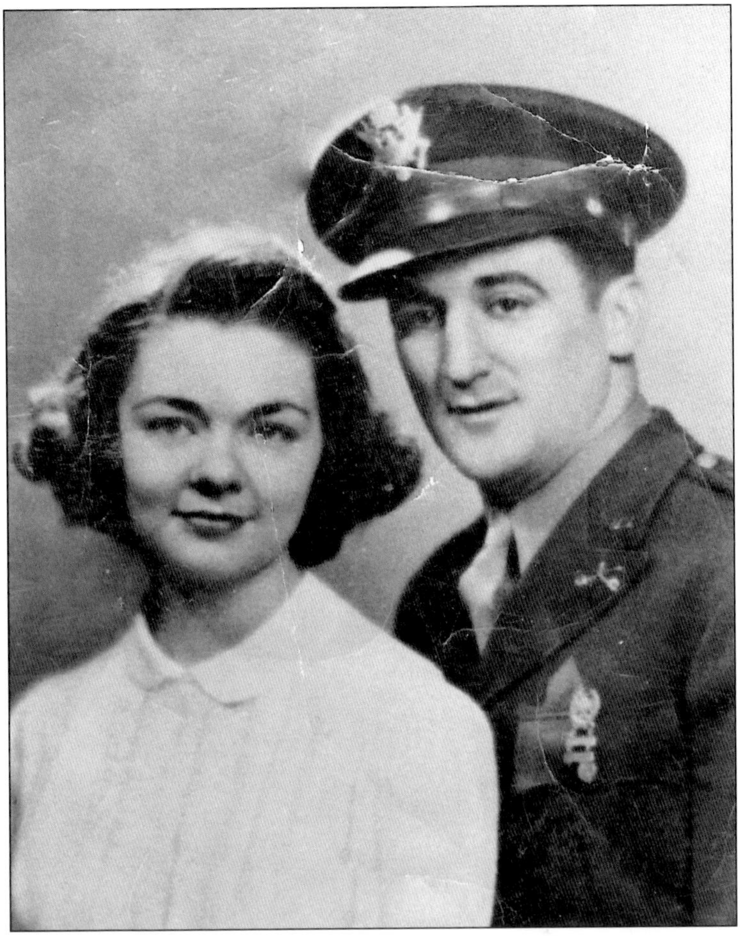

Mr. and Mrs. John J. Seery Sr. John Seery Sr. married Annette Kiskadden after attending college in Amherst, Massachusetts, where he made his mark playing football and joined the ROTC. He was commissioned first lieutenant in the 4th Cavalry Reconnaissance Squad and was deployed to England in early 1944, serving under Gen. Dwight D. Eisenhower. During his time in England, he had the opportunity to travel to Ireland, meeting many family members. While serving in France, he was killed while running for cover in a hedgerow during a German artillery attack in July 1944. He never got to see his newborn son, John J. Seery Jr. (Both, courtesy of Michael Seery.)

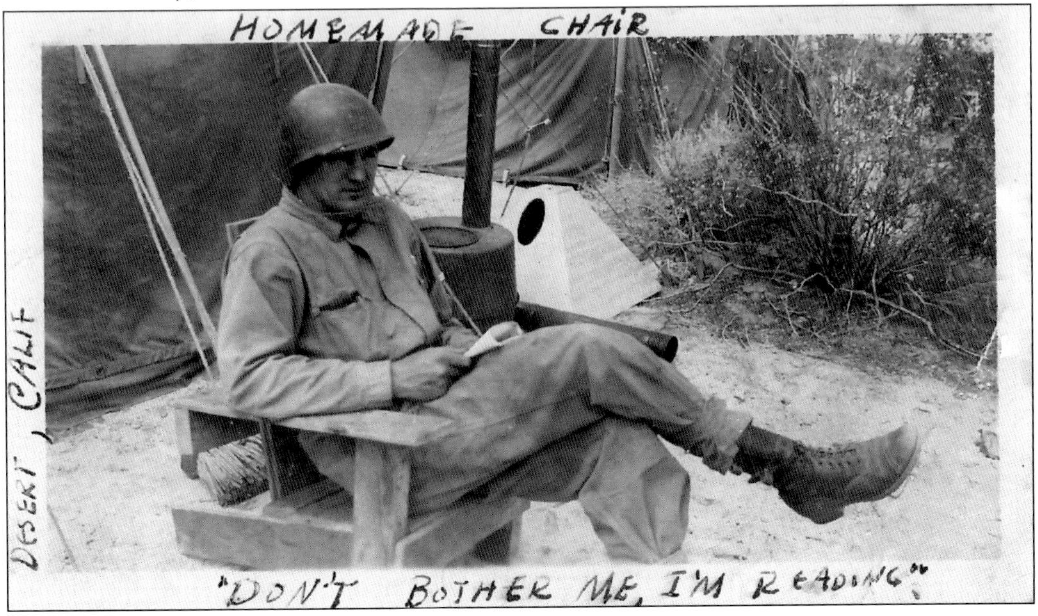

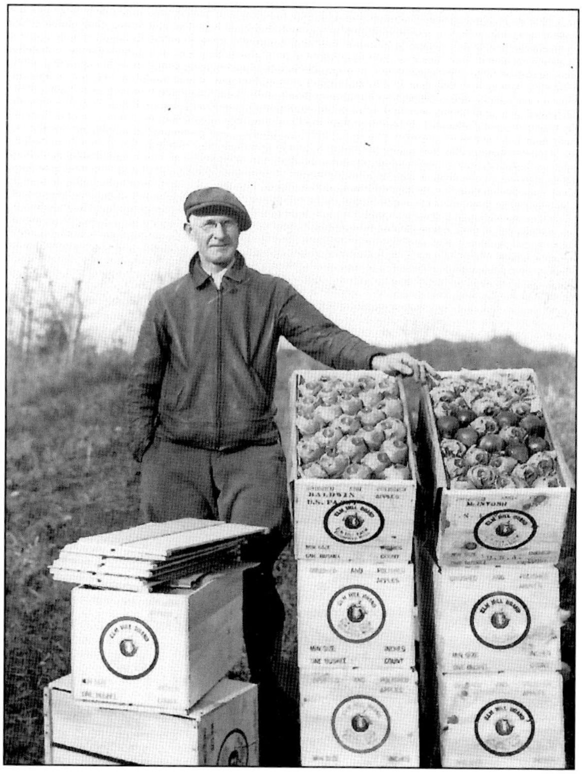

APPLES FOR THE TROOPS. Lee Boyce, manager of Elm Hill Farm, displays apples that were wrapped in special paper to prevent bruising for shipment overseas during World War II. The crates contain Baldwin and McIntosh apples, noting that they have been brushed and polished. For many years, Elm Hill Farm made apples in cold storage available for purchase at its scenic location atop the hill. (Courtesy of May-Boyce Collection.)

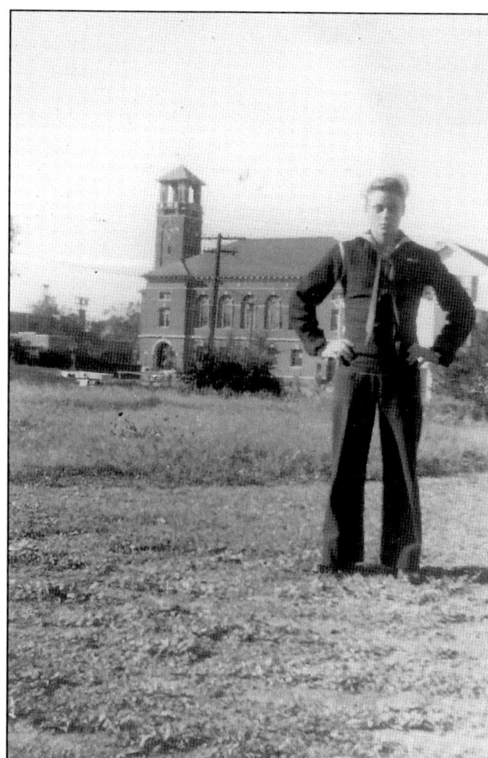

ROBERT K. RUGGLES JR. Robert Ruggles joined the Navy in 1944 while still a senior at Brookfield High School. He was sworn in and given time to complete his last months of school before reporting for duty. His discharge in 1946 notes he was a shipfitter, second class; he received the World War II Victory Medal, Philippine Liberation Medal, Asiatic-Pacific Theater Medal, and American Theater Medal. (Courtesy of Ruggles family.)

POTTER FAMILY, KIMBALL STREET. Navy radarman Milton Potter joins his family on leave from duty on the USS *Albermarle* during late summer 1944. Connie Gustin and Milton Potter are shown with their children, clockwise from the top, Jeanette, Elaine, Blaine, and Carolyn. The Potters later relocated to West Brookfield and, in the 1960s, owned the popular Uncle Miltie's ice cream stand in that town. (Courtesy of Carolyn Potter Murray.)

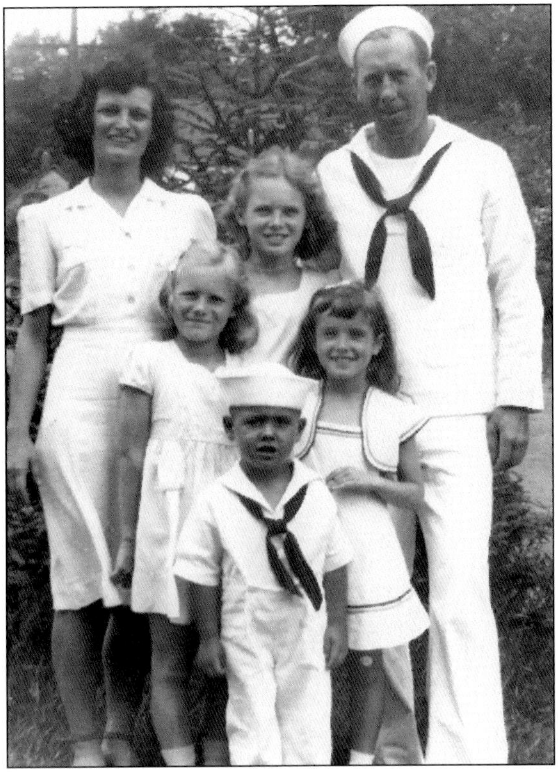

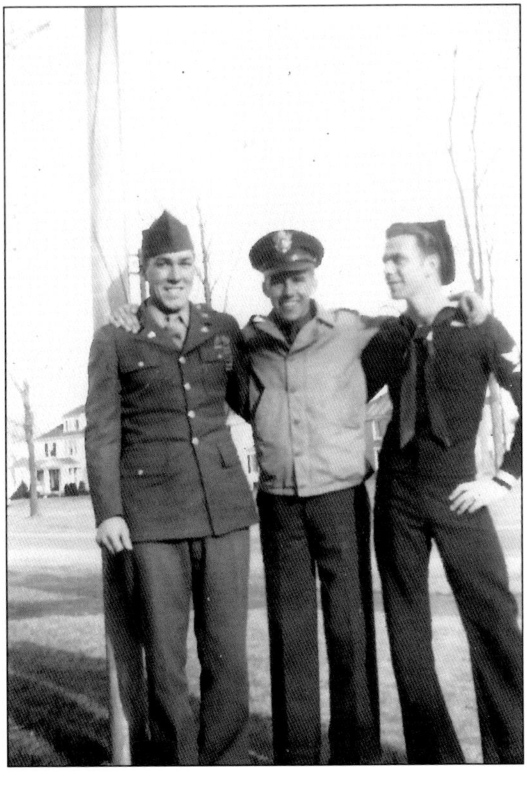

THREE NATIVE SONS. Men and women returning home for leave posed for photographs in front of the high school on River Street, as seen in this picture, with the school flagpole and town common behind them. Here are, from left to right, Richard Boynton, Philip Eaton, and Clyde Gregson, who all returned after their service was completed at the end of World War II. (Courtesy of Gloria Achilles Faugno.)

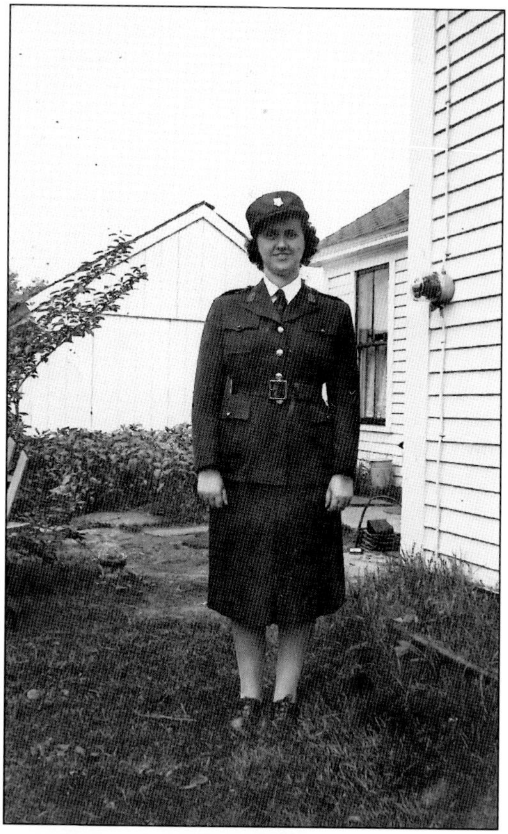

Civil Defense Warden. Mary Leach is photographed after completion of the Massachusetts Women's Civilian Defense School. Leach had a long career as an upper elementary school teacher, followed by many years as principal of both Blanchard Elementary School and then Brookfield Elementary School, where she worked the combined job of sixth-grade teacher and principal. She retired in 1973. (Courtesy of Docwra family.)

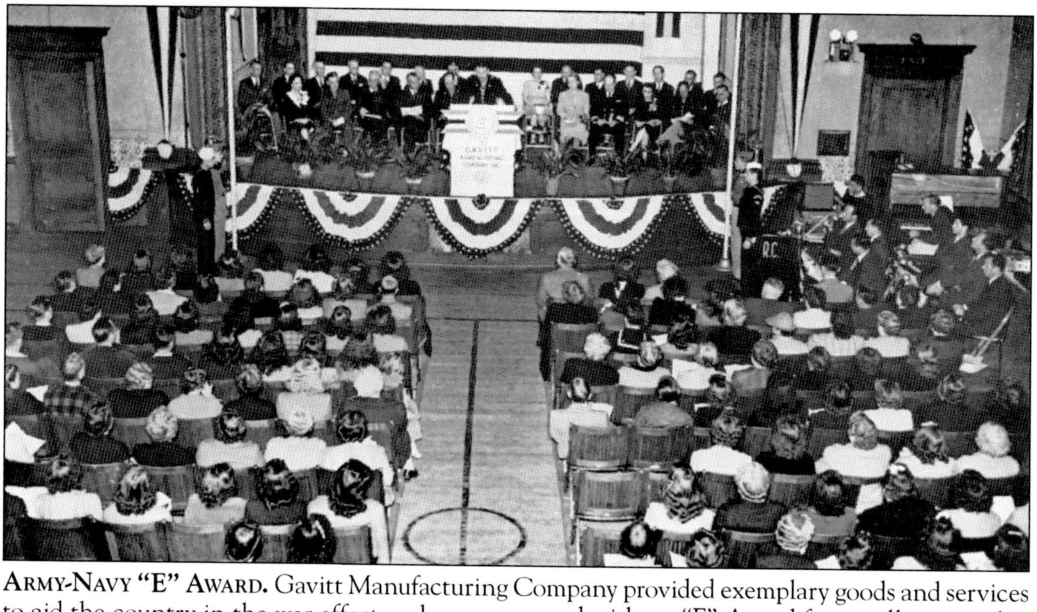

Army-Navy "E" Award. Gavitt Manufacturing Company provided exemplary goods and services to aid the country in the war effort and was presented with an "E" Award for excellence at this ceremony held on October 11, 1945, in town hall. Presenting were representatives from the armed forces to let those working on the home front know how much their contributions were appreciated by those serving. (Courtesy of Harold R. Chesson Jr.)

Korean War Veteran. Cpl. Michael J. O'Keefe enlisted in the Marine Corps from high school in 1948. He served in the 1st Provisional Marine Brigade and participated in five amphibious landings, including Chosin, Inchon, and Pusan. He suffered multiple wounds in 1950 and was reported missing in action. He received a Purple Heart and Bronze Star as well as many citations and medals. (Courtesy of Michael J. O'Keefe.)

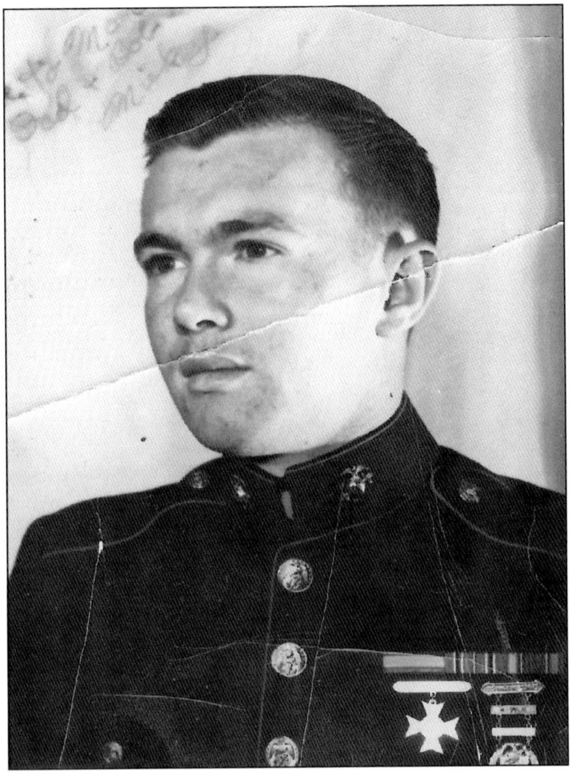

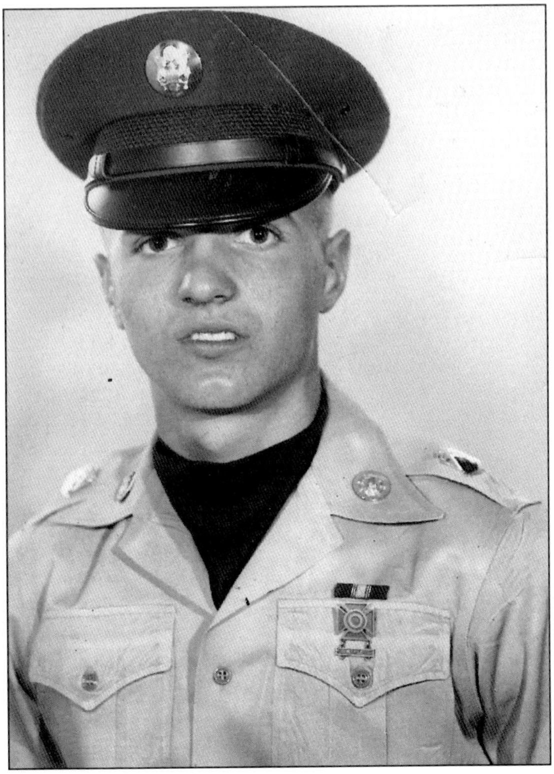

Vietnam Veteran. Teddy Lee Williams, son of Raymond Williams Sr. and Frances Robidoux Patterson, grew up on Rice Corner Road. He enlisted in the Army in 1966 and served as a private first class in the infantry for three years, first in Germany and then in Vietnam. He died at a young age after returning from Vietnam. (Courtesy of Bonnie Williams Olson.)

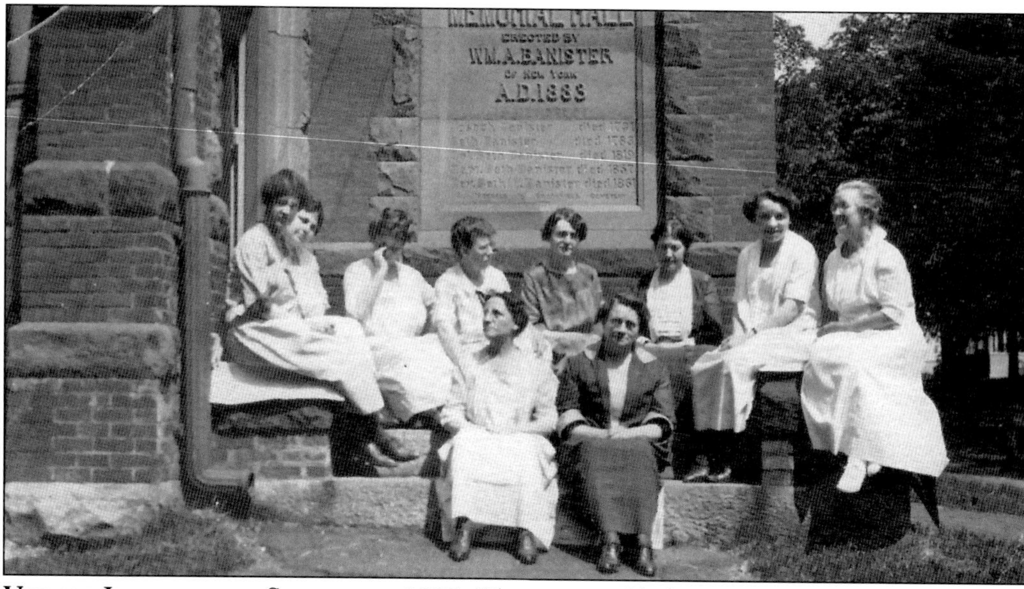

VILLAGE IMPROVEMENT SOCIETY, c. 1935. This group of ladies, among them E. Prentiss, A. Dean, N. Sweet, Jennie Pike Lamb, ? Goodwin, Jane Chapin, M. Finney, and H. Thurber, gather on the granite steps of Merrick Public Library to contemplate the need for town uplifting and refurbishing. (Courtesy of Michael Seery.)

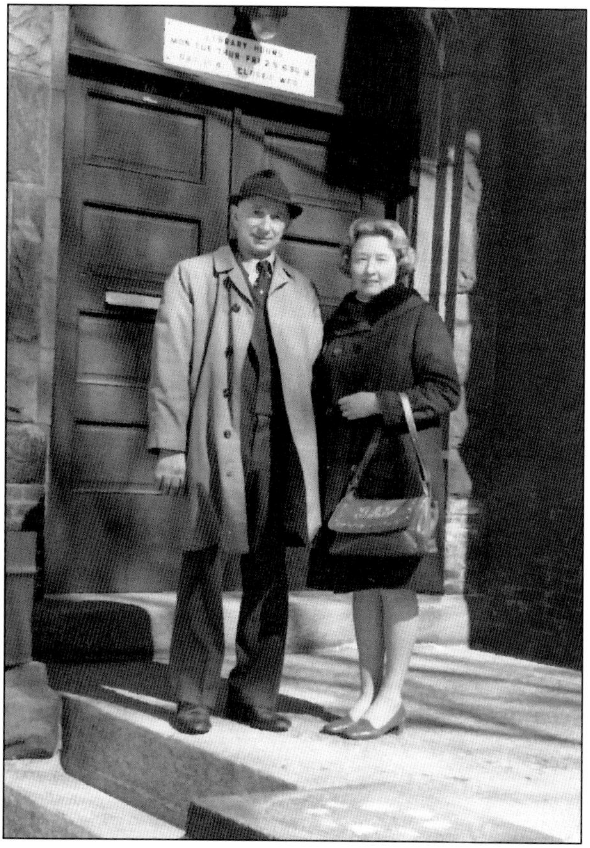

MERRICK PUBLIC LIBRARY. This 1978 photograph frames Arthur and Gloria Faugno at the library entrance. He was the library custodian and on the fire department for 54 years. She was a library clerk, later serving on the board of trustees, and also one of the original Ladies of the Lake on South Pond, whose purpose was to clean the lake and maintain its integrity. (Courtesy of Gloria Achilles Faugno.)

Bibliography

Bassett, Louise Galloway. "Living Lore in Brookfield with Ella Bartlett, New England Gentility, and Mary Ann Meehan, Irish Cook." *American Life Histories: Manuscripts from the Federal Writers' Project, 1936–1940*. American Memory, Library of Congress. memory.loc.gov/ammem/index.html.

Crane, Ellery Bicknell. *Historic Homes and Institutions and Genealogical and Personal Memoirs of Worcester, Massachusetts, with a History of Worcester Society of Antiquity*. NY: Lewis Publishing Company, 1907.

DeCelle, Kenneth F., and Philip C. Becker. "The Warren, Brookfield & Spencer Street Railway Co.," *Trolley Days in Western Mass.* 1.4 (January–December 1986): 50–68.

Dion, Michael R., and David R. Vallee. *Southern New England Tropical Storms and Hurricanes, A Ninety-Eight Year Summary, 1909–1997*. Taunton, MA: National Weather Service, 1998.

Eddy, Charles W. *Brookfield: Illustrated with Pen and Camera*. Ware, MA: 1886.

Fletcher, William G., PhD. *The Oliver Crosby House, 1797*. Brookfield, MA: Dr. and Mrs. Harlan W. Angier, 1960.

Howe, Charles Oliver. *What I Remember, 1895*. Fort Valley, GA: Annie Lyon Howe, 1928.

Marvin, Abijah Perkins. *History of Worcester County, Massachusetts: Embracing a Comprehensive History of the County from Its First Settlement to the Present Time, with a History and Description of Its Cities and Towns*. Vol. 1. Boston, MA: C.F. Jewett, 1879.

Powers, William F. *French and Electric Blue: The Massachusetts State Police: A History*. Boston, MA: Department of Public Safety, 1979.

Savoy, William. *Historic Tour of Old Brookfield, Massachusetts*. Brookfield Historical Commission, 1989.

Temple, Josiah H. *History of North Brookfield, Massachusetts: Preceded by an Account of Old Quabaug, Indian and English Occupation, 1647–1676; Brookfield Records, 1686–1783*. Town of North Brookfield, MA: 1887.

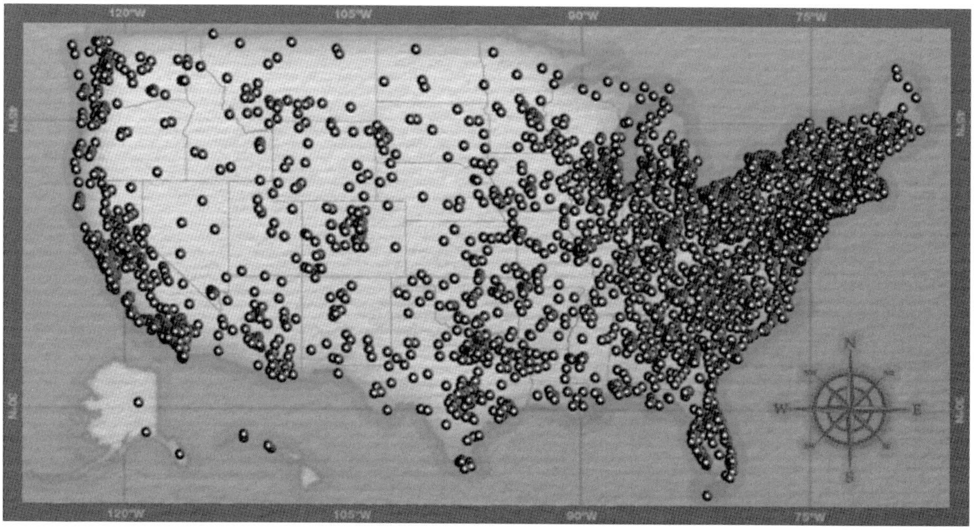